Action research and postmodernism

Conducting educational research

Series editor: Harry Torrance, University of Sussex

This series is aimed at research students in education and those under-taking related professional, vocational and social research. It takes current methodological debates seriously and offers well-informed advice to students on how to respond to such debates. Books in the series review and engage with current methodological issues, while relating such issues to the sorts of decision which research students have to make when designing, conducting and writing up research. Thus the series both contributes to methodological debate and has a practical orientation by providing students with advice on how to engage with such debate and use particular methods in their work. Series authors are experienced researchers and supervisors. Each book provides students with insights into a different form of educational research while also providing them with the critical tools and knowledge necessary to make informed judge-ments about the strengths and weaknesses of different approaches.

Current titles:
Tony Brown and Liz Jones: *Action Research and Postmodernism*
John Schostak: *Understanding, Designing and Conducting Qualitative Research in Education*

Action research and postmodernism
Congruence and critique

Tony Brown and Liz Jones

Open University Press
Buckingham · Philadelphia

Open University Press
Celtic Court
22 Ballmoor
Buckingham
MK18 1XW

email: enquiries@openup.co.uk
world wide web: www.openup.co.uk

and

325 Chestnut Street
Philadelphia, PA 19106, USA

First Published 2001

A catalogue record of this book is available from the British Library

ISBN   0 335 20761 8 (pb)   0 335 20762 6 (hb)

Library of Congress Cataloging-in-Publication Data
Brown, Tony, Ph. D.
    Action research and postmodernism : congruence and critique / Tony Brown and Liz Jones.
        p. cm. – (Conducting educational research)
    Includes bibliographical references and index.
    ISBN 0-335-20762-6 – ISBN 0-335-20761-8 (pbk.)
        1. Action research in education.   2. Postmodernism and education.
    I. Jones, Liz, 1950–   II. Title.   III.   Series.

LB1028.24 .B78 2001
371.1–dc21   2001032138

Typeset by Graphicraft Limited, Hong Kong
Printed in Great Britain by St Edmundsbury Press Limited,
Bury St Edmunds, Suffolk

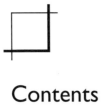

Contents

Acknowledgements

This book is the culmination of a project that has spanned some six years. The project was funded in its entirety by the Manchester Metropolitan University and the authors are very appreciative of this support. Many people have contributed significantly along the way. In particular we would like to express our thanks to Ian Stronach who has supported us throughout. We are also indebted to members of the MA in Teaching course team at the university: Andy Pickard, John Pearce, Una Hanley, John Powell and Tony Mulligan. We are also grateful to the many teachers who have followed the course and made such a strong investment in it. We would particularly like to thank those who have allowed us to quote their work in this book: Alistair Bryce-Clegg, Lorraine Dooley, Janice England, Terry Gould, Steve Grimley, Anna Perry and Mary Savill. At the later stages of preparing this book Harry Torrance offered some perceptive observations and provided some very helpful suggestions for developing the manuscript.

We would like to thank journal editors who have allowed us to quote from earlier articles in *Teaching and Teacher Education*, *Teachers and Teaching*, *Early Years*, *Educational Action Research*, the *British Educational Research Journal* and *Gender and Education*. Aspects of the theoretical work on transition were developed in the context of work for two projects with Olwen McNamara and Una Hanley, funded by the Economic and Social Research Council – project numbers R000222409 and R000223073.

Tony would like to express his appreciation of the support and love offered by his wife Alison and children Elliot and Imogen.

Liz would like to extend personal thanks to the school where her study was undertaken. Particular thanks to Kate, who in her position as head of school always encouraged the research. Special thanks must go to the children of the nursery. Thanks are also owed to a number of sterling women, particularly Sue, Seona, Lorna, Abi, Jane and Ruth. Finally, heartfelt thanks to Kerry, Joseph, Rosalind and Matthew for their love.

Introduction

Emancipation and postmodernism

Failure in emancipatory projects

We shall begin with two anecdotes that highlight the issues we wish to examine.

Anecdote 1
One day Liz found herself reminding the children about certain school rules: 'no running'; 'no hitting'. A young girl, Keeley, responded by saying 'My mum says that on the street if anyone hits me I'm to hit back'. Liz found herself lamely replying, 'At school we don't hit'. In part, the proffering of such a pat response comes from not really knowing what to say to the child. In Liz's nursery and in nurseries generally the discourse of liberal humanism prevails so that children might become civilized and rational. It is for these reasons that traits such as 'caring' and 'being kind' are privileged. Yet in this instance there is a collision between the messages that the child is bringing from home and the nursery discourse. Liz's lameness is further compounded as her response seems to conflict with her desire for children to think critically and to adopt a questioning attitude towards certain practices – including whether rules are appropriate. But on what basis can one decide what is appropriate? To whom does one appeal for adjudication?

Anecdote 2
During the early 1980s Tony taught at a large comprehensive school in London. The school combined a 'progressive' approach to education with respectability in terms of the student intake it attracted, its results and attendance levels. This was at the time of

Ken Livingstone's GLC (Greater London Council), when progressive methods had gained significant influence in London schools generally and in the university education departments which supplied many of their teachers. In the early 1990s, long after Tony had left, Ofsted (Office for Standards in Education) went in. They wrote a negative report and declared that nearly a third of the teachers were unsatisfactory. Perhaps the teaching force had changed during the intervening years, but more likely it was the broader conception of what constituted 'a teacher' that had changed. Such conceptions would appear to be time dependent. This anecdote in some ways echoes a recent account by Boaler (1997) in which it was claimed that a school adopting 'progressive' practices was significantly superior in its mathematics teaching when compared to a school that favoured more 'conventional' practices. Yet later it was the progressive school that was forced to change its methods after its own inspectorial visit by Ofsted.

These stories in some ways encapsulate the sort of difficulties post-modernist thinkers have with those assuming a more emancipatory quest for improvement in educational contexts. Any emancipatory perspective presupposes values which cannot be agreed upon universally or permanently. If we fight for something we are always working against someone else's interests and there are difficulties in creating a robustly moral perspective that will be seen as better by everyone. In saying that we are working in the children's best interests, what interests do we mean? The anecdotes pinpoint the dependency of conceptions of teaching on the ideological backdrop. Research into teaching, meanwhile, will always be premised on situationally derived assumptions. And whatever the findings of research, in many instances the researcher is unlikely to have the power or authority to have the final word.

Moreover, such research draws on an uneasy alliance of two alternative research perspectives: (a) the insider perspective of teachers focusing on their own actions; and (b) research motivated by attempts to influence policy across broader sections of the teaching force. It may work in my classroom, and perhaps even in the classrooms of the student teachers I work with, but it is a different matter making it stick as a national policy. Further, research agendas are not easily harmonized with conflicting assumptions and motivations held by different agencies, not least those assumptions built into the infrastructure within which education practices take place.

This book centres on reflexive work being undertaken by practitioner-researchers in educational contexts. It focuses on what is entailed when the move is made from common-sense understandings of what it means to be a teacher, to a problematizing about and a careful examination of the tangled complexities which lie between knowing and doing. In building this account, we use past and ongoing research activities both from our own work and from people who have worked with us.

The book explores the notion of the 'teacher as researcher' seen as the framing of relevant aspects of practice in reflective writing which enables a move from mere description to an understanding of the intricacies of such descriptions. The book also addresses the ways in which social norms and structures work at coercing these descriptions. Such an approach, however, has the potential to lead not to the unlocking of complexity but to the elucidation of rigid preconceptions which serve only to confirm injustices of the 'found' world. Hitherto, action research has assumed a reality which can be uncovered and then altered in some way or improved upon for emancipatory purposes. This however begs key questions about where our ideas of what counts as 'improvement' come from. How can the researcher both 'observe' reality as well as being part of it and thus be implicated in its continual creation and recreation? These issues are much more complex than action research has acknowledged so far. We need to move beyond the notion of the 'reflective practitioner' to encompass poststructuralism which attends more to the way in which we construct reality. Our broader understandings of the flow of time, we suggest, are conditioned by the media through which we receive depictions of it. Newspapers, for example, create as well as report news. They have considerable influence over the way in which information about the present is processed and the form it has to take to be heard. Such media channels are instrumental in our everyday construction of the world in which we live. They are part of the shorthand we all employ in coming to terms with the complexity we face. In research we are in the business of creating a similar mediating layer with many similar characteristics, and are susceptible to varying interpretations of its function. Research may be targeted at finding out how things are, how things work, or be about describing the world in some other way. But we are always confronted by the unanswerable question as to whether our language is responsive or assertive. As researchers, are we saying how things *are* or telling people how things *should be seen*? In constructing validity criteria for our assertions, whose interests are we serving? In particular, what is reflected in reflective writing produced within practitioner research? We propose that we are more than passive recipients of our supposed mirror images, and that 'reflective' writing plays an instrumental role beyond mere reflection.

In this book we draw specifically on poststructuralist theories of subjectivity, language and meaning. Because it disputes the notion that language is transparent and does not permit either accurate expositions or conclusive or definite explanations, poststructuralism allows the reflexive practitioner to see experiences, including those that occur within the workplace, as open to contradictory and conflicting interpretations. Language can no longer be relied upon for mastery or control. However, the book argues that while poststructuralism cannot give the practitioner-researcher control, it can nevertheless disrupt habitual and mechanistic ways of being. By adopting poststructuralist frameworks and by engaging with practices of deconstruction, attempts are made to break away from inappropriate and inadequate category systems.

We write at a time when education generally, but schools specifically, have been the subject of close government scrutiny and where teacher autonomy has been considerably eroded. We perceive writing this book as a move towards creating a space where we might articulate something of what it is to be 'a teacher'. We cannot presume to write what it is to be a child. What we can do, however, is write our way towards some understanding of our own complicity and culpability in relations of dominance against those that we would seek to empower. Effectively, this book is concerned with asking hard questions about our own practices, especially those which are ostensibly concerned with emancipation.

From emancipation to postmodernism

How then might school-based practitioner research enable us in capturing and guiding classroom practice? A premise of many teacher research enquiries undertaken within the context of award-bearing courses is that reflection on practice can lead to a development of that practice. Such reflection, it is purported, enables the practitioner in organizing the complexity of the teaching situation, with a particular emphasis on how 'monitoring change' can be converted to 'control of change'. For the teacher engaged in this style of research there may also be hopes that the research will result in 'better teaching' as well as a hope that the children may as a consequence of education have 'better lives'. This book questions the limits of our capacity to enter into *projects of action* (Schütz 1962) as intentional beings in this way, but acknowledges that we may suppose that we are such intentional beings and act as such. The book questions the track record of the notion of construing developing practice as 'aiming for an ideal'. The very desire for control, and the difficulties encountered in trying to document it, can cloud our vision against the very complexities we seek to capture, trapped as we are in socially derived constructions of the world we experience. Postmodernist analysis, meanwhile, offers opportunities to conceptualize the world in different ways. It insists on undercutting the foundations upon which notions such as empowerment and enlightenment rest, although some argue that this may not necessarily be a threat to such notions (e.g. Carr 1995). We shall, however, see how our initial attempt at a reconciliation of the hermeneutic underpinnings of the practitioner research enterprise with poststructuralist analyses turned into a disruption of the initial assumptions as to the purpose of research, thus moving away from a somewhat rationalist focus concerned with effecting productive change through a systematic process.

The basic task of this book is to examine some of the difficulties encountered when seeking to reconcile a postmodernist style of analysis with the intentionality ordinarily assumed in practitioner-oriented re-search enquiry. Much research has been predicated on a modernist project of the teacher wishing to examine his or her practical relation to the professional situation they inhabit. Furthermore, this is often motivated by notions of empowerment both for the children taught and for the teacher themselves, and as a consequence the research seeks to uncover, critique and challenge the structural conditions which envelop the pro-fessional tasks being faced. However, theories of postmodernism and poststructuralism have impacted on recent work in the field of educa-tion, and in very many ways they cut across and work against these various concerns. The book examines writings produced within a vari-ety of practitioner research enquiries taking place within the context of award-bearing courses. It explores the premises upon which such enquiries are constructed and questions the sorts of resolution that can be reached.

It would seem that what we are proposing is an unlikely match. On the one hand there is the notion of the subject who besides being stable and coherent can use powers of reasoning and rationality in order to understand the complexities of the world, including those which are embedded in teaching. This conception of the researcher finds favour within various examples of practitioner research paradigms. On the other hand, there is the fragmented subject, with its multiple selves, implied by poststructuralist theories. Given such incompatibilities, marriage be-tween the two seems doomed. However, it is not marriage we are pro-posing. Rather, we perceive ourselves entering into a lengthy engagement with postmodernism. It is an engagement which finds the practitioner-researcher situated within the logic which circumscribes such projects. But, by incorporating theories of postmodernism into the research practices, we are obliged, we believe, to interrogate that very logic. In this way we show how the logic is no longer a satisfactory means for addressing the complexities of social life, including those that are within the classroom.

The chosen research instrument within this book is reflective writing produced by practitioner-researchers. We suggest that the researcher needs to be self-consciously reflective and thus that they need to be aware of their own growth in this process. We prefer to argue for the centrality of the writing process rather than any supposed research process. It is through such a writing process we suggest that the researcher asserts and thus 'creates' themselves. This is rather like the psychoanalyst's client pronouncing from the couch who they are and the things in life shaping their sense of self. Such assertions or pronouncements provide frameworks against which we can choose to live our real lives. We thus understand the task of practitioner research as being targeted at producing a construction of self in relation to the professional/social context being faced. (Although most of the research to be discussed in this present volume is directed at personal and professional development, such a construction of self may still be implicated in research seeming to claim a more 'objective' stance.)

We ask how we might proceed in producing and understanding the reflective writing that might arise within such a process. Our premise is that the practitioner researching in their classroom brings about perceived changes both through acting in the classroom itself and in producing writing commenting on this classroom practice. That is to say, written descriptions of classroom practice, undertaken by the practitioner, effectively change the reality attended to by that practitioner. The writing generated in this process can be seen as both responding to past action and guiding future action. The practical knowledge derived through such a process is however both dynamic and provisional. In traditional action research there appears to be a supposition that the researcher stays the same during the research period. It also often seems that the world they inhabit 'stops' long enough for them to look at it and then act. We propose that changes in both researcher and world need to be documented within the writing process, since they are mutually constitutive. In short, in describing my classroom, I affect the way I see it, thus the way I act in it, the way I am and hence the way I subsequently describe it (since it has also been changed by my actions). In engaging in this circular hermeneutic process, teacher-researchers pass through a sequence of perspectives, each capable of generating various types of writing and each susceptible to a variety of later interpretations. However, this writing becomes detached from the person who generated it. It becomes a historical artefact susceptible to multiple interpretations as to its origins and its situation within the social sphere through which it emerged. While individuals can, if they choose, wed themselves to understandings of themselves as intentional beings as they act professionally and write about their actions, such understandings are always temporary; subject to reformulations and recontextualizations. Research enquiry can thus be revisited as a historical analysis of practitioners' writing, but a history that creates futures as well as presents and pasts (see Ricoeur 1984).

Chapter outline

The book continues with a development of these issues discussed in relation to a number of studies being carried out by teachers following masters and doctoral routes. After a brief review of the critical education foundations from which our own work springs we offer a more developed account of the hermeneutic underpinnings that provided the starting point for our discussion, discussed in relation to some teacher studies. We then offer a more detailed account of a project carried out by Liz in a nursery school in which a more poststructuralist analysis is introduced. We conclude with a discussion of how we might live with a compromised set of emancipatory values within a more postmodern frame.

Chapter 2 begins with an account of some of the factors shaping the practice of teachers in school and their associated work on university courses. It then explores the burgeoning of practitioner research paradigms within award-bearing courses for teachers and other professionals in education and the roots of this in the writings of certain key authors (e.g. Carr and Kemmis, Elliott). Such authors, it is suggested, seem to presuppose an essence (of a situation or a person) which can be revealed and improved. These issues will be discussed briefly in relation to key critical pedagogy theorists such as Freire, McLaren and Giroux. A more developed example is offered relating to feminist conceptions of emancipation. The discussion then introduces the work of Habermas, in so far as his work might be seen as underpinning contemporary understandings of emancipatory practice governed by rationalist principles. However, we then outline how postmodernism rejects the notion of a rational intentional being centred in a professional situation to be analysed and modified. We then ask how we might proceed in bringing postmodernist analyses to approaches presupposing subjects and situations in search of improvement.

Part 1 considers the hermeneutic underpinning of critical practitioner research strategies as exemplified in a research masters course for teachers. It then considers how reflective writing might provide an instrument for loosening the ties of overly rationalist research objectives. Chapter 3 examines how writing produced within school-based practitioner research can be seen as framing and guiding both classroom practice and the research process itself. It commences with a discussion of an emancipatory aspect of Habermas' work that has been influential in framing practitioner enquiry in education. It provides a brief account of John Elliott's Gadamerian objection to this approach in which *emancipation* is replaced by *evolution*. A masters course for practising teachers is described in which this objection is accommodated. This is based around a model drawn from Saussurian linguistics for analysing text, widely used by poststructuralist writers. In this model the meaning of the text depends on an evolving relationship between the words within it. An analogy is drawn with practitioner research, which is characterized as the generation and analysis of a sequence of pieces of writing whose meaning can be derived through analysis of the relation between the successive pieces of writing produced. This model is employed as a framework for understanding, monitoring and influencing changes in practice. Examples of teachers' reflective writing from the masters course are used to illustrate alternative approaches to achieving such writing-led professional change.

Chapter 4 sets out to examine the nature of time and how it is constructed within reflective teacher research. The chapter is motivated on the one hand by a belief in evolving identity but on the other it acknowledges a world where such identities are collapsing into interweaving discourses where notions of such evolution are not tenable. It draws on the classic debate between Gadamer and Habermas concerned with how we experience our living in the present, either as a 'being in the world' or as an 'end gainer' aspiring to a new structural framework within which life will be unconstrained by reifications of oppressive relations. After questioning the notion of human agency that these views presuppose, the chapter pursues a resolution offered by Ricoeur and his subsequent work on the close relation between time and the stories we tell about it. Some work arising from a masters course for teachers is described in which attempts are made to reconcile practice with descriptions of practice. In particular, issues of the teachers working with their own earlier writings are discussed. It is suggested that such writings can be used to form a reflective/constructive narrative layer that feeds, while growing alongside, the life it seeks to portray.

Chapter 5 draws on Lacan's work in psychoanalysis in seeking to locate a model for the identity of teachers working on their practice. For Lacan the human subject is always seen as incomplete, where identifications of oneself are captured in an image: as an individual I am forever trying to complete the picture I have of myself in relation to the world around me and the others who also inhabit it. I respond to the fantasy I have of the Other and the fantasy I imagine the Other having of me. The mirror image I create of myself is built through successive interpretations in such exchanges. But these interpretations are in turn a function of the language we share. In the context of practitioner research, what version of myself do I feel comfortable with – what fantasies do I have about myself, the place I work, the people I work with and the broader social context within which this takes place? What story do I tell to justify my actions? How do I frame my plans and intentions? How do I understand and depict the discourses that interpellate me? What construction of self is implicated in the models of practitioner research offered so far? Extensive reference will be made to some writing produced by some teachers for their final masters dissertation and subsequent work to illustrate how this psychoanalytical approach might be enacted as part of a professionally oriented research enquiry.

Part 2 centres on Liz's study based in a nursery classroom in which a fuller deconstructive unpicking of teacher research practices is offered. Chapter 6 introduces the conceptualization of the study which brought the two authors of this present book together. It discusses Liz's work in a nursery school and her attempts to find a way of defining the motivation underlying her own practices as a teacher. It provides an example of a transition from an enquiry rooted in emancipatory aspirations that becomes unstuck, forcing a requestioning of the motivations assumed at the outset.

Chapter 7 continues to discuss the nursery study and illustrates some of the repercussions, particularly the advantages, of adopting deconstructive approaches to those meanings which are brought to an account of young children's play within a teacher research enquiry. In describing and interpreting an example offered here the objective is not to fix a definitive or accurate explanation to it. Instead, the ambition is to disperse rather than capture meanings, to offer multiple and open-ended interpretations and in so doing disturb the equilibrium of the reported perspective which gave rise to the account. Through such an approach, it is suggested, we can challenge ingrained ways of knowing and doing which inhibit opportunities to question 'authoritarian fictions' present in the way we often describe the learning of young children, which because they are habitual and collective, have come to be regarded as 'natural' and as 'truths'.

Chapter 8 centres on power relations as they are played out within the context of the nursery. Accounts which centre on the children's play are used to illustrate not only how power circulates but additionally how it might be both resisted or tampered with. Moreover, the writing illustrates how particular discursive practices have the potential to constitute individuals into particular ways of being. Nevertheless, by taking up different subject positionings, teacher and child alike can challenge and render fragile notions of power. It is just such a play of discourses which this chapter attempts to illustrate.

Chapter 9 takes time out to consider a number of questions including: (a) is the practice of deconstructing a responsible act?; (b) should playing with texts – that are themselves concerned with children's play – be taken seriously?; and (c) can educational research which produces bafflement rather than solutions be considered as research? In her efforts to address these questions Liz's first step is to offer a rereading of a boy's game. However, she tries to centre her attention not so much on the salient features of the game but on those things which are not 'precisely' present. Such a move provokes different perspectives and it is these which allow her the possibilities to ask 'new and different questions'

(Hebdige 1989: 226), a practice which is arguably an act of responsible research. Her second move is to examine why it is she has what could be described as a 'jackboot' response to boys' play with toy guns. Using a number of texts which are concerned with 'gun play' Liz picks apart her own investments in certain ideological positionings. Such aggravations do not offer a clear-sighted vision as to where to go next. Rather, Liz is left baffled and it is this which prompts the continual critique of practice.

Chapter 10 concerns itself with notions of 'agency'. Liz takes a brief exchange between herself and some of the nursery girls. Using this as a catalyst and working from a Foucauldian perspective she ponders on the possibilities of individuals becoming 'transgressive agents'.

The Conclusion, Chapter 11, asks whether it is conceivable for the practitioner to continue to hold on to notions of emancipation when it is no longer viable to appeal to the old grand narratives, including those of universal truths, objective science and reason. The chapter assesses the attempt made in this book to revisit and question the foundations of educational practitioner research. Taking our cue from Derrida (1994), we argue that it is possible 'never to give up on the Enlightenment'. But, as he cautions, this requires 're-reading and re-interpreting . . . to raise new questions . . . disturb stereotypes and good consciences, and to complicate or re-work for a changed situation' (p. 34). By drawing on the authors' base domains of nursery teaching and mathematics education research, our ambition is to illustrate how different conceptualizations of 'knowledge' and 'understanding' can open up the possibility for a 'changed situation'. We suggest that the narrative product of reflexive research might be seen as the aspirational voice that keeps emancipatory intention alive. Thus the chapter, through revisiting some of the authors' own specific professional concerns, highlights some of the strategies suggested for grappling with the complexities of researching educational practice.

2

Research and the development
of practice

Framing the issues

As we write, there is much that is occurring and has occurred within schools and universities which both perplexes and troubles us. During recent years various shifts have taken place which effectively have diminished several notions that seemed key in earlier conceptions of professional teaching – including those of personal independence, autonomy and liberty. These shifts have been effected in several ways.

For example, in Liz's school, the staffing became heavily hierarchical. Weekly staff meetings were used less as arenas for debate and instead became occasions for informing the rank and file of those decisions which had been made by the senior and middle management teams. More generally the National Curriculum has been introduced, which teachers are legally obliged to deliver. The metaphor of a 'delivery system' (Carr and Kemmis 1986: 15) is an apt one, as it summarizes much of what it feels like to be a teacher in current times. Teachers are akin to 'operatives' who 'implement' rather than 'create' (Carr and Kemmis 1986: 47), and teaching has been reduced to being 'simply the technical mastery of a set of discrete procedures, achievement of which is readily manifested as a corresponding set of discrete behaviours' (Parker 1997: 15). In the nursery context the controls of the National Curriculum could be described as being covert rather than overt. The children of the nursery, because they were not of statutory school age, did not come under the remit of the National Curriculum. Nevertheless, it was expected that when the children left the nursery and entered mainstream education they would have the necessary foundations in order to receive and benefit from subsequent blocks of learning. To this end there were both government and local education authority (LEA) guidelines which stipulated curriculum content and defined what 'desirable outcomes of learning' should be. Learning, both within the nursery and the rest of the school was premised on the principle that 'the addition of one unit of knowledge to another cannot but precipitate a coherent result' (Parker 1997: 16). All this implies that within the nursery there were expectations that the children would be exposed to, get to grips with, and finally master or internalize certain skills or concepts.

It is this sort of technical mastery that has also become more apparent in universities, both in initial training and even in more advanced training as teachers have come under pressure to develop their practice according to government-led agendas. The apparatus of government policy seems increasingly to be shaping the college experience of becoming a teacher. Overly prescriptive policy initiatives can often squeeze out key aspects of training, including the teachers' own capacity for working on their own professional development in a way that relates to their own more personal aspirations of what it is to be a teacher. New pressures resulting from subject knowledge requirements, for example, mean that initial training courses are now over-committed in terms of content and too short (Askew *et al.* 1997). Such training also carries with it many conflicting policy messages which results in a certain amount of cancelling out (Brown *et al.* 1999a) and more reflective work, in so far as it exists, merely provides a forum in which students seek to reconstruct their own identity as they become inducted into the professional discourses required of them (see Hanley and Brown 1996, 1999; Jones *et al.* 2000). Further, such policy initiatives can result in students specifying their own needs in somewhat restrictive terms, in line with government requirements. This can result in college tutors needing to defend their own professionality, defined in terms of broader educational aspirations, against a framework that seems rather more narrow.

Aronowitz and Giroux (1986) have argued that this is a broad conservative trend in higher education. The massive expansion in higher education institutions has resulted in a reconceptualization of the job they do. It is now, they suggest, more about technical training where broader conceptions of education are reserved for those in the more élite pockets of higher education. For initial teacher training students in the UK it appears to be that training is indeed privileged over education; training from which it often appears that students emerge as civil servants of the latest government truth.

Within university courses of advanced training meanwhile our own experience suggests that teachers are increasingly governed by the need to reconcile their practices with the host of external discourses to which they need to attend in their everyday teaching, perhaps to some extent, we feel, at the expense of asserting and developing their own voice. These moves come at a time when there appears to be a more general reconceptualization of 'the professions' and their relation to the state.

The medical profession, the police, social workers etc. are all finding their respective roles as 'public servants' being emphasized as the government asserts its 'management' of these roles for the greater good of the populace.

Current government policy and its associated documentation aimed at raising 'standards' also seems to be experienced by many teachers in the classroom as having an all-embracing effect on their practice, which may be affecting the nature of teacher- and school-led continuing professional development initiatives (Bottery and Wright 1996). A longer-term view, however might see such policy as part of a perpetual readjustment in teaching styles, related to the evolution of learning theories and policy fashions (Brown 1997). As such, the attendant pressures may be in respect of relatively short-lived educational objectives.

Also, the relationship between policy and its implementation is often unclear. Just because policy is set does not mean that it is understood in the terms in which it is presented (see Millett 1996), nor that it is fully implemented before the next policy comes along. When it comes to policy, there is often a sense of a bus lane with a frequent service: 'There'll be another one along in a minute'. Frequent policy change can unsettle, and activates a responsive attitude resulting in dragged compliance rather than proactive strategies by teachers. Teachers can experience great difficulty in describing their own practice in terms of the language employed within curriculum documents. Millett (1996) and Simon and Brown (1996) offer an example in mathematics education. The much heralded notion of 'using and applying mathematics' seemed to have little impact on teachers' practice; to a large extent they used it as label for what they were already doing. There seemed to be a significant delay between the appearance of policy documents and evidence of this impacting on teachers' practice and their way of describing it. Given the rapid succession of such documents in recent years, teachers have not had the opportunity to live in a policy phase for more than a few months before yet another change was demanded. The disorientation and fatigue brought about in teachers by such rapid change resulted in a promise from the government not to change anything else relating to the National Curriculum for five years to appease a disillusioned teaching force. One would have hoped that this stability in the curriculum might in itself have brought about an improvement (cf. Brown 1997). The multitude of successive interpretations relating to the curriculum, however, have been no less pervasive, whether these come from Ofsted or advisors disseminating the National Literacy and Numeracy Strategies.

Such cases suggest that the balance in current practice tends more towards producing policy fatigue rather than to the stimulation that can sometimes be brought about by trying out new perspectives and frameworks. The institution of 'requirements' by government agencies seems to be more widespread of late. These are offered against a backdrop of improving the quality of teaching in our schools. Yet it would seem that the laying down of such requirements can only be presented as a teacher development strategy for the profession as a whole if compliance with the current policy is interpreted uncritically as displaying 'high standards' (DfEE 1998). One might suggest that such standards are derived from a very specific version of 'education'. Bourdieu and Wacquant (2001: 5) argue that this sort of pseudo-intellectual imperialism is 'increasingly crowding the autonomous and critical intellectual born of the Enlightenment tradition out of the public scene'. They suggest that intellectual argument used in the service of government initiatives itself is increasingly manufactured, whether this argument is produced by government officials offering overly technical analyses 'to justify policy choices made on decidedly non-technical grounds', or by defected academics entering 'the service of the dominant, whose mission is to give an academic veneer to the political projects of the new state and business nobility'. The production of such technical discourses and how they obscure social rituals is discussed more fully by Stronach (1999).

It is against this background, where a somewhat impoverished, means-end conception of rationality seems to hold court, that we still hold onto notions of emancipation. That is, we may, by using certain strategies, including for example 'a continuous, relentless interrogation of sedimented social practices' (Groundwater-Smith 1988: 257) then be better placed to appreciate the workings of such practices. This chapter centres on our own predicament where we are both disappointed in, and yet still find ourselves tied to, certain Enlightenment ideals.

We commence with a brief account of how practitioner research has been predicated on such understandings of intentionality, and particularly where this has been motivated by some emancipatory ideals. We discuss this in relation to féminism in particular. At this juncture, after attempting to frame the conundrum at the interface of Enlightenment ideals and postmodernism, certain aspects of Habermas' work are considered because of his commitment to 'objectivity in universals' (e.g. the good life, the better society, democracy) (McRobbie 1993: 132). However, the decision is made not to rekindle hope or belief in modernity but to remain disappointed. This 'disappointment' can then be set to work to confront those binary oppositions which have traditionally promised a number of things including an autonomous subject, a transparent language and a certainty of knowledge (cf. Stronach and MacLure 1997: 4–5). Nevertheless, we proceed with hermeneutics a little further, but with an increasing suspicion towards the linguistic ties that seem to bind its approach. We conclude the chapter with a brief consideration of how we might start to chip away at such guiding principles.

Practitioner research in education

'In the midst of the crisis which is education, and teacher education in particular, we see ourselves on the side of the angels: we are in the business of empowering good teachers by enabling them to confront, analyse and develop their practice in ways which allow them to recognize and eventually celebrate their teaching' (Manchester Metropolitan University 1994: 4). This quotation is taken from the course documentation of the MA in Teaching mentioned in the Introduction, a course that will provide much of the data for this present book. Here we propose that this quotation can be perceived as a 'representation'. This begs the question, 'What is being represented?'

The suggestion is that the quotation can be understood as a representation of those teacher-practitioner traditions and movements which have a commitment to, and a belief in, notions of emancipation. These would include the 'reflective teaching movement' which is sometimes referred to as 'action research' or 'practitioner research'. Stemming from the work of Stenhouse (1975), Schon (1983) and much earlier, Dewey (1933), current proponents of practitioner research would include Winter (1989) and Elliott (1991). Such practitioner research often accommodates an understanding of how researchers are practically related to the situations they investigate, where their actions, as teacher-researchers, are seen as an essential part of the situation being described (see, for example, Schon 1983; Adler 1993; Elliott 1993a: 193–207; Brown 1994a; Lomax 1994). Also, such research paradigms are increasingly being employed in programmes of professional development within both initial training (e.g. Francis 1995; Hatton and Smith 1995; Hanley and Brown 1996, 1999) and masters-level work (e.g. Cryns and Johnston 1993; Brown 1994b, 1996). Associated with these moves is a burgeoning literature on teacher narratives, emphasizing the teachers' perspective as represented through the accounts they give of their professional situations (e.g. Connelly and Clandinin 1988; Weber 1993; Beattie 1995; Olson 1995; Brown and Roberts 2000). Such approaches are also increasingly influential for other professional groups (e.g. McLeod 1997; Titley *et al.* 1999). Ricoeur (e.g. 1984) and Cavarero (2000) offer more theoretical treatments of narrative.

Similarly, the quotation could also be a reference to those educational theories and practices which are drawn from and influenced by 'critical theory'. Critical theory is rooted in both Kantian and Hegelian philosophy as well as the critical theory of Habermas and the Frankfurt school. Critical theory finds application in education through the work of many practitioner-researchers including, among others, Carr and Kemmis (1986) and Young (1989, 1992).

The quotation could also be a reference to 'liberatory education', 'emancipatory education' or 'critical pedagogy'. Derived from the liberationist philosophies of Freire (1972), 'emancipatory' work is fairly widespread within education and finds resonance in, for example, the work of Bowles and Gintis (1976), Aronowitz and Giroux (1986) and McLaren (1995). Feminism can also be located within the 'emancipatory tradition'. Thus, although the quotation does not make any direct reference to feminism or indeed to any of the other movements, nevertheless the suggestion is that it can be read as a representation of them.

However, there is no implication that by seeing the quotation as a representation of several movements they are, therefore, all more or less the same. On the contrary, each of these movements and traditions have particular ideas, structures, claims, concerns, histories and backgrounds. However, they do share certain characteristics and features, including:

> a commitment to the authority of reason; rejection of a means-end conception of rationality and of a technical-rationalist view of human worth; a commitment to personal autonomy and its rational components of honesty and sincerity; emancipatory concerns, liberal and democratic politics, an idea of genuine knowledge as essentially purposeful rather than inert; a transcendental justification.
>
> (Parker 1997: 32)

Significantly, it is within this theoretical background that this book can be situated. That is, we seek for ourselves and the students we work with both 'empowerment' and 'emancipation'. We want to learn to 'think critically' so that we are then able to recognize the ways in which dominant ideologies and social structures work at coercing and oppressing. Moreover, from a feminist perspective we are prompted to work at securing gender equity, autonomy and liberation both within and outside educational contexts.

But how may such things be achieved? Effectively, the quotation maps out a methodological procedure. First, a 'beginning' is established. This could centre on a 'crisis'. The focus might be on the difficulties of incorporating personal politics, including feminism and socialism, within the restrictions of centralized and conservative educational policies. The story could then be developed further by offering descriptions of reflective practice. As a consequence of 'confronting' and 'analysing', opportunities are then made possible in order to 'develop' practice in ways which are 'empowering'. Finally, teaching can be 'celebrated'. It is interesting to note how Christian terminology works at both mirroring and thus heightening the notion of the pilgrim making 'his' way along the path to salvation.

In all, reflective teaching aims to develop rational persons by rational processes. This is not a one-sided affair in which the teacher lays down the rules of how to reason. Rather, it requires the initiation and complicity of the children so that they too may become critical participants (see

Peters 1966; Carr and Kemmis 1986; Siegel 1988). For example, within Liz's nursery, through a topic such as 'People who care for us' the children and the teacher might consider notions surrounding 'families' and 'family life'. By various means – for example, through one-to-one teacher-child encounters and small group discussions – views could be exchanged. This would include drawing out the different ways that families can be constituted and would involve the teacher as well as the children sharing their ideas concerned with domestic life. Additionally, a range of stories could be read in which the characters and household arrangements are much more representative of the ways in which the children live out their lives. In these ways there would be some resistance to external ideology and cultural values where the notion of the 'family' is construed in very particular ways.

We have, then, strong attachments to notions of emancipation. Furthermore, it is a commitment which is fuelled by socialism and feminism. Accordingly there is a preoccupation which centres on how research and practice can effectively challenge relations of dominance.

On the other hand, we have become increasingly attracted to theories of postmodernism/poststructuralism. Writers such as Foucault, Derrida and Lacan have given a new prominence to the role of text and discourse analysis in building understandings of human action. But in an interesting twist, especially present in the work of Foucault (e.g. 1991), there has been a shift to an analysis of the relationships between discursive and non-discursive relations, as located in social institutions and the practices they engender (Smart 1985: 43). An important thrust of this work is that the categories implicit in the use of language itself reveal much about the community which generated it and the perspective of the individual user. In describing the world I say a lot about myself and the way in which I see my actions gearing into the world. Similarly, there are cultural conventions in describing the world, which reveal the culture's understanding of the world and hence something about the culture itself. As Coward and Ellis (1977: 1) put it, 'the study of language has opened up a route to an understanding of mankind, social history and the laws of how a society functions'.

The emphasis in recent studies concerned with language has been on how language is used, by individuals and by societies. That is, the performance of language has taken precedence over the study of the structure and system of language *per se*. The world is increasingly seen as being understood through the filter of socially derived words which individuals use to describe it. Conversely, in seeking to change their actions, both individuals and societies can, in the first instance, work on changing their use of language. For example: individuals undergoing psychoanalytic therapy seek to change their actions through reframing in words the way in which they see these actions; similarly, recent change in educational practices within the UK was brought about through introducing a curriculum which reorganized the way in which learning was spoken about.

Postmodern thought has affected literary theory, feminist theory, psychoanalytic and cultural critique (Shapiro 1991: 112). However, its impact on education generally, but critical pedagogy in particular, has been and continues to be a more cautious affair. Perhaps this is because particular theories of postmodernism(s) appear to offer very little in the way of hope that liberating human or social transformation is a possibility. How, for example, is it possible for individuals to engage in various forms of rational critique (one of the hallmarks of modernity) when the world has collapsed into 'an implosion of the real' and when it is 'no longer a question of a false representation of reality (ideology), but of concealing the fact that the real is no longer real' (Poster 1988: 171)?

Later we will draw a little more on certain key writers whose writing have suggested an interesting challenge to conventional wisdom within educational research – that the task is to resolve meanings and strategies in a definitive way. These writers range from radical educational theorists (e.g. Henriques *et al.* 1984; Davies 1989; Walkerdine and Lucey 1989; Lather 1991; McLaren 1995; Stronach and MacLure 1997) to feminist theorists (e.g. Moi 1985; Hekman 1990), to literary and cultural theorists (e.g. Eagleton 1983; Hall *et al.* 1992; Barry 1995). However, in very many ways these writers present theories which go against and work at undercutting the foundational knowledge which gives impetus and strength to emancipatory movements, including feminism and those engaged with 'emancipatory education'. Effectively this places us in a conundrum. What follows is an attempt at giving some meaning to this position in ways which allow it to move beyond being an academic exercise.

Feminism and the Enlightenment

We have alluded to personal disappointment in the Enlightenment epistemology. To take the case of defining feminist perspectives, one of the defining characteristics of modernity is its anthropocentric definition of knowledge. As Hekman puts it: 'since the Enlightenment, knowledge has been defined in terms of "man", the subject and espouses an epistemology that is radically homocentric' (1990: 2). Thus, while the likes of Descartes, Locke and the other seventeenth- and eighteenth-century philosophical 'founding fathers' attempted to develop an intellectual movement which would lead society out of the darkness of irrationality and superstition that supposedly characterized the Middle Ages, their efforts never disturbed the centrality of 'man'. Instead, this was reinforced.

'Man' was to be no longer dependent on the guidance of 'another'. Rather, by his own capacities he could progress and, as it were, become an angel in this world rather than wait until the next. These 'capacities' included a faith that rational knowledge of society could be attained and that this knowledge was universal and thus objective. Knowledge that is acquired from the right use of reason is truth, in that it represents something real, unchanging and universal about the hu(man) mind and the structure of the natural world. Such knowledge, being grounded in reason, can both disperse and overcome the conflicts which lie between truth, knowledge and power (Singh 1995: 202). As a consequence, truth is able to serve power without distortion; in turn, by utilizing knowledge in the service of power, both freedom and progress will be assured. Knowledge can be both neutral (e.g. grounded in universal reason, not particular 'interests') and also socially beneficial. In other words, rational knowledge, because it is both rational and neutral, can lead to mental liberation and social betterment among humanity (McLennan 1992: 330).

Hence, the promise of the Enlightenment movement centred on a coherent and stable self, and one where this self or subject can be the self-conscious guarantor of all knowledge, or, as Taylor puts it: 'When the subject totally comprehends the object and the object is perfectly reflected in the subject, the doubt and uncertainty with which modern philosophy begins are finally overcome' (1987: 3).

Furthermore, language is, in some senses, transparent. As Flax (1990: 42) writes:

> Just as the right use of reason can result in knowledge that represents the real, so, too, language is merely the medium in and through which such representation occurs. There is a correspondence between word and thing (as between a correct truth claim and the real). Objects are not linguistically (or socially) constructed; they are merely made present to consciousness by naming and the right use of language.

These beliefs, which are concerned with identity, truth, knowledge and power, are the basis for many assumptions and serve as legitimation for contemporary western culture.

Any outright rejection of the ideals of the Enlightenment project leaves both feminism and projects such as emancipatory education in a curious and anomalous position. On the one hand, because all forms of feminism take the concept of 'woman' as a necessary point of departure for any feminist theory and feminist politics, the fundamental and homocentric assumptions of the Enlightenment project have to be questioned, challenged and disputed (Alcoff 1988: 405). But, on the other hand, the feminist movement is itself both historically and theoretically rooted in the Enlightenment project (Hekman 1990: 2). For example, nineteenth-century feminists such as Mary Wollstonecraft and Harriet Taylor looked to and depended on the theories of liberal humanism, and under the panacea of acquiring the vote aspired to be like men, and as a consequence 'be free and equal and able to determine their own fates in a civil society' (Nye 1988: 3).

Similarly, it is possible to discern within the Enlightenment project certain objectives, including the desire for a better and more just society, as being the underlying impetus from which was spawned a number of counter or oppositional enterprises, including, for example, neo-Marxist emancipatory projects and Freirean participatory research. What unites these movements is an assumption that the world is not a fair place and that there is unequal distribution of resources and power. However, it is possible to transcend this injustice if people first comprehend that they are oppressed and, further, understand how this oppression functions and operates. This then opens the way for resistance and, as a consequence, greater self-determination is achieved (Fay 1987). Similarly, practitioner enquiry projects including action research (Elliott 1991) and 'self-reflective enquiry' (Kemmis 1985), have similar aspirations:

> Action research is a form of self-reflective enquiry undertaken by participants (teachers, students or principals, for example) in social (including educational) situations in order to improve the rationality and justice of (a) their own social or educational practices, (b) their understanding of these practices, and (c) the situations (and institutions) in which these practices are carried out.
>
> (Carr and Kemmis 1986: 162)

It is evident, we believe, that while there may be differences in methodological procedure, all the approaches mentioned above hold a commitment to notions of emancipation involving 'a freeing of the mind from the distortions of ignorance, ideology, irrationality, tradition and habit so that the beneficiary is able to become properly rational and see the world right. It entails commitment to individual autonomy and democratic principles of equality and justice' (Parker 1997: 41).

Hence, on the one hand both feminism and emancipatory or critical/reflective enquiry seek to unmask the lies, myths and distortions that construct the basis for the dominant order (see Giroux 1983: 109), but on the other hand, besides both being products of the 'dominant order' they both additionally have some residual and lingering investments in it. Reflective practice, for example, is both driven by and embodies the liberal, meliorist sense of the infinite perfectibility – through the application of reason – of humans and their institutions (cf. Gray 1995).

For feminists, the Enlightenment notion of the 'subject' has to be challenged because it is gendered. As a consequence, the oppositional binaries of modernist thinking, including the dichotomies of rational/

irrational and subject/object and where 'man' is situated both as 'rational' and 'the subject', are no longer tenable. The vexing question of where to go to next then emerges. If for example feminism joins and allies itself with a movement such as postmodernism(s), the question then arises as to whether it is possible to have an adequate politics of subjectivity when there is no longer, as it were, a 'viable subject' with fixed capacities and a stable sense of identity.

For oppositional initiatives, including critical and emancipatory educational enquiries, the critique of rationalism and its promise of certainty unsettles one of the hopes of such initiatives, which is that individuals can, as a consequence of consciousness-raising practices, come to 'know' and 'understand'. In effect, this places oppositional social science programmes and the efforts of natural (positive) sciences on the same side of the coin. Hence, while social science programmes argued that their goal of 'understanding' was distinct from that of the natural sciences, which is 'explanation', what the social sciences failed to challenge was that which lies at the root of both positions: Enlightenment epistemology (Hekman 1990: 4).

From many positions, including those of 'woman' and 'feminist teacher' the Enlightenment project can be read as a series of disappointments. Hence, while it masqueraded itself as 'universal, rational, scientific and objective' (Singh 1995: 184) it was, and in many arenas still is, essentially masculinist. To put it slightly differently, disappointment in the Enlightenment resides in its own failings to realize its many desires, including those for 'certainty, clarity, illumination [and] generality' (Stronach and MacLure 1997: 5). In seeking to both respond to and oppose Enlightenment thinking, contemporary feminists have since the late 1960s, but more significantly during the 1970s, attempted to develop theories which would give fresh insights into a variety of organizational mechanisms. These include those that work at excluding and oppressing women within the social domain. Hence, for example, radical feminists looked to Marx in whose terms aspects of women's lives such as domestic labour as well as procreative and sexual work could be viewed and understood as 'value producing' and therefore subject to Marxian analysis (e.g. Dalla Costa and James 1975; Jagger 1983).

However, although the oppression of women is a material reality, this is perhaps a too limiting view and one that fails to encompass the question of sexual ideology. A material view, we believe, fails to make inroads into those ways men and women 'image' themselves and each other in a society where men are still the primary force (Eagleton 1983: 149). If feminist Marxism works only on a material basis and as a consequence does not engage with certain personal dimensions of human life, including sexism and gender roles, this, we feel, both weakens and deeply flaws its efforts to alleviate the subjugation of women.

Meanwhile, certain cultural feminists (e.g. Daly 1978) sought to invoke a universalizing conception of woman and as a consequence offer an essentialist response to misogyny and sexism through a conception of 'woman'. However, Alcoff (1988: 421) warns:

> Cultural feminism has provided a useful corrective to the 'generic human' thesis of classical liberalism and has promoted community and self-affirmation, but it cannot provide a long-range future course of action for feminist theory or practice, and it is founded on a claim of essentialism that we are far from having the evidence to justify.

The successes of cultural feminism is that it imbued and gave vigour and strength to certain traits which within the Enlightenment project went unrecognized – including, for example, the ability to nurture. But no new conceptions of 'woman' were offered. Instead, energies have been directed into challenging those definitions of 'woman' which were born out of male presumptions.

As Alcoff (1988: 407) says: 'For feminists ... it appears we have nowhere to turn'. So, where do we go next? Do we, for example, follow Habermas' suggestion, where we 'try to hold on to the intentions of the Enlightenment, feeble as they may be, or should we declare the whole project of modernity a lost cause?' (1985: 8–15).

Framing the conundrum

The belief in rationality, both a legacy of the Enlightenment project and a cornerstone of humanism, is a central target for postmodern thinking. The debate that was begun by Nietzsche is continued and developed further by postmodernists. In general terms, postmodernists propose that the foundationalism and absolutism of modernism is no longer an acceptable or appropriate way of understanding a world which has witnessed many changes. These include economic changes (the move from mass production to flexible specialization), political changes (the collapse of the Eastern European block and a lack of confidence in Marxism) and social changes (the so-called fragmentation of social classes as a consequence of marketing lifestyle niches). Furthermore, these upheavals, when combined with the communication explosion, particularly in the visual media of film and television, work at splintering social cohesion and coherence. This is replaced by 'cultural images and social forms and identities marked by fragmentation, multiplicity, plurality and indeterminacy' (Thompson 1992: 223).

In rejecting the privileging of rational thought as being the sole avenue to truth, theories of postmodernism argue against meta or grand narratives including the:

overarching philosophies of history like the Enlightenment story of the gradual but steady progress of reason and freedom, Hegel's dialectic of the Spirit coming to know itself, and, most importantly, Marx's drama of the forward march of human productive capacities via class conflict culminating in proletarian revolution.

(Fraser and Nicholson 1988: 86)

Not too surprisingly, in addition to rejecting the rational/irrational dichotomy, postmodernism also attacks all other dichotomies on which Enlightenment epistemology rests, including subject/object, reason/emotion and language/reality. Inevitably, what is also repudiated is the assumption embedded in these dichotomies – the idea of a 'coherent, unified self, a rationalist and individualist model of knowing and the possibilities of a metalanguage' (Hallberg 1992: 374).

Given such an assault on the discourse of progress, how is it possible to sustain projects such as educational action research and critical pedagogy? Does the embrace of postmodernism necessitate an abandonment of the emancipatory impulse? In other words, how can theories which make a point of both incorporating and accepting ephemerality, fragmentation, discontinuity and the chaotic (Harvey 1992: 258) contribute to a project which has as one of its concerns some notion of liberatory thought and action? Furthermore, if it is no longer tenable to aspire to a coherent and unified representation of the world, then what are the possibilities for developing an adequate political programme? As George McLennan asks, what is the point in doing social science at all when it all seems so purposeless? He writes: 'It seems to me that without some universal concepts, without some attempt to see the social world as an evolving totality, without some aspiration to better humanity through improving knowledge, I see no purpose whatever in doing social science at all' (1992: 353).

Following Habermas: holding on to the threads of rationality, hope and emancipation, or letting go?

Habermas' early work has had some influence on theoretical work on practitioner-oriented educational research, understood from a critical perspective (e.g. see Carr and Kemmis 1986). This perspective has since been challenged by Elliott (1987) who assumes a more Gadamerian perspective. For the moment we focus primarily on Habermas. In the next chapter we consider what a more Gadamerian approach might look like. In the subsequent chapter we hold them against each other as a prelude to challenging the supposed dichotomy and moving to a more fluid conception.

Habermas himself is all for trying to shore things up. Rather than abandoning the Enlightenment, he insists that it can be revisited: 'We think that instead of giving up modernity and its project as a lost cause, we should learn from the mistakes of those extravagant programmes which have tried to negate modernity' (1985: 8–15).

Accordingly, he has sought to outline a fundamental framework within which rational practical discourse can take place, by articulating the basic presuppositions of speech acts. He proposes a theory of communicative speech action. Thomas McCarthy (1982: 60) offers an overview of the theory:

> As Habermas sees it, the basic idea behind this approach is that speaking and acting subjects know how to achieve, accomplish, perform, produce a variety of things without explicitly adverting to, or being able to give an explicit account of, the structures, rules, criteria, schemata on which their performances are based. The aim of rational reconstruction is precisely to render explicit the structures and rules underlying much 'practically mastered, pre-theoretical know-how', the tacit knowledge that represents the subject's competence in a given domain . . . if the tacit, pre-theoretical knowledge that is to be reconstructed represents a universal know-how . . . our task is the reconstruction of a 'species competence'. Adopting this approach, Habermas advances a proposal for a universal or formal pragmatics.

McCarthy (1982: 255–6) continues:

> Communication that is orientated towards reaching understanding inevitably involves reciprocal raising and recognition of validity claims. Claims to truth and rightness, if radically challenged, can be redeemed only through argumentative discourse leading to rationally motivated consensus. Universal-pragmatic analysis of the conditions of discourse and rational consensus show these to rest on the supposition of an 'ideal speech situation' characterised by an effective equality of chances to assume dialogue roles.

Elsewhere, Habermas (1990: 89) spells out some of the 'rules' of communicative action. These include:

- Every person with the competence to speak and act is allowed to take part in the discourse.
- Everyone is allowed to question any assertion whatever.
- Everyone is allowed to introduce any assertion whatever into the discourse.
- Everyone is allowed to express his [sic] attitudes, desires and needs.
- No speaker may be prevented, by internal or external coercion, from exercising his rights as laid down (above).

Given all these procedures it is then possible, so the argument goes, to have understanding, truth, sincerity and correctness (Safstrom 1998: 3), and thus let the best idea win.

It is, we think, apparent from this brief excursion into aspects of Habermas' work why his theories hold appeal to practitioner research enquiries. Habermas clearly holds onto modernity's quest for the 'good life'. Additionally, he maps out both the route and the vehicle – that is, language – towards attaining those prerequisites (understanding, truth, sincerity and correctness) which characterize 'goodness': 'The speaker as well as the spoken to, must both embrace these rules in order to be able to reach intersubjective understanding. This is the goal for conversation' (Safstrom 1998: 3).

However, does the communicative thesis hold? Can emancipatory potentials be built within the very structure of language? Can language redeem the project of modernity? Is a theory which has a preference 'for a kind of argument which places logic over rhetoric, the rationalistic over the metaphorical' (Rasmussen 1990: 111) able to accommodate the challenge of 'the diverse and disorderly others' (Hartsock 1987: 195)? Can the 'Enlightenment project', which is after all a metaphor, be redeemed by logic? Can communicative action accommodate the complexities of difference?

Safstrom (1998: 3) thinks not. In his view Habermas' theory:

tends to deal with difference as a prerequisite for conversations. While it does so, the difference is supposed at the same time to vanish, to be dealt with and to be exceeded in favour of a harmonisation of opinions and stands. This is accomplished through the generality of communicative rationality and its universalism . . . [theory] on this stand is risking to violate difference through treating it as a temporary state of affairs which by necessity should be unified and transgressed. The question of what, for example, are being excluded in the process of unification becomes secondary in relation to this very unity.

Clearly, notions of 'difference' are highly problematic. Flax (1990: 42) argues that feminist notions of self, knowledge and truth are too contra-dictory to those of the Enlightenment to be contained within its categor-ies. She writes: 'the way(s) to feminist future(s) cannot lie in reviving or appropriating Enlightenment concepts of the person or knowledge'.

In a similar vein, Huyssen (1981: 38) offers the following succinct critique:

The critical deconstruction of Enlightenment rationalism and logocentrism by theoreticians of culture, the decentering of tradi-tional notions of identity, the fight of women and gays from a legitimate social and sexual identity outside of the parameters of male, heterosexual vision, the search for alternatives in our relationship with nature, including the nature of our own bodies – all these phenomena, which are key to the culture of the 1970s, make Habermas' proposition to complete the project of modernity questionable, if not undesirable.

Within the traditions and movements of action research and reflective practice, becoming aware or critical (Carr and Kemmis 1986) is a prerequisite to resistance. What this necessitates, however, is an acquiescence to the consequences of the rule of reason (Parker 1997: 44). Then the thinking and actions of the autonomous individual will be independent of the prescriptions or arbitrary directions of authorities 'and based instead on reason' (Dearden 1968: 46).

However, one recurring and nagging question, which is asked throughout this book, is whether there are possibilities for other stories to be told. Must there only be linear narratives where the 'beginning, middle and end' schema works at bringing stories to a close? What other options are available within critical education besides victory or liberatory narratives? Put a little differently, can we, as Derrida (in Kearney 1984: 122) suggests, have 'another language besides that of political liberation' and one which is not driven by the powerhouse of rationality? It seems clear from Derrida's remark that he feels that there is such a need, but what does he mean by 'another language'?

Derrida's question can, we believe, be perceived as a representation of 'another language besides that of political liberation'. It is a language of possibilities rather than certainties, where the task of bestowing meanings is left to 'anyone' rather than the authorial 'one'. Language, as we have tried to illustrate, is problematic. Its meanings are neither singular nor straightforward. Yet it seems that in order for language to be used to secure rational ends, all the illogical and unruly aspects of its nature have to be subsumed, kept covered or ignored. Derrida's question can be read, we are suggesting, as a plea or maybe a demand that there are other ways of 'languaging'; ways which refuse to be closed off or bounded by those binary oppositions that have 'traditionally promised the comforts of certainty to philosophical thinking' (Stronach and MacLure 1997: 5).

But what is meant by 'another language'. Does this imply a complete abandonment of the 'language of political liberation'? The meanings which surround 'another' make, we believe, a yes/no answer impossible. Perhaps what Derrida is implying is that we have to be mindful of all the meanings that are carried by 'another'. Maybe 'another language' does not infer a complete break; rather it implies a form of departure where there is then the space 'to question the assumptions which a discipline or field takes to be self evident' (Stronach and MacLure 1997: 3). This would include the field of political liberation. Hence, when working within the language of political liberation, a task would be to seek out and identify those ways in which the text works at glossing over or repressing the unruliness of language in order to sustain the univocal reading.

As an example, many teachers in the UK recently spent a week of their vacation preparing an application for an extra allowance in their salary. They needed to prepare their case within a framework outlined by the DfEE (Department for Education and Employment). This resulted in them reflecting on and describing aspects of their practice, but through an externally provided filter which understood teaching in the way that the DfEE preferred teaching to be understood. In a subsequent conversation with a DfEE official, Tony questioned whether the week, spent by so many teachers in preparing their case, could in itself be seen as a valuable staff development exercise. The official's response unsurprisingly was in the affirmative. Our caution would first be in questioning whether such compulsory exercises can be seen as development. Second, we would see the exercise as the DfEE seeking to assert more control over how teachers describe their practice, whether this be restricted to filling in a form, or perhaps applying and being interviewed for a job, or partaking and being successful in other government sponsored staff 'development' exercises. Were we to import into this question the issue of 'political liberation' we might understand it in terms of how teachers detect and resist the conception of teaching embedded within the DfEE framing of the job of a teacher.

But what are the methodological implications as a consequence of this 'departure', this 'other language'? How does the practitioner-researcher proceed if not along the straight and narrow path? Perhaps the answer is to undertake further play with the line which works at separating out the subject from the object, the rational from the irrational and the logical from the illogical. Maybe the scenario is not one where the practitioner turns their back on notions of political liberation, but rather turns because it allows different perspectives to emerge. Our approach is not characterized by linearity. Rather, its features can be caught by expressions such as 'toing and froing', 'back and forth' and 'in and out', all of which could put us in mind of weaving.

For now, we wish to pursue the hermeneutic foundations of action research a little more to see how they might be responsive to a little nudging and poking. In the next chapter we introduce an approach leaning on Gadamer, a figure famous both for his key work in contemporary hermeneutics and for his capacity to have disputes with both Habermas and Derrida, while somehow mediating the ground (or absence of ground) between them.

Part  1

The hermeneutic backdrop: narrating the researcher

3

Creating data in practitioner research

From Habermas to Gadamer

Socialism, feminism, equity and improving teaching cannot just be thrown out as impossible dreams. We find ourselves still wanting to hold onto our emancipatory aspirations despite knowing about all of the flaws. Similarly, we cannot 'just say No to the postmodern subject, the one in whose fragility and fragmentation so much energy has been invested' (Steedman 2001: 45). It seems that as researchers we may need intermediate aspirations to hold on to prior to pursuing broader deconstructive ambitions. For example, in working with masters and research students it seems appropriate to engage with existing practitioner research approaches prior to examining how they do not function in the way they may first appear. Critical aspirations examined through an action research frame provide a good backdrop to a more radical reappraisal of educational research practices and the outcomes of such work. Thus with misgivings about Habermas on the table we pursue him a little further. First we examine his impact on educational practitioner research via a key textbook for practitioner researchers. Second we consider a critique of this book, influenced by his key adversary within hermeneutics, Gadamer. It is through Gadamer, and his famous dispute with Habermas, that we begin to loosen the shackles of a critical hermeneutical project and enter a more fluid linguistic realm (cf. Brown 1996, 1997).

In an influential book, Carr and Kemmis (1986) applied Habermas' early work in examining how teachers might define critical education ventures. This provided an approach to analysing attempts by teachers to articulate their understanding of their own practice with a view to creating strategies for developing this practice and moving to new ways of understanding what they are doing. Habermas (1972: 308–11) identified three 'knowledge constitutive interests' that operate in making sense of one's task, and for Carr and Kemmis this framework provided a way of viewing the levels at which a teacher can intervene in his or her practice. The first of these is the interest of achieving *technical* control. This relates to 'means-ends' strategies (e.g. 'If you set homework for students they will understand the classwork better'). However, this sort of control has limited value in so far as it comprises techniques supposedly available to everyone. Habermas, while recognizing the power of such a scientific approach, claimed that theoretical stances need to offer more than a technological control over practice, since the individual needs to understand the functioning of such techniques within their own personal style of practice.

The practical interest arises in a practitioner getting to know their professional situation through being involved in it. This entails both increasing familiarity and personal reflection, where the practitioner seeks to understand how they are functioning within their specific job. This *practical* knowledge of teaching is embedded within a history of understanding teaching practice, and the specific strategies that the practitioner employs within it. Developing practice requires a reconciliation between new understandings of what the practitioner is currently doing and the practical modifications these may imply.

Finally, the *emancipatory* interest may be seen as the quest to break free of the ideological distortions intrinsic to the language itself. Habermas was influenced by Freud in his understanding of how language sometimes has an uneasy relationship with the reality it seeks to portray. As Habermas (1976: 349) puts it:

> Freud dealt with the occurrence of systematically deformed communication in order to define the scope of specifically incomprehensible acts and utterances. He always envisaged the dream as the standard example of such phenomena, the latter including everything from harmless, everyday pseudo-communication and Freudian slips to pathological manifestations of neurosis, psychosis, and psychosomatic disturbance. In his essays on cultural theory, Freud broadened the range of phenomena which could be conceived as being part of systematically distorted communication. He employed the insights gained from clinical phenomena as the key to the pseudo-normality, that is to the hidden pathology, of collective behaviour and entire social systems.

The emancipatory interest adopts a critical attitude to the language that we use in describing our professional practice. We must be sensitive to how certain styles of speech display the 'hidden exercise of force' (Ricoeur 1981: 78). For example, in so far as recent government reforms in the UK have affected the language which teachers use in describing their teaching, an emancipatory aspect of knowing may be the attempt to step outside of this frame to view alternatives and perhaps critically examine how such a language serves the people who created it.

John Elliott has responded to Carr and Kemmis's (1986) formulation. Unlike Carr and Kemmis however, Elliott (1987) prefers to follow Gadamer. Habermas and Gadamer were engaged in a long-running and very famous dispute that will be discussed in more detail in the next chapter. Elliott follows Gadamer in rejecting the notion that one can step outside language to do a critical take on it. He prefers to see teacher development as an ongoing hermeneutic process reconciling experience with ways of describing it. While embracing technical and practical interest, he replaces any notion of an emancipatory quest with the notion of an *evolutionary* interest (Elliott 1993b: 197). The teacher cannot merely operate on the classroom situation with a view to changing it. The teacher is necessarily integral to that change – immersed in the very discourses which describe the change. In addressing specific professional concerns the teacher may choose to introduce theoretical perspectives, but for theory to be used in a meaningful way there is a need to build in a self-reflexive dimension which positions the evolving individual in their evolving professional situation. Within this frame, theoretical understanding might be seen as both informing and being derived from this reflective (hermeneutic) process. As Winter (1989: 261) puts it, ' "theory" cannot simply be derived from data, but is always the outcome of a process in which researchers must explore, organise and integrate their own and other's theoretical resources as an interpretive response to data'.

In this way, Elliott (1987, 1993b) criticizes Habermas' model which, he suggests, implies a motivation of moving from a bad state of affairs to a good state of affairs and replaces it with a model more focused on an ongoing hermeneutic process of substituting successive accounts. We are not so much concerned with emancipation from a particular social tradition to a new one free of ideological distortion but rather involved in the rewriting and reconstitution of the tradition in an ongoing way. This avoids the risk present in Habermas' approach where the individual is simply initiated into another 'distorted' ideology, or the risk of setting up idealism as an unachievable goal. The task for Elliott is to construct stories which resonate with the ways in which things are seen. In addressing the changes in practice the central task is not to learn new techniques but rather to locate oneself in one's own current practice and build a notion of a way forward. As such we are not engaged in a project with an end but rather in a process that always moves forwards, built around a dialectic of action and description of it (Brown 1997: 175–6).

Elliott's approach will be helpful in pursuing our analysis, not least since we propose that for an idea to be more than an ideal we need to have an understanding of how its own implementation is built into it.

Theory generation is often about establishing ideals to aim for. An altern- ative is to emphasize and problematize the immediate; deciding how to shape the next step from the one we are currently taking.

In this chapter we work from our initial premise that the practitioner researching in their classroom brings about changes both through acting in the classroom itself and in producing writing commenting on class- room practice. That is, descriptions of classroom practice, made by the practitioner, effect changes in the reality attended to by the practitioner. We suggest that actual professional practices, and the ways in which these are described, influence each other. The writing generated in this process can be seen as both responding to past action and guiding future action. In engaging in this circular hermeneutic process, teacher-researchers pass through a sequence of perspectives, each capable of generating various types of writing and each susceptible to a variety of later interpretations. We examine how such writing can be seen as data stimulating this process. In particular, we show how writing produced within such work itself becomes scrutinized as an integral aspect of practice and instrumental in the process of self-reflexive practitioner-led change. In doing this we employ a method based on the linguistic model of Saussure ([1959] 1974), an approach often referred to by poststructuralist writers – for example, Derrida and Lacan (cf. Brown 1996). In this model, absolute understandings of any individual piece of writing are not sought but rather each successive piece added modifies the flavour of the growing collection. We show how this emphasis on writing can be instrumental in promoting the development of professional practice (cf. Elliott 1987, 1993b: 197). Further, we offer examples of how the seeking of future pieces of writing can heighten awareness of significant moments of prac- tice as they arise. We suggest that this offers a first step in distancing the subject depicted in the writing from the 'being' generating it.

A chain of stories

In engaging in educational research we are invariably engaged in a task of capturing the experience of the research process in some tangible and collectible form. Depending on the style of research in question this might include: extracts of people's speech, statistical analyses, lesson plans, examples of children's work, presentations or critiques of theoretical positions, interpretations of data, etc. In developing or reporting on a research enquiry there is a need to find ways of looking back on this tangible product in deciding how best to select and combine components of it in creating further tangible product. We wish to propose a model for describing the research process based on the notion of it being seen as the production of a sequence of pieces of writing. This is based on the premise that the accountability of research activity, and the orienting and fixing of statements made in respect of this activity, is closely associated with the production of writing. The task of this chapter then is to focus on the generation by the researcher of this sequence of pieces of writing.

In examining this model we introduce a theoretical framework based on Saussure's model of linguistics. For Saussure ([1959] 1974: 120), working at the turn of the century, a word in a text does not have meaning in itself but rather derives its meaning from its relation to the words around it. To understand the meaning of a text we need to understand how the individual words interrelate. Saussure takes as his unit of analysis 'the word'. Meaning is derived from a succession of words and so is defined relationally where the meaning of words depends on the words around them – for example, Sarah *Green, Green*peace, the grass is *green*, he's a little *green* in such matters (cf. McNamara 1995). Seen in this way, particular words are not held in stable meaning relations with particular things.

This idea has become a guiding principle within some poststructuralist writing. Derrida's use of this notion is encapsulated in his use of the term *differance* – a play on the French words for deferral and difference. For him (e.g. Derrida 1992: 101–32), the meaning of a text is always *deferred* since the play of *differences* between the terms is never finally resolved. Derrida (e.g. 1978: 278–93) seems to be suggesting that since long ago we have been describing the world such that our way of describing has taken on a life of its own. We always end up describing previous descriptive structurings. Within more traditional hermeneutics (e.g. Ricoeur), although we can build a picture of reality, we can never access this reality directly; language always intervenes. Derrida meanwhile dispenses with such understandings of reality since for him they are meaningless without the linguistic layer, created as it is presently but according to inherited categories. For example, Derrida (1994) has discussed how our understandings of the present are conditioned by the media through which we receive depictions of it. He claims that actuality is *made* and that virtuality ('virtual images, virtual spaces, and therefore virtual outcomes' – 1994: 29) is no longer distinguishable from actual reality: 'The "reality" of "actuality" – however individual, irreducible, stubborn, painful or tragic it may be – only reaches us through fictional devices' (1994: 2). Nevertheless, he carefully distances himself from the more extreme position of Baudrillard whose stance is encapsulated in *The Gulf War Did Not Take Place* (1995). Here Baudrillard argues that the war as understood by most people became a media event largely unhinged from the suffering of the participants.

In this chapter we are experimenting with making an analogy between the sequence of words in a text and a sequence of pieces of writing produced within a research enquiry. That is, the meaning of a research enquiry is a function of how the different pieces of writing are seen as interrelating. Thus seen, the process of building a research enquiry is inextricably linked with the process of generating new pieces of writing. This strategy promotes a multiple play of meaning derived through juxtaposing the various written accounts offered (Urmson and Ree 1989: 311). Absolute meanings are not sought. Rather, meaning evolves or gets generated differently as new contributions are introduced. Clearly, this sort of approach is not about 'picturing' reality in the way of Russell (e.g. 1914) or the early Wittgenstein (1961). For those engaged in practitioner research this textual analysis can offer an instrument for monitoring practice and an approach to uniting thinking with action through reflection (cf. Silcock 1994: 278). Writing has a tangible product and offers an approach to accounting for the reality to which we attend.

The parameters of the space for professional action are negotiable, as is what can be done within them. Both this space and how it is seen are governed by the language used in describing it and, we will argue here, this can be operated on through the medium of text. Writing can be used to tell a story about what is going on. There are, however, many ways of doing this and practitioners can seek to be creative in developing productive ways of seeing their practice through this medium. Nevertheless, although such an approach has a liberating feel to it, there is a sobering aspect to this account of poststructuralism that we need to guard against in examining the relationship between a text and that which it seems to describe. As indicated above, any accounts offered by individuals *speak* the society from which they come and have, built within the language itself, layers of assumptions endemic in that society's view of the world (cf. Foucault 1972; Habermas 1985, 1987). The social values we may wish to bring into question can be embedded deeply within the fabric of the society's way of talking about things. There cannot be a clearly defined boundary between creating and inheriting ways of seeing things. The parameters individuals confront and the way they are understood are conditioned by social norms. These norms might, for example, embrace the tradition of understanding teacher practice through positivistic models (Olson 1995). Such norms can serve to constrain the individual's sense of what is possible, or realistic, in their own particular situation (cf. Buchmann 1987).

The meaning of a story

Here we propose the hypothesis that the meaning of a story is dependent on its usage, by someone, in another story. If, as a researcher, I produce a piece of writing, its meaning is dependent on how it relates to other pieces of writing collected in the enquiry and to the enquiry as a whole as it currently exists. This relationship, however, is not resolvable in an absolute way. The way in which any two pieces of writing relate to each other is dependent on my understanding of my current task. This will evolve through time as I pass through a variety of perspectives on what I am doing. In his discussion of Ricoeur's work on hermeneutics, Thompson (1981) suggests that the meaning of an action is related to how it is described. The sort of actions we wish to focus on are the productions of pieces of writing within practitioner research. Following Thompson we suggest that the meanings of such productions are dependent on how they are understood and referred to in other pieces of writing. Each piece of writing produced functions in a particular way in relation to the others. None has an absolute meaning since another story can always be placed alongside. They support different new stories according to how they are used subsequently (cf. Sanger 1994). A space is inserted between the event and the description of it. By creating sets of stories relating to practice, the author produces points of reference which enable them to orient subsequent practice in relation to characterizations of past practice.

Framing in the voice of another: creating and validating data

In discussing the issue of generating pieces of writing as data within practitioner research we wish to offer some examples resulting from work by students on the masters course, described earlier, at the Manchester Metropolitan University where we both now work. Our particular concern is with how pieces of writing reporting on practice become data within practitioner research enquiry.

The course does not have a syllabus as such, given its intention of enabling teachers to develop their own framework of analysis. This is expressed clearly in the course documentation:

> The course ideology is concerned with what Aristotle called phronesis – practical knowledge or wisdom. Such understanding is not reducible to technicalities or technical knowledge because praxis cannot be reduced to means/ends analyses. Because the course experiences are radically constrained by *concepts* of practicality its intellectual origins lie in pragmatism and in continental philosophy in its concern with the phenomenology of lived experience. The hermeneutic enterprise has to begin, we believe, with 'finding one's own experience'.
>
> (Pearce and Pickard 1994: 34)

This attitude is reflected in the approach taken to assessing students' written work where there is an attempt to minimize imposed structures and assumptions. For example, the assessment of the final dissertation attends to criteria where the emphasis is on students building their own defence of their work through what is intended to be a relatively neutral frame:

1 *Conceptual understanding:* the student's capacity to understand and explain their own professional beliefs and practices.
2 *Research methodology:* the student's enquiry is systematic.
3 *Intellectual context:* reference to relevant debates in current educational research and related fields in analysing the student's own specific concerns.
4 *Local professional situation:* pertinent analysis of the student's own professional situation – for example, their school.
5 *Broader professional context:* pertinent analysis of the student's broader educational context.
6 *Strategic implications:* evidence of developmental engagement with practical professional concerns.
7 *Professional intent:* evidence of the student identifying his or her own wider professional development within the course and outlining the implications this has for future practice.

Teachers attend one evening a week over a three-year period, working closely with a group of a dozen or so peers. Teachers entering the third year of the course will have compiled a huge body of writing – a mixture of small and big pieces, formal and informal, transcripts, lesson plans, anecdotes, responses to reading, responses to sessions, etc. A principal task during this year is to consolidate and extend this work so that it becomes more clearly targeted on a specific theme for focused enquiry. The task of constructing such a theme serves as a guiding principle for third-year work and, in particular, in the production of a dissertation at the end of the year. A strategy employed in the first few weeks of the third year is specifically directed towards the clarification of this theme and with how pieces of writing function within it.

First, the teachers are requested to choose a small piece of work (maximum of one page), written in the past, which they see as having some resonance with their chosen theme, as they currently see it emerging. Second, having selected this they are asked to set up a situation in their teaching during the following week which will result in another piece of writing which they see as being about working on this theme. At the following week's session they bring the two pieces, old and new, together with their proposed title as they currently see it. The next session begins with these pieces of writing being circulated to all sub-group members. Each person is asked to write a paragraph about the three pieces which explains how the reader sees the two pieces of writing being concerned with working on the given title. Upon receiving these paragraphs the writer is asked to make a statement about their proposed theme, and how they see themselves working on it in a way which makes explicit reference to the comments made by their sub-group colleagues (cf. Francis 1995: 235–6). This statement then forms the basis for the next cycle. It is through this process that the structures inherent in the writing become *realized* in *formatting* actual practice.

Below are pieces of writing produced by teachers working within this frame. First we offer pieces of writing by Terry Gould (1995): an old and a new piece, the title guiding the selection and production of these; a tutor response; an example of a peer response; and a revised statement with a comment on it.

Extract A (from the old piece)

Susan's mum and I chatted whilst Susan selected a felt pen and began to write her name on our Welcome Board. Susan's mum and I watched and after showing interest in her writing Susan's mum initiated further conversation with a comment about how well she felt Susan was doing with her writing, saying she could see a substantial improvement in the way she was forming her letters.

There is a traditional expectation . . . that teachers are a little reserved and unapproachable, except on their terms, which is considered part of the institution of teaching and its professionalism . . . Even though I feel more traditional teachers would prefer me to remain shackled by this tradition within the profession I want to, and feel the need to, shake off part of it which keeps parents and teachers at a distance.

Extract B (from the new piece)

Parent: He keeps on wanting me to get him a kite.
Teacher: Have you thought of making one with him?
Parent: I did but I haven't got any stuff and anyway, I'm not sure how you do it. With him having no dad it's a bit awkward for things like that.
Teacher: Well there are lots of ways of making kites and you don't necessarily need lots of expensive materials. You could even make one out of an old newspaper, some Sellotape, string and a plastic bag.
Parent: Do you hear that Nigel, Mr G is going to show us how to make a kite!
Teacher [*Thinking to myself what a big mouth I've got and I am really in a hurry tonight*]*:* Well all you need is to roll up a newspaper in thin tight rolls like this and use sellotape to fix them. Then you cut out a kite shape such as a large diamond out

of an opened out plastic bag and fasten them all together with Sellotape.

Parent: You couldn't make one for us could you? I'm not very good at practical things like that . . . Nigel would really love that . . . Wouldn't you Nigel?

Title

'United we stand, divided we fall: An exploration of dialogue between parents and teachers'.

Tutor response

The first piece is written in fairly general terms which means we can only talk about what you might do next in similarly general terms. The second piece however, is much more specific and we can become much clearer about your use of wording and the sort of effect it has and how you might work on changing it. The second piece offers real substance that you can refer back to and helps me be clearer about your task which seems to be to do with developing ways of talking to parents so as to enable them to participate more fully in the schooling process for their child.

Peer responses (extracts)

The little chats are about you controlling the agenda – trying to get parents to think your way . . . The mother in the new story has turned the tables on you. She has you hooked rather than you being in control . . . You will need to rely on others' perspectives much more than your own. Transcripts seem a good starting point in this area but how you can take the matter forward seems quite difficult . . . where are you coming from?

Revised title

Action research to illuminate and problematize the main areas involved in developing home-school communication with particular reference to dialogue between parents and teachers at the nursery stage.

Comment

I feel my revised title now gives more insight into the research being undertaken. I realise the difficulties (as identified) as the research involves accessing the perceptions of others and analysing these in a very clear and objective way.

In this process the author uses earlier pieces of writing, and responses to them by peers, as points of reference in creating new pieces, under the umbrella of the revised thematic title. By reassessing past writing in the light of peer response he becomes clearer about the way in which he might generate, and work with, new pieces.

The act of writing is inevitably associated with an act of reading. In writing, this student needs some understanding of how his writing will be read and understood by others. In conversing with others, resonance is important and feedback is valuable in building one's research findings with an audience in mind. I show my understanding of your story by offering a related story. I substitute your example for another in an attempt to emphasize and extend your point, but also to see how it fits with my own experience. In doing this I bring meaning to your story for myself and perhaps, in revealing my perspective, shift the way in which you understand the significance of your own story (cf. Cryns and Johnston 1993: 149–52).

Such a dialogue conditions the way in which subsequent action is planned and reported on. Another technique employed within the course described above is to examine how ideas sound through the voice of another person. Subgroup colleagues are frequently invited to make comments on someone's writing or verbal delivery so that the writer/speaker can hear themselves being 'played back' through the voice of another. It may also be that someone from another subgroup or a 'spare' tutor might be 'borrowed' to witness this summary and to write a one-sentence statement which for them encapsulates the summary. The original speaker is then asked to make a statement saying how they see their original statement differing.

The function of these exercises within the research process is to integrate writing into the framing of the research enquiry. The writing produced in respect of the enquiry is not only about mapping the action on the ground: 'reporting' what 'is happening'. Writing is an integral part of the action being described. It provides a way of framing experience in a fixed form so as to pin down some aspects of this process with a view to orienting the process. In doing this the writing itself becomes part of the substance of the research enquiry. Like the actions in the classroom it becomes part of the 'thing' being reported on. The conceptions in the writing become *realized* as they frame actual practice. Further, writing *formats* the reality attended to for future action (including future writing). As a consequence, classroom practice by the individual becomes increasingly conditioned by the linguistic framings being brought to it by them (cf. Schon 1983). For example, in having selected an old piece of writing with a view to creating a new piece the teachers are structuring a piece of actual practice for the purposes of creating a new account. There is embedded within this an attempt at creating a resonance between actual practice and ways of describing it. Practice and description of it become mutually formative in a hermeneutic relation. This will be developed in the next section where we explore further how practitioner research might be oriented around change in this way.

Understanding, monitoring and influencing change

Another important function of such exercises is to enable the researcher to become aware of how their research is developing. Of particular concern to someone in the middle of action-oriented research is where to go next. It entails going through a sequence of different perspectives, where each perspective is informed and flavoured by those which have preceded it. The next step cannot be preplanned since, often, I will not understand the circumstances until I am confronted by immediate possibilities. In practitioner research, which downplays any notion of a detailed over-arching plan, I need to be rigorous in making the next step. Mason (e.g. 1992) has, for example, completed work directed at the task of being *inside* a problem. He has addressed a variety of types of problem, both within mathematics and within practitioner research and professional development. In particular he has worked on the task of 'deciding what to do next'. A key aspect of his work is learning to recognize in current problem situations characteristics one has experienced before. This might be seen as being a task in assessing the environment in problem situations so that features of current situations might be associated with past ways of reaching a resolution. In this chapter, pieces of writing are being offered as a way of marking the environment of the teaching problem and thus providing an orienting framework. This is akin to the work of Dockar-Drysdale (1991: 98–111) with emotionally deprived adolescents (cf. Brown 1994b). For these children, who experienced difficulties in orienting themselves in their everyday lives, the teacher employed a technique of helping them create and remember stories to which they could return, so as to provide points of reference for new stories. Employed within practitioner research this technique provides textual constructions against which the meaning of new stories can be constructed – the meaning of the new stories being relational to those already in place. Such a framework can become instrumental in understanding how practice is changing.

A formulation offered by Schütz pinpoints the different sorts of motivation underpinning such change. Any action can be seen as having both a responsive and intentional component. That is, any action simultaneously has a cause and is a cause. In dealing with this, Schütz (1962: 21–2) draws a distinction between 'in-order-to' and 'because' motives to separate two different sets of concepts:

(a) We may say that the motive of a murderer was to obtain the money of the victim. Here 'motive' means the state of affairs, the end, which is to be brought about by the action undertaken. We shall call this kind of motive the 'in-order-to motive' . . .

(b) We may say that the murderer has been motivated to commit his deed because he grew up in this or that environment, had these or those childhood experiences etc. This class of motives which we shall call '. . . because motives' refers from the point of view of the actor to his past experiences which have determined him to act as he did.

It is often tempting for teachers to emphasize 'because' motives in describing their professional situation. Here the emphasis is on the situation as they see it; how the school operates, what the teachers and children are like, their views on the school administration, how they judge themselves as teachers, etc. The school is constructed according to the categories through which it is perceived by the practitioner as an observer and participant. Such accounts are perhaps seductive, especially for in-service practitioners on an evening course wishing to offload after a hard day teaching in school. Such accounts tend to locate the teacher as a recipient of a given situation. In the turmoil of things happening in a stressful day, accounts of how the world appears seem more immediately pressing than a reflective response concerned with identifying the intentional component of what the teacher did. The fatalism endemic in such teacher accounts can be seen as disempowering where the teacher is passively receiving what is thrown at them. Their accounts emphasize their response rather than their resolve.

How might we enable the practitioner to redescribe their situation in terms of what they can do about it? This is to do with building a more assertive voice, categorizing their practice according to the control they see themselves having over it. Given a particular situation, how do I act now? The focus moves towards responsibility and control. The task for the practitioner becomes more to do with learning about how they do things in certain situations. Accounts now capture the practitioner's view of their intentional and potential actions rather than descriptions of arbitrarily chosen situations. The picture the practitioner constructs of themselves becomes one of someone making decisions about how they need to act, 'in order to' bring about a certain state of affairs.

To pursue a developmental path within practitioner research there is a need to build an understanding of change. We suggest the task of such practitioner research enquiry might be seen as first to conceptualize this change, second to monitor it against this conceptualization and third to influence it. We propose to address this here by positing a notion of change as evidenced through markers separated by time. Such a marker in this instance will be a piece of writing within the research process.

For the classroom practitioner there are many strands evident in change. Further, the researcher's perspective of this change is susceptible to change, as is their way of describing it. In the classroom the children change because they get older, because of changes of teaching style, because ways of monitoring their progress change. The teacher changes because they get better (or worse!) with practice, because they bring new structures to their ways of describing their lessons, because the children change etc. For the teacher-researcher, change is something of which you are part, something you observe and something you report on. There is a need to experience yourself as part of it before you can report on it. Making sense is done retroactively. Pieces of writing can function as markers in time, capturing how things are seen at a particular moment. By comparing pieces of writing produced at different junctures the writer can understand how certain things have evolved. As an example we offer three extracts appearing together in the final dissertation of Anna Perry (1994).

Extract A

I want the children to do well at school. I want them to achieve the goals of reading, writing and arithmetic. I want them to gain social skills too and be able to cooperate and express themselves ... Children who are still struggling to form letters or read simple words cause me concern. I feel as if I cannot be doing my job properly at times, not reaching them.

Extract B

We operate in different discourses depending on need. On my part, the need to be seen as a teacher with good control, or, and often at the same time, the teacher who fosters discovery through active learning and rationality. As a result I categorise children according to that need. My guilt comes from the fact that I recognise when I am not operating as the passive, facilitating teacher and feel that the way I am behaving is therefore wrong. It is wrong because I am operating more within the shadow side of child-centredness, that of the old pedagogy of chalk and talk and authoritarianism. I see this behaviour of mine as a danger sign which threatens. It threatens because it goes against the morality of child-centredness – the fair equal way, where the teacher does not have the right to oppress the children.

Comparison of the two pieces

The most obvious change I see in these two pieces of writing is a move from looking purely at what I do or do not do towards an attempt within a theoretical framework to explain my actions and feelings. The first piece of writing places me immediately within the feelings I had about my classroom and teaching at that time. It feels anxious and angst ridden, the latter piece reads far more object-ively, the self condemnation replaced by a more analytical attempt to understand.

In the first piece, the teacher grapples with her perceived difficulty in managing a child-centred environment. In the second, the philosophy of teaching underpinning the first description is examined. In the third, the two earlier pieces are compared and contrasted as pieces of writing. A new meaning is brought to them by a teacher now able to say more about the limitations of her earlier perspective. Taken together the three pieces evidence changes in writing style, changes in her perception of her teaching, changes in her perception of how her writing functions. There is an ongoing attempt to switch between adopting an insider stance on how things are experienced and giving a retroactive account of how earlier first person accounts arose. The teacher is concerned with understanding a more sophisticated version of self; a self understood as evolving through time. Linguistic instability is a necessary consequence since the evolving subject cannot see herself from a fixed point.

In another example, Lorraine Dooley focused initially on her ques-tioning strategies within her mathematics teaching (cf. Brown 1997). The work for this took place over just one term. Lorraine documented aspects of her teaching strategies with a particular emphasis on possible connections between her teaching style and the nature of pupil inter-actions. Dooley (1994: 38–40) sets out her stall by introducing her con-cerns over her teaching of mathematics:

> The tension which emerged is that although I feel I encourage children to exercise some control in certain areas of the curriculum, I assume tighter control, mainly in mathematics. So there are times when the way the curriculum learning is managed blatantly denies the children a sense of ownership. Do these instances contradict, and therefore counteract, what I am trying to encourage and are there-fore, equally or even more important aims that I feel take priority? Do I believe that there is a curriculum which exists independently of the children? . . . If I value responsibility and ownership in other areas . . . How can I enhance the development of these desirable qualities in other areas of the curriculum over which I have tighter control?
>
> I made the following statement, after producing evidence and talking about situations in the classroom which I perceived as children developing autonomy: 'There are still things I need to teach them (the children) especially in Maths'. This was quickly jumped on by the tutor when he asked 'Why? Why do you feel you need to

"teach" them?' The question stupefied me somewhat, but I answered: 'Because by teaching the children "new" mathematical concepts, which sometimes has to be didactically, they would have a good grounding or base for the more open-ended mathematical activities and problems presented at a later stage'. The discussion progressed and I argued that I did encourage thinking in the children, by my use of questioning, which I viewed as more 'open-ended' than 'closed' type or reversing questions asked. However, I was encouraged to explore the notion that children can find things out for themselves, even in maths and therefore create opportunities for extending these boundaries that I had erected for myself. I therefore started to look closely at my teaching practices in maths and explored the different ways I could influence the nature of the decision making process, with particular reference to my interactions with children.

Dooley (1994: 40–50) offers some transcripts capturing some of her dialogue with children:

Teacher:	What number do you multiply first?
Lisa:	The 2.
Teacher:	Why the 2 Lisa?
Lisa:	Because the 2 is in the units column, so we multiply the units first.
Teacher [*nodding*]:	Good.
Kim:	Can you see whether I'm doing this right . . .
Teacher:	Can you tell me what you've been doing with the ones you have already done?
Kim:	Well, for these I set them out on some paper like this [*starts to write H T U*] . . . then I put the numbers in under here like this . . . then I added them . . . like this.
Teacher:	That looks fine to me Kim. How could you check them?
Kim:	Use the calculator.
Teacher [*smiling*]:	There you've answered your problem yourself, haven't you?
Kim:	Yes.
[A little later]	
Teacher:	Well remembering what you've just done for 76 × 4, can you do the same for 76 × 20 here?
Ben:	Yes I know . . . we can put the 1520 here and then put an arrow showing 76 × 20 here. Is that right?
Teacher:	Good. Well done!

These brief extracts show children asking direct questions and being given more direct answers, utterances and positive gestures (e.g. smiling or nodding of the head) and showing my approval at what they have done (e.g. Good! That looks fine to me. Well done!). In these instances I cannot really gain an understanding into what the children are thinking because they are answering direct questions.

This material was brought to a college session and discussed with colleagues. Here is another extract from Dooley's dissertation (pp. 42–4):

As I begin to modify my teaching style, I adopt a different questioning technique and it becomes a more powerful tool for encouraging children to think, calling for more thought and explanations, calling for analytical reasoning and informed judgment. Some data collected a few weeks later, illustrates this.

Some examples of teacher speech from a long transcript

– How are you doing these Kim?
– Why? Tell me why you thought that?
– . . . but how did you arrive at 11×11?
– Yes, I understand that but . . .
– So what's a square number?
– Well, David said that 11 is a square number. Do you agree with him?
– Can you tell David what you think a square number is then?
– Do you understand that David?
– Fine. Just see if you can discover what a square number is and what isn't . . .
– So what have you found out about square numbers?
– Can you tell me a bit more?
– Why?
[A substantial discussion between pupils follows this.]

A discussion of this transcript appeared in the dissertation. Dooley seems to become somewhat captivated by what she appears to view as an emancipatory quest, immersed as she is in seeking to 'improve' her practice:

This transcript has brought me to a clearer understanding that the way children think and learn, in a mathematical activity, can be influenced by the teacher's questioning technique. The children de-centre, think about and reflect upon their thoughts and explanations, and consequently become more analytical, less impulsive and achieve more effective control over their learning. By modifying my own teaching style to adopt different questioning techniques, I am giving the children time to elaborate and reason out loud, learning how to express their ideas, formulate their thoughts and say what they know, providing opportunity to regulate, reason and explain themselves, so improving their level of performance . . . I am now beginning to see my role changing from that of a person who imparts knowledge to that of a person who is responsible for carefully structuring the learning experience of the children, only intervening where necessary. I am now inviting interaction, negotiation and shared constructions of experiences which will enable the children to learn. Although I have not taught these children anything 'new' about this mathematical concept, I have encouraged them to use skills and knowledge they already possess to understand more clearly. I see my role as now challenging the thinking going on instead of explaining how I think it should be done. I can also see the changes with the children to which I am giving more status. So this is where I have got to, which I feel is more successful. Earlier I was speaking in negative terms – 'I can only teach maths this way'. By monitoring changes – hence raising the question I was asked a few months ago – Do values shape our practices, or do practices shape our values? – I am beginning to think the latter could be true!

(Dooley 1994: 46–7)

Dooley (pp. 49–53) follows this with a detailed description of some work with a child in her class. We offer a very brief extract from an extensive transcript provided by Dooley to capture the flavour of her new approach to questioning:

Teacher: You look happy about something, David!

David: Well, I got the shape like you said and I measured all the sides. But I knew they'd be the same length. Then I thought, well the angles must be the same. I mean, even though I was making a bigger one . . . this is just the same only a shrunk down version, the angles will be the same.

Teacher: How do you know they are all the same size, David?

David: Well . . . I know an angle of a square is always 90° – it doesn't matter about the size and a triangle with all the sides the same is always 60° so I thought this is a regular pentagon, the same will apply to this.

Teacher: So what did you do?

David: So then I measured up all the angles and I marked it down as 70 at that stage, but David O'Shea asked me how I did it and then I said I just measured the angles like this [*picking up his protractor*] . . . and then, I saw then that they were all slightly above 70°, so I added them all together. Actually they were 72°.

Teacher [*confused*]*:* How did you get 72°, David?

David: Well I just measured them again to show David and I saw that the protractor . . . this bit on the bottom here [*the protractor base line*] and it wasn't straight, so then I measured it again and it came up as 72°.

Teacher: And what made you think this was right?

David: Well, I thought 360° is a full turn and I thought well this round the edges here is nearly a full circle with the edges cut off and I thought well it loses some as you cut off the rounded part and it gained some as the turning is sharper. Then I thought, well it's logical. It's 360° . . . so then I measured all the sides again on my drawing and they were all the same.

Teacher [*confused by David's explanation*]*:* Show me which angle you measured.

David: This one here . . . look, it's just of 72° [*measuring outside angles*] and I worked it out – 7 by 72° is 360°.

Teacher [*still a little confused*]*:* Oh, I see now.

David: But also . . . if you measure this here [*inside angle*] that comes to 108° so it must be right, because if you think about it, this here [*putting his ruler across the shape*] is a straight line and 72° and 108° is 180° which is a straight line.

Teacher: Right I understand now. What did you do then?

David: First I decided the length I wanted my sides and then, working with the angles, I worked out the pentagon.

By allowing David to reflect on his experiences and the kind of thinking he was engaged in, he became more aware of the activity in which he had been engaged. Tackling a new problem, he brought his own past experiences to bear on it and made productive use of them. He invented a workable method to solve his problem, a method which I couldn't have envisaged and one which had confused me initially when he was explaining the process he went through to arrive at his answer . . . When I began this chapter, my belief was that mathematics was something which was outside independence and autonomy, but I now realise that this was an indication of my state of mind, my attitudes, my values and beliefs about mathematics. But is it also a general message I have, of what children are capable of? . . . My own notion was that the conceptual structure of mathematics as a subject was one where certain mathematical content had to be 'taught' in a linear way. In other words, I felt that 'basic' concepts had to be taught and learned before more difficult concepts could be tackled. This therefore limited the range of my practices, which then served to define and reaffirm the academic nature of the subject. If I believed that children needed a structure, I therefore questioned their ability to create structures of their own . . . Being somewhat forced to experiment with maths has made me peel back old beliefs in order to examine previous assumptions. But what are the beliefs and values I hold, in particular to the teaching of mathematics, and from where have I got them? I showed earlier that my beliefs and values came from a variety of sources, which included my own education in school, college training and my experiences in different schools. How then have these influenced my beliefs about teaching mathematics?

I now know that it has nothing to do with techniques I use in the classroom, it is not just me coming up with some good questions as far as maths is concerned, it is about me opening up and creating a set of possibilities for children to explore the world in all kinds of significant ways and to be objective about themselves, their role, their conduct and who they are.

In a further example we offer some writing from a teacher examining how the analytical frame he has built up can assist him in modifying his practice in specific situations. Steve Grimley (1995) worked in a centre for children with special needs. However, a lot of his work involved visiting students in other schools. His early writing centred around the mismatch between his understanding of his role and the expectations of his colleagues and the teachers in the schools he visited. He sought to focus on the difficulties he experienced in resolving the disputes which ensued. This writing helped him, with the aid of fellow course members, to identify the way in which his own actions exacerbated some of the disputes. The following extract focuses on a dispute, involving Steve, concerned with the process through which a school had referred a pupil to the centre. Steve uses his writing about this dispute to assist him in clarifying the process through which he is examining and seeking to develop his practice.

Having worked through a process of development based in meeting the course criteria I had reached an auspicious moment within my chosen research methodology, I had:

• Analysed my professional beliefs and practice.
• Gone through a data collection process.
• Validated what I had done through a validating group.
• Focused on changes over the period of time of the process.
• Begun to identify an area of concern with implications for future practice.

The new objective was the planning of and implementation of changes to my practice in my professional context. How was I to move forwards? I decided to collect some more dialogue as data, not a random piece but created with the specific intention of collecting to complete a picture of my dissertation. My focus became clearer: 'My ways of presentation, how they communicate my intentions in my range of professional interactions'. I wanted some data generated to do with my focus and I began looking for situations which could provide opportunities to generate such data. Within two days such an opportunity developed. I decided to act on the basis of collecting specific data within a plan of trying to re-frame the discourse whilst remaining in [the mode of] Transactional Analysis 'adult' [Berne 1964]. I then reflected on the data as I recorded it, but first the 'Allocation Transaction'.

18/5/95 Allocation Transaction

The Centre staff meet weekly to discuss allocation of training, new cases and change of provision for schools and pupils. A referral came up for a school I am the link teacher for. This is what I wrote and reflected on:

'I asked, "Where has this come from?"' A brief public argument followed between me and Colleague 1 about whether the school was using a back door method to gain extra provision.
Colleague 2: I don't think it is useful to go into this now, we have other things to discuss.

The meeting continued and I decided to follow up the discussion later. It was an unproductive argument and afterwards I checked that interpretation with colleagues which confirmed it. There had been a misunderstanding and I had responded negatively to what I perceived as aggression. I decided to follow up according to my planned shift by an intervention where I changed my approach by clarifying and re-framing what I had been saying whilst trying to see what had been the perceptions of others. As I said at the time: 'Here was a chance to re-frame my approach and have a different outcome which meant applying a planned and controlled change. Which was . . . try to re-structure the Transaction by pausing and trying to explicitly clarify what sort of problem it was and to try to redefine it.'
  I wanted to collect some more dialogue as data, not a random piece but created with the specific intention of collecting to complete a picture of my dissertation to do with my focus of my way of talking and how it communicates my thinking and meaning. At this point I asked 'How am I going to act from here?'. Shortly afterwards I met Colleague 1, bearing in mind my planned shift:

Me: I want to check what was going on at the allocation
               meeting. It seemed you thought I was being critical of
               you, why was that?
Colleague 1: You were saying I had not used the proper system.
Me: No, that's not what I was trying to say. What I was
               meaning I think was annoyance at what I thought was
               another example of the school trying to avoid doing
               things properly. I think you do a good job of ensuring
               the link teachers are not ignored. I was expressing my
               annoyance with the school and apologise if you saw it
               differently as that was not the intention.
Colleague 1: That's OK.

We then discussed other things and I needed time to reflect on the
outcome and significance of the fairly brief attempt at the planned
intervention. My plan had been an attempt to halt the transaction
and re-frame my presentation. I had noticed my anger rising in the
original Allocation Meeting as a response to what I felt as aggression, not an intellectual response but an emotional one . . .

In recording and reflecting on the dialogue, two ideas primarily
began to seem important in terms of the task I had set myself.
Firstly, the idea that the initial aggressive interaction could have its
origins elsewhere, i.e. in the school not following systems and wanting back door access to the service. Secondly that there could be a
chain of causes and effects within these actions. I could begin to see
where to collect my next piece of dialogue. I was going to plan an
intervention with the senior teacher I liaised with at the school.

Steve then plans for an encounter with this senior teacher, records his
conversation when it takes place and uses this data as a focus for further
analysis. Increasingly, the writing he produces is directly a consequence
of his professional actions and also part of a guiding framework for
subsequent practice (cf. Brown 1994b). The research process becomes
an integral part of his actual professional development. In meeting the
senior teacher at the school the teacher-researcher is targeting a particular
encounter, about to happen, with a view to understanding it, and indeed
acting within it, in line with his current research agenda. The outcome
is that he builds not only a sense of 'how things might be seen' but
also of 'what might be done'. In doing this the practitioner synthesizes
'description-led experience' and 'experience-led description' (Hanley and
Brown 1996). He acts on the basis of meanings he has given to earlier
accounts of his professional dealings. But each new professional encounter helps the practitioner to modify his sense of what needs to be done.
The above piece appeared in Steve's final dissertation as an illustration
of the process he went through. Looking at the entire piece retroactively

he brought new meaning to it, through reconciling his post-experience understanding of the process with the words contained in the piece, which had sought to capture how he understood his actions at the time. The older writing, now separated from the person who wrote it (since that person has moved on), is scrutinized for its implicit qualities as evidence of past perspectives (cf. Sanger 1995: 90–1).

Conclusion

In this chapter we have sought to emphasize two key aspects of the role of writing in practitioner research:

- writing as an integral aspect of the classroom action being described;
- writing as an important marker of time in monitoring change.

In producing writing as part of the practitioner research process we are creating part of the reality to which we attend. Further, we construct an understanding of time through selecting and composing sequences of pieces of writing. Consequently, the process of research becomes a task of, first, positing a way of doing things in writing and, second, assessing this writing in relation to how things are then experienced. Neither of these can be understood independently of time. In order to capture time, moments in time are characterized through pieces of writing which serve as position statements for those moments. These pieces of writing, however, become anchorages for the constructed reality simultaneously capturing the past and positing the new, according to their particular usage in newly generated stories, constructed by the researcher, as they move between being a writer and being a reader in response to, and in creating, their evolving research interest. And as we have seen, this evolving research interest may at various points be specified in terms of emancipatory ideals being sought by the writer. After all, we cannot abandon all sense of hope and aspiration merely because it is philosophically implausible! However, Steedman (2001: 48) cautions that the identities revealed in the stories we tell may end up far from substantial reality and enter more into the realm of desire: 'Not a question for philosophers' she guesses, although one might ask how humans assert their credentials as worthy philosophical subjects.

We shall briefly take stock of where we are at this early stage in our journey through the pages of this book. While our hermeneutic credentials have remained at the fore in this chapter, we suggest that a little slippage has commenced between the writer and the way in which they are depicted in their reflective writing. Writing has become a sort of posture that the writer seeks to fulfil or claims has been fulfilled. The writer never quite catches their own tail, never landing where they aim, nor ever quite reoccupies the same spot. Whether we nudge towards Ricoeur (e.g. 1966) and seek an individual will, or towards Derrida where such notions seem to get left out of the picture, our central object has become the writing rather than the writer – and how that writing interacts with the other actions of that writer. We shall stretch this sort of notion a little further in the next two chapters.

4

Transitions: issues of temporality and practitioner research

And because the stories were held here in fluid form, they retained the ability to change, to become new versions of themselves, to join up with other stories and so become yet other stories.

(Rushdie 1990: 73)

... narrative is able to sustain desire rather than as is generally supposed to fulfil it.

(Lapsley and Westlake 1996: 193)

... for nothing is more necessary today than to renounce the arrogance of critique and carry on with patience the endless work of distancing and renewing our historical substance.

(Ricoeur 1981: 246)

This chapter builds further on the notion of how we might construe time as practitioner-researchers. It questions the limits of our capacity to enter into *projects of action* as intentional beings (Schütz 1962), embedded as we are in socially derived constructions of the world we experience. It offers alternative versions of how we map out time into the future and how we situate ourselves as beings derived from our pasts. It hints that construing practice as 'aiming for an ideal' has a questionable track record, but also that we necessarily experience difficulty in making sense of the present since we understand our present through cultural filters to which we contribute. As researchers this contribution is instilled with our specific research attitude as to whether we see ourselves as 'beings in the moment' or as those seeking to achieve a better world at the end of the day. Finally, we turn to see how Ricoeur's work on time and narrative can be applied to some writing produced within another practitioner-oriented study. We argue that his emphasis on narrative offers a productive approach to conceiving of reflective writing generated within practitioner research as being instrumental in revitalizing and renewing the research situation being examined.

The linguistic layer

Issues of how language is related to the world we experience underpin a substantial part of contemporary philosophy. We restrict ourselves in the first instance, in this chapter, by returning to a particular manifestation of these issues as they have arisen in a dispute between two leading contemporary writers, Gadamer and Habermas.

Gadamer's (1975) analysis sees tradition and language as fundamental constraints to any hermeneutic process. So viewed, the practitioner-researcher would be seen as being steeped in tradition and in language which prevent action that can be seen as in any way independent. Yet at the same time the researcher is responsible for constructing this very tradition which constrains them. Any creative linguistic offerings a researcher might make are always already partly constituted by virtue of being in an inherited language: 'we can only learn about the unknown by recognising it as something already known' (Gallagher 1992: 68). We are always immersed in meaning and are unable to enter any situation free of the traditions that gave rise to us. Gadamer firmly asserts the centrality of the individual human in the creation of meaning while on the one hand seeing the world as something of which they are part, or on the other seeing it as comprising elements upon which they can operate. Here, learning can be seen as comprising 'self-learning', a learning coming about through experiencing oneself operating on and in the world. In this paradigm, practitioner research would be principally concerned with enabling the researcher to construct meaning. The emphasis would not be on the researcher recreating the reality of the world they face in any sort of universal way but instead would be on the researcher's production of meaning in respect of their given task. As an example, Tony was rather surprised when a cousin of his wife, Michael, evaluated the picturesque Peak District landscape that they were both walking through from a military perspective. Michael was seeing completely different things to what Tony would see in his normal guise as an unathletic rambler motivated by nice views and proximity to a pub. A 'pretty red bush' to Tony was a 'point of cover overlooking the valley entrance' for Michael. With this in mind, any interpretation underlying a research enterprise is seen as producing something new, shaped around the perspective of the person looking. As seen in the last chapter, this Gadamerian stance has been pursued in the field of practitioner research in education by Elliott (e.g. 1987, 1993b).

Meanwhile, Habermas' (e.g. 1972) analysis aims at unconstrained communication which seeks to avoid reproducing the structures of society and the ideological distortions that go with them. Within such an understanding the task of practitioner research might be seen largely as a transformative process. The scope of Habermas' enquiry extends beyond the universal linguistic dimension which characterizes Gadamer's version of interpretation and addresses extra-linguistic factors such as economic status and social class which it sees as distorting interpretations. As in Gadamer's hermeneutics, Habermas' critical social theory presupposes a truth which can be found. Habermas' approach has also been pursued explicitly within the domain of practitioner research in education (e.g. Carr and Kemmis 1986; Zuber-Skerritt 1996). Carr and Kemmis, for example, seek to activate movement towards a better situation in which particular conceptions of 'educational values' might flourish. In particular, they examine:

> the different views of educational reform implicit in different views of educational research and [defend] the idea that the teacher is a member of a critical community made up of teachers, students, parents and others concerned for the development and reform of education. The professional responsibility of the teacher is to offer an approach to this task; *to create conditions* under which the critical community can be galvanized into action in support of educational values, to model the review and improvement process, and to organize it so that colleagues, students, parents and others can be actively involved in the development of education.
>
> (Carr and Kemmis 1986: 5, emphasis added)

Here, in line with Habermas, good education seems to be a promise for the future rather than part of a process taking place now.

Ricoeur (1981: 78), in comparing Gadamer's and Habermas' arguments suggests that they are premised on different assumptions. Ricoeur suggests that:

> [1] Habermas' account is based on an overly singular account of history. As such a specific interpretation of the present, and what is wrong with it, is overstated. Gadamer accepted more the inevitability of his own prejudices in creating historical accounts . . .

> [2] . . . Gadamer appeals to the *human sciences*, which are concerned with contemporary reinterpretation of cultural tradition, [while] Habermas makes recourse to the *critical social sciences*, directly aimed against institutional reifications . . .

> [3] . . . whereas Gadamer introduces *mis-understanding* as the inner obstacle to understanding, Habermas develops a theory of *ideology*, construed as the systematic distortion of communication by hidden exercise of force . . .

> [4] . . . For Gadamer the hermeneutic task is based on a 'dialogue that we are' whereas Habermas has a quest for 'an unrestricted and unconstrained communication that does not precede us but guides us from a future point'.
>
> (Ricoeur 1981: 80–1)

If we take examples of each of these concerns in turn, within the context of practitioner research in education, the difficulty of taking sides is further problematized. In terms of (1), as practitioner-researchers what assumptions do we make about the situation we are researching? Through what process do we establish the categories through which we organize the questions we choose to ask? For example, Walkerdine (1988) argued that many advocates of Piagetian-oriented child-centred learning made particular assumptions about what a 'child' was and what needed to be seen as the 'natural' way of learning. These assumptions then guided the way in which research was pursued. But how do we understand the creation of these assumptions as being an intrinsic part of a research process evolving through time?

Turning to (2), as teacher-researchers should we focus on the cultural understandings of the subjects we teach or on the way in which these are understood in the specific educational context? For example, within the UK mathematics understood as a traditional discipline is rather different to its reification in the National Curriculum. Where should we begin in delineating our assumptions as to the thing we are researching?

As far as (3) is concerned, hermeneutic enquiry, we suggest, is directed at the mutual co-formation of nature and institutions. That is, attempts at describing nature construe subsequent observations (cf. Eger 1992; Heywood 1999). Our attempt to describe the world always results in a formulation that is an approximation to the world being described. Put simply, the difference between Gadamer and Habermas is whether this formulation should be seen as a misunderstanding or as an ideological distortion. To pursue the example of school mathematics: the attempt to describe mathematics in a curriculum inevitably results in a caricature of traditional understandings of mathematics as a discipline. However, this caricature can be viewed variously – for example, as a serious but imperfect attempt to describe mathematics to guide school instruction *or* as a cynical ploy to make teachers and children more accountable according to a particular institutionalized account of mathematics, *or* as a reconfiguration of the discipline itself to meet contemporary needs. Ricoeur would downplay intent in the construction of the formulation and see it more as a matter of subsequent interpretation, and action on the basis of this, as to whether the formulation was a misunderstanding or an ideological distortion.

Finally, (4). In Carr and Kemmis' account above (1986: 5) it is assumed that we do not yet have the 'conditions under which the critical community can be galvanized into action in support of educational values'. This assumption triggers a particular research orientation. We suggest that Gadamer would have a different attitude as to how the researcher's assumptions trigger, and assume a place within, a research process. For him, we suggest, the building of the assumptions would be given a higher profile and be seen as integral to the unfolding research enquiry.

A key aspect of this debate for our purposes here is the extent to which one can distance oneself from the use of language one is seeking to reflect on. For Gadamer we are immersed in language and so we cannot assume any distance from language to inspect how it functions. We understand ourselves through the categories of language which simultaneously describe and create the world we inhabit and our relation to this. Within this version of hermeneutics, although we can build a picture of reality, we can never access this reality directly. We always end up describing previous descriptive structurings.

For Habermas, systematic distortions have occurred in the social fabric which distance language from the reality it seeks or purports to capture: in principle reality, truth could be apprehended if ideology did not intervene. Ricoeur (1981) is suggesting that resolution of these two perspectives lies in recognizing their alternative conceptions of the scope of language. For Gadamer, the emphasis is on seeing oneself as part of language where language is all-embracing. For Habermas it is possible to distance oneself from language and operate on it to correct its distortions.

For the remainder of this chapter we develop an account of Ricoeur's alternative course as manifest in his later work and align ourselves with it. This course rests on a more overt account of time in which past, present and future are all understood as being filtered through the medium of narrative. We suggest that this approach reduces the implicit conservativism in the position of Gadamer with its gravitation to existing ways of seeing things. It also avoids Habermas' dual insistence that we work from an assumption of troubled beginnings and that effective action is conditional on getting somewhere first (behold the revolution), with the risk of infinite deferral that this implies. We partially accept Elliott's (1993b: 197) Gadamerian stance in which he suggests that we can be critical of the traditions through which we emerge. Nevertheless, while the practical reflection Elliott advocates can be seen as a critical instrument, we suggest Ricoeur's analysis offers a radical reconceptualization of where such critical analysis is centred. In this way, Ricoeur supplies a more powerful effacement of the potential dichotomy between the work of Gadamer and Habermas.

Time as narrative

As researchers, how do we depict the reality we experience? In which senses is this depiction time dependent? How do notions of future, present and past figure in the understandings of time we conjure in this depiction? Whether we aim for some ideal structure in the future (as does Habermas) or focus more on rereading the present (as does Gadamer) we need to work at how we mediate past, present and future. In the context of practitioner-oriented research we also need to concern ourselves with how we construct ourselves as future, present and past beings in this depiction. In this section we look at how narratives are constructed as accounts of the passing of time. We then connect this with the task of pinning down bits of experience faced by teachers carrying out reflective practitioner research, where the person speaking sits inside the situation being described.

Within practitioner research, how do we build a sense of our own identity? We shall explore this question a little here and in more detail in the next chapter. For a teacher engaged in reflective research over a period of time, pieces of writing often get created. In this sense these teachers can be seen as being responsible for creating their own identities, in so far as any statement predicates a perspective which provides a snapshot of how the researcher makes sense of a situation. Sometimes this also provides an explicit account of how they see themselves within this situation. Nevertheless, while some writers (e.g. Lacan) might claim that identity is an effect rather than an origin of linguistic practice, one's own identity can still be something one asserts and deploys rather than merely discovers:

> Identity should not be seen as a stable entity – something that people *have* – but as something that they *use*, to justify, explain and make sense of themselves in relation to other people, and to the contexts in which they operate. In other words, identity is a form of argument. As such it is both practical and theoretical. It is also inescapably moral: identity claims are inevitably bound up with justifications of conduct and belief.
>
> (MacLure 1993: 287)

We argue that this construction and use of identity by the researcher is not pinned down to a time and place. Rather it is a function of a more fluid reflective process. In this process practitioner-researchers implicate themselves in the situations they describe. Further, narratives as generated from these reflective writings can form a layer that conditions the research situation from which they are generated. Yet these narratives are susceptible to ongoing renewal as their relationships to the research situation which generated them are reevaluated.

Ricoeur (e.g. 1984) argues that the passage of time does not lend itself to being described as a sequence of events, features or stages but instead needs to be understood as being mediated by narrative accounts of such transitions, relying on interpretations which at a very basic level cannot be seen as comprising phenomenological features. Ricoeur's analysis begins with an account of Augustine's twelfth-century work *Confessions*.

Ricoeur (1984: 4) suggests that in Book 11 of this work Augustine 'inquires into the nature of time without any apparent concern for grounding his inquiry in the narrative structure of the spiritual autobiography developed in the first nine books of the *Confessions*'. He then follows this with a discussion of Aristotle's *Poetics*, written some 1500 years earlier, in which he 'constructs his theory of dramatic plot without paying attention to the temporal implications of his analysis' (p. 4). Ricoeur then combines these themes of the two works in his own thesis within which time and narrative are mutually constitutive, whereby 'time becomes human to the extent that it is articulated through narrative mode, and narrative attains its full meaning when it becomes a condition of temporal existence' (p. 52).

Following Aristotle, Ricoeur suggests that 'Plot' is the *mimesis* (imitation) of an action. We take this to mean that to imitate an action in words is to offer an interpretation of an event, in which some causal relationships might be postulated in the form of a plot. Such interpretations, however, can always be revisited. Although as Ricoeur frequently reiterates in his earlier work (e.g. Ricoeur 1981) such interpretations are never final, some however may be closer to the truth than others. But in his later analysis Ricoeur (1984: xi) introduces three distinct senses to the term *mimesis*, namely:

- *mimesis 1:* 'a reference back to the familiar pre-understanding we have of the order of action';
- *mimesis 2:* 'an entry into the realm of poetic composition';
- *mimesis 3:* 'a new configuration by means of this poetic refiguring of the pre-understood order of action'.

We understand these as follows.

Mimesis 1 applies to our existing common-sense view of the world in which we have gained experience of organizing events in a particular way in making sense of that world. For example, if we show a video of an everyday classroom scene to a group of teachers in an in-service training session we might expect some commonality of interpretation. Teachers will have developed some sense of how a classroom is organized and have some understanding of how different features are related (e.g. 'the teacher misjudged the level of work which led to some restlessness').

Mimesis 2 applies to unfamiliar situations in which normal ways of working are modified or disrupted through some sort of new initiative. For example, within many action research enquiries, teacher-researchers seek to try out new ways of characterizing their professional practice and also new forms of actions are attempted as professional objectives are modified. *Mimesis 2* can be seen as an experimental phase in which new ways of describing and new forms of actions are explored.

Mimesis 3 applies after the experimental phase has been assimilated into normal practice. Here past struggles have become dissipated as they lose their experimental edge with the new forms of practice that have been tried out becoming familiar components of everyday practice or otherwise consigned to the scrap heap of failed attempts.

Ricoeur places these phases under the umbrella of what he calls 'semantic innovation'. At the level of a sentence, a new word or metaphor places stresses and strains on the existing words as they accommodate the new member. Ricoeur offers the example of 'Nature is a temple where living pillars . . .' (1984: ix). Here each word tugs at the conventional meaning of the others to produce a novel effect. The poetic or novel usage of certain terms takes them away from more mundane meanings towards a more expressive style that perhaps loses its charge with repeated use. Existing words hold onto meanings in a modified way and new words come to the fore in orienting our experience. At the level of narrative, new stories result in a reconfiguration of the way in which the world is experienced and acted in, as older stories are repositioned.

Narrative within practitioner research

It seems to us that this style of analysis readily lends itself to a closer examination of how teachers engaged in reflective writing over a period of time construct their own notions of transition. In saying this we are making the assumption that this writing itself is a key instrument in renewing understandings of who one is and how one is. Nevertheless, at any point in time writing can provide a snapshot of an individual's concerns, their way of seeing things and the way in which they see themselves. Each piece of writing produced along the way within reflective practitioner research provides a caricature of particular concerns being addressed at different points in time, which reveal aspects of the story the researcher wants to tell. Yet for most of us it is slightly embarrassing to look back at personal writings we produced a little while back, and so our past gets accessed through the rather awkward medium of writings we now feel uncomfortable with. We can no longer quite connect with the issues as we saw them then, past tangles having been resolved with new ones entering present concerns. Past incidents and ways of life have been preserved as explanations offered at the time or later. Earlier we discussed the creation of meaning within practitioner research as being analogous to how meaning arises within contemporary understandings of language (e.g. Saussure). Here the reflective practitioner produces a chain of pieces of writing over time and that meaning is derived from the succession of pieces of writing, where no individual piece has meaning in itself but rather depends on its relation to other pieces. The creation of meaning within a practitioner research enterprise can thus be seen as being dependent on the management of collected writings. As we have already suggested, the meaning of any story depends on its use in another story. However, we also wish to problematize how we understand the commencement of any research enterprise and suggest that we cannot easily define a starting point from which we can simply map out a possible future as a continuation of a singularly defined past. Events as depicted in any particular piece of writing can always be revisited and reorganized in relation to each other in positing any newly supposed causal sequence.

In examining this sort of process we shall look at an example drawn from an enquiry carried out by Lorna Roberts within the MA course. The programme of study comprised three years of producing reflective writing examining aspects of her professional tasks. Her study spanned two successive work situations; as a teacher in further education and then as an access tutor at a university. The final dissertation comprised an account of the transition she experienced in her own professional functioning as an individual within various institutional settings. For much of her time on the programme, Lorna described herself in the role of someone experiencing difficulties as a result of people marginalizing her contribution. Her work for the course aspired to the modernist plot of making things better, a would be 'victory narrative' (Stronach and MacLure 1997), but within a Kafkaesque world of infinite deferral. The stories documented difficulties as successive conceptualizations of ways forward floundered. Lorna's conception of community was one where she was situated as a participant on the fringes. It was this recognition that brought about a change in her approach. The sequence of extracts below, taken from her reflective journal but then reproduced in her dissertation (Roberts 1997), provide a taste of this transition, in which successive pieces of writing produced over the course of the three years, according to specific concerns at the time of writing, are repositioned in new accounts of how the transition as a whole might be seen.

> I have been experiencing some difficulty with one of the women students. I believe there is a personality clash which I feel affects the teaching/learning relationship. The situation has got me thinking about my interaction with individuals and groups in a classroom setting and how the dynamics can facilitate or impede learning. I am particularly intrigued by my role in this situation.
>
> (1997: 13, journal year 1994)

> I believed I could understand my practice – what was happening in the classroom – simply by focusing on myself and my interaction with students. I ignored other contextual features – my relationship with colleagues, the structure of the organisation and the wider

social context. As far as I could see the issue was my classroom practice and nothing else was relevant. I needed to know why my methods were not having the impact I wanted with certain groups, therefore my focus should centre on the classroom and myself.

(1997: 12, journal year 1996)

It was ridiculous to say that I am not part of the world. My personal beliefs and values may be different but I am tied into the daily rituals and practices and this is recognised by those I come into contact with – hence the tensions I experience in those interactions – i.e. I represent the institution. That is why I am able to speak with the institutional voice. Even though I may be at odds with certain practices or beliefs I adopt the rules of the organisation.

(1997: 58, journal year 1997)

When I review my experiences within the institution and account for the problems as being the result of institutional racism I am inscribing myself (paraphrasing Zizek 1989) as a subject in a particular symbolic chain whose signifier is racism . . . I have positioned myself in a particular discourse and have taken the identity such a discourse allows . . . When I review my accounts of practice what is revealed is my sense of hierarchy and lack of control in the situation. The journal entries . . . provide some evidence of this. Use of passive tense removes all notion of actor. This gives a sense that the structures are some unseen force over our heads guiding our every move. I speak in terms of 'the unit', 'the project' and 'the programme' as though they existed as concrete entities with the power of action. War-like – 'bombarded', 'firing', 'barrage' reveal the extent to which I feel I am under attack.

(1997: 63)

The later style of writing armed Lorna for her own 'attack'. It seemed that the very apparatus within a course designed to liberate gave rise to the frame which constituted her oppression. Her self-reflection on practice conjured as a strategy for progress resulted in a particular version of self, trapped within certain conceptions of practice and of potential conceptions of progress within them. Her attack took the form of resistance against the modernist conceptions of supposed emancipatory moves embedded in the course's own self-image (to improve one's teaching, to unfold the picture one tells, etc.). Her critical stance, this 'critical' strategy which had become part of her lived tradition, enabled her to distance herself from these conceptions. In doing this she seemed, intentionally or otherwise, to be redefining her community as the course team and fellow students and succeeded in rattling the cage to make the course team feel uncomfortable about the assumptions underlying their own teaching strategies.

Lorna's examination of her own past writing revealed a pattern; stories formulated in this particular way always gave rise to a particular conception of herself. It revealed itself to be a caricature, a façade which itself needed to be rejected. Her study instead became an account of how such caricatures are produced as a consequence of particular conceptions of practitioner research.

In deploying Ricoeur's analytical frame, how might we capture the transition being supposed here? *Mimesis 1* might be seen as the first world Lorna sees herself occupying where she is situated as weak, in a world resisting her attempts to impose some sort of modernist plot. Such accounts are derived from her everyday style of reflection on her practice, laced with the analytical approach developed within the course. Within this frame both her professional institutional setting and course structure were seen as non-negotiable. Only her actions could be changed. *Mimesis 2* derives from her recognition that the style of story frame she uses is inhibiting. It feels as though she is always returning to the same frustrating starting point. Her stories are thus reevaluated and new ones are tried for size. Her recognition that she was speaking with the institutional voice rather than against it repositioned her with a resulting shift in perspective, revealed in her writing. Thus she developed a critical stance towards the course strategies while also changing her understanding of her relationship with her professional situation. *Mimesis 3* is the calm attitude, almost detached from the former state, where she is knowingly living in the new realm where the new brand of stories are seen as fitting better with her new understanding of her professional role. The former stories have become mere history, preserved as quotes of herself.

This account of Lorna so far, however, was created by her tutor for the purposes of writing a paper (Brown and Roberts 2000) and now being reproduced here. The tutor selected what he saw as four poignant extracts from Lorna's final dissertation and spun a yarn around them consistent with the assertions he was making within the paper. Lorna and Tony would however, as co-authors, like to distance themselves from research traditions that deny research subjects a right to reply. Fortunately Lorna retains a live voice and has responded to the choice of extracts through which she has been characterized, and to the story that has been built around them:

> This brings to mind earlier discussions with my tutor where I did not recognise my intentions or myself as revealed in his interpretations of my writing. Although these particular extracts do capture the essence of my evolving thoughts as I sought to make sense of my world, they do not capture the full flavour of my position at the time of writing. I am struck by the strident character of Lorna going on the attack, 'redefining her community' and 'rattling the cage'.

This Lorna appears self-assured and quite deliberate in her actions. As I remember it when I wrote the dissertation these extracts were presented to tell the story of my transitional shifts as I saw it looking back to the past from the vantage point of the present. I was writing as someone trying to make sense of how I came to frame my experiences during the course of the research. Elements of this new story do resonate but this is no longer the story of my tortuous journey. But I am reminded of a quote I used in the dissertation: 'There are no "final" stories but each story reflects our own way of organising and understanding the social world' (Jennings and Graham 1996: 169).

Conclusion

Empathetic historical analyses (e.g. Collingwood 1994) focus on understanding why the actor acted in the way they did. But then the actor might have been deluded, pursuing some unrealistic fantasy of what they wanted to achieve. So where is history located – in the supposed truth then, the whole truth, or nothing but the particular truth you have in mind right now? Ricoeur (1984) talks of fragmentary temporalities whereby temporality defies phenomenology except at the level of narrative. That is, the process of history cannot be fully captured in the stories about it but instead we employ a form of phenomenological highlighting. In teacher education, for example, we mythologize certain expressions, points of reference which become socially constructed phenomenologies which serve as anchorages for given communities (e.g. 'levels of attainment', 'failing schools', 'reflective practice'). Official languages become an imposed form of anchorage which taints the space people see themselves working in (cf. Bourdieu and Wacquant 2001). Developmental practitioner research is thus always conditioned by the discourses which surround it – sometimes pulling, sometimes pushing, where any notion of an underlying truth is the *myth* that gets told at the time (Barthes 1972).

What then is the main function of practitioner-oriented educational research and how is it associated with revisions of practice? Within this chapter we have sought to reconceptualize the task of the practitioner-researcher a little further. We have nudged away from Habermasian-style victory narratives in which research is targeted at creating a better world, as conceptualized from specific interpretations of the present. We have also more cautiously rejected the 'being as we are' stance of Gadamer. We would however, accept Elliott's defence of Gadamer in so far as it sees practical reflection both as a critical instrument of traditions *and* as a critical instrument of the perspectives from which those traditions are successively viewed. In line with Ricoeur, however, we claim that we need to focus on the key role of narrative in building an account of the passage of time and to understand research as a mechanism present within a process of change through which we distance and historicize ourselves. Ricoeur's analysis suggests that narratives might be seen as always imperfect accounts of time, but a time that depends on these very narratives. Thus, Ricoeur seems to give a higher status to narratives in the construction of time than does Gadamer. He also demonstrates the rather fine dividing line between historical and fictional constructions (Ricoeur 1985).

We have suggested however that narratives are always susceptible to reformulation. We cannot suppose any finality in the authorial construction of the events described nor in the position adopted in making this construction. Nevertheless the author may recognize this and be always on the lookout for more captivating descriptions. This search however results in the object of the search being reconfigured and reconceptualized which invalidates past attempts by the (now changed) author at pinning down this (now changed) object. Research discourses inevitably create the analytical frames that we use, which in turn create the objects we research; objects that grow and evolve whether we acknowledge this growth or not. In this way these discourses reinvigorate and renew both object (the researched) and subject (the researcher) of research. As such, research becomes the instrument through which we build and understand our practice, not to reach some higher plane of perfection, nor to be more in touch with where we are in life, but rather to make explicit a reflective/constructive narrative layer that feeds, while growing alongside, the life it seeks to portray.

On identity

> Stories are precious, indispensable. Everyone must have his history, her narrative. You do not know who you are until you possess the imaginative version of yourself. You almost do not exist without it.
>
> (*Time* magazine, quoted by Zizek 1993: 11)

> When the patient says 'I', the analyst should be mistrustful.
>
> (Leader and Groves 1995: 64)

The research masters degree described earlier enables practising teachers to examine aspects of their own teaching. A key aspect of this work centres on developing understandings of why the teachers see their practice in the way they do and how this governs the way in which they act. In this sense the course engages teachers in the creation of autobiographical writings. Thus, teachers on the course describe themselves in their own specific professional situations. But is this portrayal of self really convincing? Or rather, for whom is this portrayal created? This chapter focuses on the nature of such self-portrayals. It suggests that the author's habitual ways of describing their practice can squeeze out more difficult self-awarenesses, as discussed in Habermas' (1976) reworking of Freud. This chapter builds on the theme of the last two chapters by examining how the writing produced in practitioner research contexts can be an instrument through which such habitual practices can be identified and seen alongside alternatives. Consequently, our notions of subjectivity get entangled with the linguistic approaches we are accustomed to following. We understand ourselves through the categories of language which simultaneously describe and create the world we inhabit and our relation to it.

As seen in the last chapter, Ricoeur (1984, 1985) suggests that narratives might be seen as always imperfect accounts of 'action in time' but of a time that depends on these very narratives. He seeks to give a higher status to narratives in the construction of time and thus in how we organize our lives into related events, themes etc. He also suggested a rather fine dividing line between historical and fictional constructions. A key aspect of this chapter is an attempt at showing how we use narratives, anecdotes or 'stories' to depict our practice in which history and fiction, reality and desire, are blurred. However, we shall now endeavour to build a more sophisticated account of the subject involved in this process. In tackling this we shall lean on the work of Jacques Lacan and his present-day disciple, Slavoj Zizek.

Building stories of self

We begin with the first of a few brief anecdotes often used in MA sessions in tackling some of the issues resulting from attempts at encapsulating oneself.

Anecdote 1: A self I can live with
In the film *Walkabout* an adolescent girl and her younger brother get stranded in the Australian outback. They meet an Aborigine boy on walkabout who looks after them. During this encounter the Aborigine makes various advances to the girl which she resists. This rejection leads to the Aborigine's suicide. It transpires that they had been close to a town throughout and that the Aborigine had been concealing this fact to prolong the courtship. The film concludes with the girl, now a woman, living in a dreary suburb, greeting her husband who is boasting of an exciting new pay rise. The camera focuses in on the woman's disappointed face as the film slips into a dream sequence idealizing the passionate relationship with the Aborigine that never was. The past seems to be remodelled to meet the woman's current needs of what she wanted it to be (or perhaps the sequence of how she actually remembered it). It was as if she needed to remodel the past to justify her feelings of dissatisfaction now.

The suggestion here is that we create an image of ourselves that we can feel comfortable with. The aspirational critical educator might, for example, ask what personal needs are being met by alliance with critical education objectives. In producing reflective writing as part of a research process we provide an account of our past that makes sense of our current actions. In the context of the masters course described however, these accounts are presented for closer scrutiny within small cohorts. Alternative accounts are generated and considered. This leads to attempts at building a firmer understanding of how such accounts are related to the events they seek to depict. In some sense this might be seen as an attempt to move to a fuller account of the individual's teaching practices and the rationale behind them. But in a more important sense this leads to a recognition that there is no final story – rather, we have stories that help us for the present, as we make sense of the past, as we nudge to the future. Such approaches are however not restricted to research aimed at personal and professional development for the researcher. Any research perspective presented is inevitably to some degree a function of the researcher's interests or those of their sponsor. The things the research notices and chooses to identify are further conditioned through the accepted routes for dissemination, whether this be a journal, a government-sponsored evaluation report, a public lecture etc.

In the writings of Lacan the human subject is always seen as incomplete, where identifications of oneself are captured in an image. Lacan places particular emphasis on the child's early encounters with a mirror in which they recognize themselves: 'We have only to understand the mirror stage as *an identification*, in the full sense that analysis gives the term: namely, the transformation that takes place in the subject when he assumes an image' (Lacan 1977: 2).

As an individual I am forever trying to complete the picture I have of myself in relation to the world around me and the others who also inhabit it. I respond to the fantasy I have of the Other and the fantasy I imagine the Other having of me. The mirror image I create of myself is built through successive interpretations in such exchanges. But these interpretations are in turn a function of the language we share:

> Though the subject may speak, it does so only within the terms which the laws of language allow. Just as Saussure had argued that language does not simply name a reality which pre-exists it, but rather *produces* the concept of reality through the system of differences which *is* language so Lacan argues that the position of the 'I' within language does not simply represent the presence of as a subject which pre-exists it, but rather produces the concept of the subject through a process of differentiation between the 'I' and 'not-I' of discourse.
> (Easthope 1992: 68)

Lacanian analysis distinguishes between the 'I' which looks and the 'I' which is seen, including the 'I' that is seen by me. Zizek's (1989: 87–129) discussion of Lacan suggests that I notice what I do in so far as my actions inhabit my fantasy frame of who I am, but that this noticing is haunted by the bits I choose not to see. At the same time I have to reconcile this with the image others seem to have of me and how my tasks seem to be framed for me by others. I am trapped in having to constantly ask the question: Why am I what you (the big Other) are saying that I am? (Zizek 1989: 113).

Lacan's analysis introduces what he calls the 'graph of desire' to examine the interplay between self-perceptions and the perceptions one assumes others to have (Lacan 1977: 292–325). Lacan however does not privilege clarity in his writings. His 1990s successor, the Slovenian writer Slavoj Zizek does not do much better but at least Zizek offers countless playful anecdotes that assist the reader in engaging with the ideas being offered. Here we shall draw (crudely) on his analysis of Hitchcock's film *Rear Window* to draw a picture of how the researcher and researched perceive each other (Zizek 1991: 91–3). The reader is also urged to refer to his fuller discussion of the graph of desire (Zizek 1989: 87–129).

Anecdote 2: Rear Window

In *Rear Window* Jeff (James Stewart) finds himself occupying the classic stance of the uninvolved objective researcher. A broken leg consigns him to endless days looking out of his apartment window towards the adjacent block, observing the various activities of his neighbours who 'live their quiet ordinary lives (eating, sleeping, dancing, partying, making love and killing each other)' (Dolar 1992: 144). Using evidence collated in his waking watchful hours he builds a picture of the lives his neighbours lead. Mr Objective Researcher eventually concludes that a murder has taken place while he was asleep one night. And he gathers yet more evidence to validate this initial conjecture but is still restricted by what is accessible to him visually by way of the window. Meanwhile he seems relatively oblivious to the room he is in and the people who share it with him, most notably the beautiful Grace Kelly, working harder than she might be accustomed to in her real life persona at attracting attention to herself. Eventually, Jeff starts to include her in his speculations about the murder and she becomes increasingly intrigued. First, their conversation becomes just a little more animated when she begins to share his tedious obsession with the lives across the block. Jeff's engagement with her is intensified as she starts to conduct more ethnographic enquiries of her own, following the suspected murderer around a bit. But Jeff only seems to really notice her when she appears as a vulnerable figure as she enters his fantasy space for real when she breaks into the flat of the suspect. It is at this point that Mr Objective Researcher's feelings have some impact on the empirical observations being carried out as he realizes that he loves her. This becomes more acute as the murderer returns to his flat now occupied by the curious Ms Ethnographer. Mr Research Subject (the murderer) begins to suspect that he is being researched. He looks out of his window trying to catch sight of Mr Objective Researcher. Mr Research Subject then leaves the fantasy space with a view to sorting out Mr Objective Researcher and his somewhat dodgy ethical research stance. Mr Research Subject enters the apartment of Mr Objective Researcher, ill-equipped for a rather abrupt paradigm shift. Mr Research Subject looks Mr Objective Researcher in the eye and

says repeatedly, 'Who are you? What do you want from me?'
At which point Jeff falls through the window that has hitherto
facilitated his gaze, symbolically entering the world from which
he had been excluded. This, however, results in him acquiring
a second broken leg, thus postponing his date with Ms.
Ethnographer for another day. But it seems that she will be
waiting!

Mr Research Subject thus gets forced into a confusing exchange in which
he needs to know which part he is being assumed to be playing in Mr
Objective Researcher's script. And poor Ms Ethnographer has to make
do with only being noticed so long as she occupies the specific fantasy
space being encapsulated by this script. Jeff it would seem is clearly
examining the research situation on his own terms. His examination is
in the first instance a function of a particular imposed perspective. The
story is shaped on the assumption of his own exclusion from the events
being observed. He is also seemingly oblivious to how others might
make sense of the situation. For example, his understanding of the
murderer (Mr Research Subject) is as a person who is unaware that he
is being observed.

The stories that Jeff constructs around the murderer do not include
Jeff. Thus we have a fairly crude depiction of traditional 'objective'
research. However, the limits of such research have been questioned
extensively for quite some time now in educational research literature.
Ms Ethnographer bows to some of the more recent conventions in action
research by getting involved in the situation she is observing. This has
the effect of disturbing the situation being observed, thus enabling her to
evaluate her own actions within the situation. She is problematizing the
situation with a view to seeing what she can do about it. The supposed
dichotomy between objective researcher and ethnographer that this points
to, however, is still rather limited for our purposes here. Jeff, for example, is somewhat shocked when his own assumptions regarding his
research perspective are shown to be so glaringly off the mark. His pose
as an objective researcher was challenged but this did not result in him
becoming an instant convert to ethnography. It is more of a disruption
to his conception of research and of how one controls a situation through
one's actions and thus one's relation to the world. Such a disruption
may have caused Jeff to reflect, to look at himself and consider how
he might change in a more fundamental way. Seeing the Grace Kelly
character as a victim in his previously supposed story changes him as
well as her. It also seems to result in him changing his understanding of
how she saw him. The change in the terms of his participation results in
a shift in his own self-image and of the images he supposes others to
have of him.

Anecdote 3 examines another film clip in which we have an alternative take on an actor unknowingly working to someone else's script.

Anecdote 3: I think therefore I am
The film *Bladerunner* begins with Deckard (Harrison Ford) being picked up off the streets by the police in a futuristic Los Angeles. We are told that after a spell out of the police force he is being brought back for a special mission. Los Angeles is depicted as a rather uninviting environment, largely depopulated with many gloomy uninhabited skyscrapers darkening the permanently wet cityscape, brightened only by high-tech paraphernalia floating around advertising various lifestyle accessories. Apparently, the quality of life on earth is so poor that most people have left to inhabit other planets. On these planets menial tasks are performed by so-called 'replicants' – androids manufactured to be identical to humans in physical appearance, but programmed to survive just four years to avoid them developing overly human aspirations. Deckard's mission is to terminate (*kill*) four replicants who have escaped from their life of servitude and have arrived in Los Angeles in search of their maker, with a view to persuading him to reprogram their life expectancy. But along the way, he meets Rachel, the secretary of Tyrell, the megalomaniac behind the operation. Rachel, it transpires, is a replicant who does not know she is a replicant. She has the appearance of a woman in her mid-twenties but is actually only a few years old and her memories of her own childhood are mere recordings of Tyrell's daughter's childhood – memory implants fed into her brain, supplemented by a few key treasured possessions. Deckard, who is an expert in identifying replicants, gently demonstrates to Rachel that she is indeed a replicant but he falls in love with her all the same. It later transpires that this match, while not made in heaven, does at least have a certain compatibility to it when Deckard (homophonous with Descartes) begins to question whether he also is a replicant, previously unaware of this. (He is!!!)

In Zizek's (1993: 1–44) analysis of *Bladerunner* there is an attempt to examine the association between memory and identity. He discusses this in relation to the bizarre case of Deckard for whom 'the recovery of memory deprives him of his very self-identity' (1993: 11). But in which ways are we different? He argues that 'even the mass media is aware of the extent to which our perception of reality, including the reality of our innermost self-experience, depends on symbolic fictions' (p. 11).

What intrigues us in this story is the idea of memory implants. What do we need to convince us that we have a past? How do we build a sense of our own identity through the memories we hold onto? A teacher engaged in reflective research produces pieces of writing over a period of time. In this sense teachers can be seen as being responsible for creating their own memory implants – that is, the stories they hold onto around which they orient accounts of their professional lives. While Lacan might claim that identity is an effect rather than an origin of linguistic practice, one's own identity can still be something one asserts and deploys rather than merely discovers. This is pinpointed in one of Tony's recent attempts to recover a memory, recounted in Anecdote 4.

Anecdote 4: Cider at Butlins
There are very few photographs of me as a child and until
recently I had not seen any of these for over 25 years. But
for some reason I retained a memory of a particular family
photograph. It was taken at Butlins by a photographer with black
hair and a foreign accent. My father, my mother, my sister and I
were all seated around a table. My mother wore a red dress.
When we collected the photograph my mother expressed
disappointment because the dress did not look red in the picture.
The photographer said, 'Yes, it was a beautiful dress'. But until
rediscovering the photograph recently I was a little confused
about the circumstances. I associated this event with having my
first ever half pint of cider but I had also kept a badge saying
'Butlins 1964'. In 1964 I was only 8 and surely I was not bought
cider at that age. The photo confirmed that I was probably around
14 and I did indeed have half a cider in front of me. It transpired
that the badge was from another holiday. It also confirmed that
my mother's dress did not look that red. But never mind the
dress, it also reminded me of that awful brown polo-neck pullover
I used to wear all the time.

How has this event been created? It has been held in place by a photo, maintained through memories of this photo, connected to a spurious badge, associated with memories of Tony's first half pint and his mother's dress, recreated by the rediscovery of the photo. It is an event which has been preserved through having been marked in a number of ways, marks which simultaneously distort and immortalize. It is the only photograph that was taken of Tony at that age. Few other relics pin down his life at the age of 14. It is rare tangible proof of him existing at the age of 14. In what ways are these relics different to the memory implants in *Bladerunner*? But more interestingly, in what ways are they the same? What things does Tony (or indeed any of us) need to convince him that he existed as a 14-year-old? How do these things contribute to his understanding of himself as a 44-year-old now? How do such things provide anchorage for such memories?

Normally, people are not really that bothered about this sort of thing but practitioner-oriented research often projects us into such issues of reflexivity. Teachers engaged in reflective research can revisit and reconstruct their histories through reinterpretations of earlier writings. Each piece produced along the way provides an insight into particular concerns being addressed at different points in time.

Anecdote 5: Aimee
In Lacan's doctoral thesis he tells the tale of 'Aimee' who hit the Parisian headlines after stabbing a famous actress. Lacan argued that she was hurting herself in that she simultaneously admired and hated the actress with whom she identified. The actress was the person Aimee wished to become: 'free' and 'admired'. Lacan talks of identity as something located in the symbolic social network rather than in the biological body. The actress has a symbolic existence in that network and becomes the identity assumed by Aimee through her identification with the actress.

Anecdote 6: Krapp's Last Tape
After watching *Krapp's Last Tape* I was quite moved by the senile character trying to identify with his youthful and lyrically fluent past, self-recorded on audiotape. He was simultaneously despising and admiring this past self; seemingly adopting the self-defence mechanism of seeing his past self as inferior while struggling to understand what his past self was saying.

In what ways can we distance ourselves from past/present/future selves in this manner? In writing for a book we are offering a version of our professional selves as a posture in highlighting/creating aspects of our practice for public perusal. We are selective for effect but there is never a total truth to our practice. In the last chapter Tony forced his agenda into the work of one of his students (Lorna) – providing a reading which the student herself only partially recognized. There remained a distance between his reading of the student's writing (read according to his own agenda of how she had responded to his teaching) and her own reading, based around her perceptions of both the professional and course-related demands she faced. There is an ongoing feeling of inadequacy in attempting to describe our practice as tutors. But to describe the minutiae of this goes only so far in depicting the shape we see. In reaching forward to the complex world of psychoanalytic theory to assist us in building this shape, our chosen strategy is to offer metaphoric representations as fictive devices to highlight features we see in our everyday professional experience which might otherwise be lost in the mundanity of straight description. Ricoeur (1984: ix) suggests that the use of a metaphor activates strains and stresses throughout the whole sentence in which the other words function in emphasizing the 'impertinence' of the new metaphor. These strains and stresses project us out of the realm of familiar literal meanings towards creating a meaning effect unattainable within the parameters of the previous realm. Thus we seek to provide a rationale for practitioner research commensurate with our practice.

Teachers' writing of self

In understanding the task of practitioner research as a construction of self in relation to the professional/social context we face, how might we proceed in producing and understanding the reflective writing that might arise within such a process? To conclude this chapter we offer three extended examples from senior teachers who have worked within the context of the MA but who are now shifting towards thinking about how such perspectives might be developed within doctoral-level work. They discuss their work in relation to their early attempts at making sense of the work of Lacan and Zizek. The first extract looks at a headteacher's re-examination of his past writing for the course. In the next example the teacher's own changing professional role is evaluated when her school is formally closed but then actually amalgamated with another, forcing her from a senior management position into less familiar territory as a classroom teacher governed by new policy requirements. In the final example, a teacher documents her observations of how her school seems to conjure an image of the pupils that it serves which is quite at variance with how the pupils see themselves.

In the first extract Alistair Bryce-Clegg (2000), a primary headteacher, reviews his work for the MA course in the light of his recent grappling with Lacan's writing.

> When I embarked on the course I felt that I was enthusiastic, committed, fair, just able and most of all trapped within constraints that were placed on me by what I saw as the 'system'. I would later discover that these constraints were as much about me as they were bureaucracy.
>
> . . . Lacan following Freud argues that we all have an almost infinite capacity to deceive ourselves especially when contemplating or describing our own image. It is at this point that ego comes into play to negotiate between the reality of the situation and the unconscious desire to achieve the ideal. The MA process encourages self-analysis of the practice and the practitioner to pre-empt the ego and seek the reality.
>
> Looking back on my journal entries and data presentation in year one and year two, it is clear that I am making various biographical

claims as to the teacher I felt that I was . . . a great deal of my writing was seeking recognition for what I had done in the classroom. I reflect very much on systems rather than the individual. Yet I was gaining a great deal of knowledge about myself as a practitioner. Initially this was very subconscious and evidence of the changes that were taking place in my practice are not recognised by me as the writer at the time. It is only now that my understanding of theory and practice has evolved through the MA process. I can see that I have gained more experience, and the ability to reflect after the passage of time has proved invaluable.

In light of Lacan's view I now must reflect on the place of that knowledge in the network of self-construction. This is a drawn out and complicated process which can never be completely accurate in its conclusions as we can never totally eradicate the presence of 'ego'.

I wanted to look back on some of the work that I had presented during the first two years of the course and see if I could identify any of the 'myths' or 'images' that I was presenting about my own practice and to see if I could identify any truths or patterns of myself coming to terms with the practitioner that I really am. The most blatant piece of self-proclamation within my writing occurs in the first line of my policy document (Year 2) where I write: 'I am a child centred practitioner'. Here I am making a very bold statement about my view of me with little grounding in actual fact but based mainly on my understanding. I have to question now what made me feel the need to make that statement in the first place.

The answer to this may well be linked to my writing in Year 1, some of which I have already outlined . . . The whole of the year's writing was focused around recognition and perhaps more poignantly approval.

In my previous writing I have made reference to a comment made to me by a parallel teacher when discussing the limitations of shared planning. After one such planning session I was told by a colleague 'We don't all swing from the light fittings with a paintbrush between our teeth!' Initially I was angered by that statement because I felt that it was said in a sarcastic manner. Then I was secretly pleased because this meant that she saw my teaching in this way, as dynamic and exciting.

This writing was originally presented in the context of writing about a child-centered approach to teaching and learning. The point that interests me most is why I chose to present this piece of writing as data.

I can see three definite strands running through its content. The perception of me that I wanted others to see, the perception that I felt others had of me (the other teacher present) and the ego.

I am presenting myself to the reader as someone who finds year group planning restrictive because I cannot go my own way. The image to the reader is one of someone whose practice is then perhaps a little out of the ordinary, unusual. I present the other practitioner in this scenario in an unattractive light. My interpretation of her comment is of it being cutting and sarcastic. Then the most important statement of the piece, that I was pleased with her comments because they confirm exactly what I want others to think about my practice. The fact that I said that I was 'secretly' pleased indicates subconscious desire to achieve my ideal by convincing myself that not only did I see myself playing out this idealistic practitioner role but that others also did. Even if they did not say so, that is what they meant. The Lacanian conception of ego seems ever present.

By looking back at this data I can now see clear patterns emerging that help me to gain a better understanding of myself as a person as well as myself as a practitioner. What my analysis cannot do is to give me definitive reasons as to why I presented myself in the way that I did then or do now. My own ego would never allow myself to see absolute truth, but the process can help me to gain a better understanding of my own actions and an insight into possible reasoning behind them.

My role as an educator has changed on an almost annual basis throughout the three years of the MA, moving from class teacher to deputy head, to headteacher. The ability to recognise elements of self in practice and to examine their reasoning has proved invaluable in the execution of my various roles.

In the second extract Mary Savill (1999) contemplates her changing understanding of her own teaching as she moves voluntarily from a senior post to a classroom teacher role following the amalgamation of her school with another. Since writing, she has become head of learning support in the same school.

I embarked on the MA hoping to find solutions to the words I heard all around me, permeating my consciousness, of the need to be a 'good' teacher. Such words seem political in origin, coming from the educational media into an everyday world where teachers are to be judged either 'good' or 'failing'. My initial standpoint may be about a need to fulfil the expectations of others. Gaining another qualification could become part of my protective armoury. Answers however are not so easily come by and more questioning became the norm. The MA has provided the opportunity for me to gain sufficient confidence to stand back and review my beliefs about my role as a teacher and to make strategic decisions about myself and my practice, based on personal fulfilment, as opposed to fitting into a purely political mould. For a large part of this experience I am concerned with attempting to understand images of self and to discover the depths of my context. In trying to discern what are the features that I hold dear, I will look at micro situations, which have resonance with typical frustrations I experience. The account reveals my attempts to engage closely with that which I have come to take for granted . . .

In my previous post, I was Head of Technology and also Head of Year. My school was identified as one of two to close, due to falling rolls. After some time, it became accepted that a new school was to open. This was a direct result of strongly focused action by some Governors, staff, parents and pupils, channelled through the Head. The experience of feeling part of such a dynamic group, stung into action to prevent the inevitable, irrevocable closure was exhilarating. There was the implicit suggestion of reduced numbers denoting a failing school, with poor teachers. The fact of the matter being that a subsequent Ofsted and HMI visits presented a very supportive, positive view.

As the closures went ahead I chose to apply for teacher of Home Economics, having discussed with my Head my possible position in the new school. I thought at the time of making the decision, that such a step would free me to a large extent from the hated administrative task that impinged upon the time I wanted to spend teaching and with my pupils. I wanted to be in real classroom contact with my pupils understanding the inevitability of my working with disruptive pupils, rather than being in a 'status' position in dealing with them . . . I recognised I was at variance with a widely accepted view of teacher success. It isn't usual to cast off 'status'. My values are at question here, will I be other's view of accomplished teacher or my own? I had a sense of needing to move on in the personal development of my teacher being. What was this view of teacher to which I was subscribing? It held notions of active, curious children engaged in positive activities of enjoyment not conflict, of building self-esteem and mutual respect.

I wish to examine ways in which personal identity may be constructed. From my reading of Lacan, I became aware of discourse centred round a network of symbols. A body of knowledge is signified by the language surrounding it. Such a body of knowledge might be my construction of myself to myself. From my history I have come to hold beliefs about myself. Some of these beliefs have been inner ones, never before given voice. As I begin to use language to describe such beliefs, my reading of Lacan suggests to me that I am making a demand. I am asking that you accept what I am saying, while in reality I may be actually aiming at something else. Such a notion might be saying I am a shy person. An outsider meeting me in my own environment, where I feel secure and in control, might have difficulty believing such a statement. In saying I am shy I might be aiming at something else, it may be to get the other person to take the initiative in an ensuing discussion, until I work out what is the appropriate tack to take. I may not have admitted that to myself before, preferring others to accept my label of shy to avoid my feeling embarrassed. [My] 'Drive', in Lacanian terms, is [encapsulated in] my ensuing act of thinking and writing about my demand. I am to face the teacher I am and persist in unwrapping such notions of self. In discussing the distinction of there being one [demand] without the other [drive] Zizek cites the example of '*The Terminator*'. In the film, Arnold Swarzenegger plays a cyborg, who returns from the future to contemporary Los Angeles. His task is to kill the mother of a future leader. The element of horror in his character is that he holds true to his function of programmed automaton and even when all that is left of him is a metallic, legless skeleton, he persists with the demand and continues, uncompromisingly in pursuit of his victim. Thus the Terminator becomes the embodiment of drive, devoid of desire. Drive and Demand go hand in hand in my present tasks . . .

The next series of data extracts are taken from my being out in the corridors of school during a non-teaching period. The time was within the space of one lesson and each of the pupils was out of the same lesson.

Me: Why are you out of class?
J: Miss, I feel sick.
Me: You don't look sick to me. Hurry up.

Me: What are you doing out of class?
B: Miss, I'm going to the office.
Me: What do you mean?
B: I've got a pass.
Me: I don't want you out of class. I don't want you to be the one that offers to do jobs. Stay in class and make sure you take every opportunity to improve.

Me: Where are you going?
C: Miss to the toilet.
Me: You're the third Year 9 pupil wandering about this lesson.
C: Miss, I've got girl's problems.
Me: I don't care. You've got lunchtime to sort that out. The rest of us have to manage. I don't want you out of class again.

In each of these three instances I was concerned with my own form and my functioning in the role of the school representative. Upholding the 'rule' that pupils should not be allowed out of class – my pupils – my form. By the end of the third situation, I had in my mind a view that pupils in my form were disproportionately out of class and I had a partial responsibility for this. If any of them were to get into trouble it would come back to reflect on me.

There is an increase in my interaction with each consecutive instance. J got a direct question, an implication from my response 'You don't look sick to me' that I was prepared to doubt his reason, and an instruction to hurry up and disappear back to his correct place.

I implied that B should not have been put out of class. He knew as he offered me his pass to add validity to his being there. Direct speech said to B that his place was in working hard and not wasting time wandering, and by implication I had inferred that I had higher expectations of B staying on the 'right side'.

C could have elicited sympathy, but instead got a rejection: 'I don't care'. In my classroom, would I have reacted differently? Would I have seen her as a young girl learning to cope? Instead I inferred that the world of school/work made no allowances for the biological inconveniences of being female . . .

Where am I now? In this most recent data, I consider that the situation typically characterises both my practice and the children's responses. In this context, the school corridor, interaction with the pupils is brief and, by my agenda, to the point. Each pupil was legitimately out of class and I felt time-wasting opportunism was their aim . . . I was not in a position to order their immediate return to class, but could refuse to condone the pupils' actions . . . 'You don't look sick to me. Hurry up.' I felt this was initial disapproval. J is often late to class and able to cause distractions at will. I wanted to let him know that he would have to be very convincing to be ill in my class. B recently joined our school. I wanted to reinforce my perceptions to him of the school's way of being. Pupils wandering about in corridors are not encouraged. I am aware of an historical culture where pupils 'arrange' to leave class and meet up, their resulting behaviours can disrupt other teachers' lessons or even set off fire alarms. I wanted B to know I did not approve of him putting himself in this position. He has his own reputation to build and I expected it to be one that complemented my form's performance. C had everyone over a barrel, there was no legitimate way I could prove or disprove her reason. I chose through empathy to indicate that her personal problems had to be included in her planning of the day and in no way detract from her purpose in being in school. These initial comments on looking at the situation all derive from my inflexible views. I would in my value system avoid unnecessary interruption to my work. I would prefer to have control over my own actions and as far as possible not allow interruptions to what I see as important. These are reactions to the view I hold of the work ethic. My way of being cannot be isolated from earlier or subsequent experiences. This is where I begin to unwrap notions I hold of myself, as I move between roles. No longer viewing myself as only teacher, but person, form, tutor, mentor and school representative.

Personal constructs

In my view of this there is a sense of conduct, career, values and circumstances. At this point I am trying to say what I see in this reflected image. In no particular order I believe myself to be:

- middle class;
- family centred;
- satisfied with my age-view of some experience of life;
- sympathetic – good listener;
- a respecter of tradition;
- boring, shy, no good at gossip;
- conscientious;
- at the end of ambition;
- a teacher (full time, long term, identify strongly with role vocation);
- quite energetic, purposeful, self-motivated, tenacious;
- independent, self-contained;
- non-competitive;
- opposed to mixed ability teaching;
- intolerant of those who don't do the right thing;
- caring, kind, sincere.

I don't feel alienation from values and practices of the institution or in fact to any great extent from the wider political education debate. I find as time goes on, my career story gets more difficult to tell. It is no longer a chosen strategic path, it's almost in regression. Under contemporary pressures the only way forward is in reward for good classroom practice. I am content with that. I am not experiencing a crisis of identity or career. Rather a pervasive preoccupation with adequacy of self, linked to teacher identity in evaluation appraisal.

What professional identity is available to me?

I don't know if it's achievable through the organisation of school. Unease with the present notion of teacher identity – 'constrained by the culturally available iconographies of teacherhood' (MacLure 1993: 320).

Lacan's view of the 'imaginary' phase presents me with a notion that my sense of self has arrived externally from the imaginary. My identity comes from a MIS-REPRESENTATION, a false persuasion of self which will stay with me as the ideal ego for the remainder of my life. The reflection therefore presents me with the signified and myself, then acts in it becoming the signifier. I through language enter the social world and have constructed it around me. I thus produce a fiction of myself, the unconscious being, as structured as a language. The signs and symbols by which the unconscious functions in a sense is 'like' language. Lacan is saying that this unconscious comes to exist after language is acquired.

Foucault's view persuades me to 'develop action, thought and desires by proliferation, juxtaposition and disjunction' and to 'prefer what is positive and multiple' (Harvey 1989: 44). Thus will my view of self inevitably be centred in a specific course of action in time and one that I can only make temporary claims to.

The truth of myself cannot be specified, as it has by its nature a plurality of formations. Of necessity, use of extracts of data is selective, producing 'not one, but many silences and they are an integral part of the strategies that underlie and permeate discourses' (Rabinow 1991: 310).

Freud's views . . . add a wider angle on my image of self for he presents the position of the ego adapting to different cultures being tantamount to survival. A child's self-education is about what they learn despite the adults, not because of them. The paradigm encompasses a child finding out in his own way according to his own individual needs at the time. Therefore I have been subconsciously selective in what I have absorbed from my cultural contexts through life's journey, taking and weaving particular truths from unconscious desires. Our own ways of being then, link us to the past. Ironically, what is absent is perhaps what I should be interested in, but the ways in which each makes their own out of what they are given, are unpredictable . . .

Reading Zizek and Lacan had an impact on my way of thinking and my way of writing: 'The analysis of ideology must then direct its attention to the points at which names which prima facie signify positive descriptive features already function as "rigid designators"' (Zizek 1989: 109).

I aimed to achieve some identity with self, to become myself, once I have finally matured. Zizek's interplay of imaginary and symbolic identification was useful to enhance my integration into the social field. I am still aware of a gap between utterances and their enunciation, as I become increasingly enabled to listen to others and question 'Why are you telling me this?'

In the third extract Janice England (1999), a head of languages at a secondary school, provides some exploratory entries from her PhD research diary. Her specific theme is a consideration of how black children are accommodated within her own school. She examines terms such as 'inclusion' and 'disaffection' with a view to examining how these issues are understood within the school and more broadly. This work has led to a paper being published in the journal *Educational Action Research* (England and Brown, in press). Some extracts are published here with permission.

> The fourth planet was a businessman's. He was so busy that he didn't even look up when the little prince arrived.
>
> 'Good morning,' said the prince. 'Your cigarette's gone out.'
>
> 'Three and two makes five. Five and seven, twelve. Twelve and three, fifteen. Good morning. Fifteen and seven, twenty-two. Twenty-two and six, twenty eight. No time to relight it. Twenty-six and five, thirty-one. Phew! So that makes five hundred and one million, six hundred and twenty-two thousand, seven hundred and thirty one.'
>
> 'Five hundred million what?'
>
> 'Eh? Are you still there? Five hundred and one million . . . erm I forget. I've got so much work to do! I'm a serious man I am. I don't idle away my life! Two and five, seven . . .'
>
> (Antoine de Saint-Exupery: *The Little Prince*)

Circular 10/99 [DfEE 1999] Social Inclusion: Pupil Support (Extract from Chapter 3)

Minority ethnic children

3.6 Rates of exclusion among Black-Caribbean pupils, especially boys, are significantly higher than those of other pupils. Governing bodies and head teachers should monitor the use of sanctions against pupils of ethnic minority background and reassure themselves that the school's behaviour policy against racial prejudice and harassment is being fully enforced. Where there is unjustified over-representation of Black-Caribbean pupils, a strategy should be implemented to address this. Staff need to take particular care if there is a possibility that an incident was provoked by racial harassment. Teachers also need to ensure that they avoid any risk of stereotyping and that they are alert to cultural differences in manner and demeanour. Good connections between schools and community groups can help in this process.

3.7 Some minority ethnic groups attain extremely good results at school. But others do not. Schools should be aware that so-called 'colour-blind' policies can lead to the persistence of inequalities between ethnic groups. Successful initiatives designed to address under-achievement include:

- ethnic monitoring of achievement;
- community mentoring schemes;
- high quality home-school liaison work;
- the development of a Black perspective in the school curriculum;
- focus on minority pupil achievers; and
- effective links between mainstream and supplementary schools.

The reason I turn to this now is that I was struck so strongly by an image in the corridor today that it took my breath away. A couple of boys were tossing and batting a blown-up condom back and forth to each other as they stood outside the respective classrooms they had been thrown out of, presumably for messing about in class or, as they would say, having a laugh. As in a dream the image of a memory was superimposed for me of my cousins kicking a can up and down the alleyway outside the back of my grandmother's house when I was a small child. One of the boys in the corridor had a slight look of my older cousin, the tilt of the head, that's all, but the image would not disappear once it had struck me. Then I thought, what are these children doing here? They should be outside having fun, climbing trees, kicking cans, chasing about . . . Why are we doing this to our children? Most poignant of all in this story I am choosing to tell you is the fact that it was a blown-up condom, a sordid remainder, a symbol from the adult world, used as a toy.

I am beginning to ask the question 'What is childhood?' and also 'What is a child?' In my masters dissertation I had begun to explore myths surrounding childhood. But I didn't at that time question my understanding of the words 'child' or 'childhood' themselves. These are fundamental, everyday understandings and notions, which I have so far taken for granted. I now feel drawn to explore them further. Is childhood about survival of smaller people in an adult world? Looking at children's books, such as Roald Dahl, Harry Potter or some of the fairy stories I grew up with it might seem so. What do I mean when I refer to my pupils as 'children'? Are they practising for adult life in their games and playground activities, in their relationships and their conversations? I have assumed so. I have taken a fairly biological view about it so far; I have seen children as undeveloped adults on a progression through puberty to adulthood, preparing for maturity through roles that they take in their social interactions. What if I looked at them differently, as a group apart, with their own lives, priorities, social structures?

The extract from the story at the beginning of this writing is from *The Little Prince*. A small child is wandering from planet to planet trying to make sense of the adult world. In this particular extract he meets a businessman who is so wrapped up in counting that he has forgotten exactly what it is he is counting or why. I chose this piece because it makes me think of the national education policy makers with their psychotic logic of target-setting and measuring which they are imposing upon schools and ultimately on children's lives.

Are we putting our children through all of this simply because we adults just cannot stand watching them have the fun we have lost? When the government sets us targets to raise standards in our schools or issues guidelines to promote social inclusion in our system it is using the rigorous psychotic logic of our time. This is an attempt to provide meaning to society's perception that there is something terrifying out there threatening its stability for which it can offer no sense or meaning. As teachers we in turn blame the government which is giving us orders to behave in this way, or we blame black kids because they won't stop trying to have fun in our classrooms. When we do this we too are behaving like automatons and locating our terror outside ourselves. The businessman in the story seems to represent the adult world bereft of its *jouissance*. He is a Lacanian automaton driven by the big Other located outside himself who has given him his orders; he is driven, without desire, to count and count for all eternity enveloped in the fantasy he offers the little prince of himself as a 'serious man'.

There's an advert for a car on the television at the moment. The car is white with black windows and as it swoops past a house the camera focuses on a small black child dressed all in white blowing bubbles into the air. At the beginning of my writing I alluded to a notion of wanting to explore the idea of childhood and the fantasies that surround it. In the advertisement we are offered an image of pure childhood *jouissance* in the figure of the child blowing bubbles. This is used to link with the shiny fast motor car of the adult world; a hint of our lost desire perhaps which might be retrieved with the purchase of that same car. It certainly functions as a very powerful image at this level. I am intrigued by the choice of the black child dressed in a white garment. Lacan urges us to scrutinise the unnecessary details. Why a black child? Why all in white? White is the stuff of fairy tales, lost innocence and purity. So does a black child really represent the ultimate *jouissance* the middle-class white car purchasing public has lost and must desire?

My first response to reading the DfEE extract was from the title itself 'Social Inclusion' which for me constructs a social norm within which it is desirable to be included. There is a great universal 'We' which ethnic minorities are excluded from. This is a better and more desirable level of reality to which access is denied. And so here we are offering our excluded neighbour 'support'. The headteacher is expected then to put in place measures, from identifying specific problems of black pupils to policing the institution to avoid racial harassment or stereotyping ('monitor', 'behaviour policy', 'reassure themselves', 'fully enforced', 'strategy', 'implemented').

The Bible teaches us to love our neighbour. A disciple asked Jesus: 'Who is my neighbour?' and so Jesus told the story of the Good Samaritan. This interests me simply because the Samaritans were themselves a much despised and socially excluded group, and the story tells us that it was this representative of an ethnic minority group in fact who set the example of biblical good practice. The victim in this story is empowered. This document, conversely, constructs a powerless victim whom we must patronise and draw into our universal 'good'.

The problem of constructing the black child as a victim here is that this child is then perceived to have a lack or a problem to overcome ('ethnic monitoring of achievement', 'community mentoring schemes', 'focus on minority pupil achievers'). The problem is never located within the universal 'We' from which this Circular springs. And so because the problem is located outside of us, it is not uncomfortable. The black child joins the other disadvantaged groups in society such as the homeless, disabled, mentally ill, homosexual, female . . . These groups all have a lack located firmly in their social identity and our own liberal white educated identity remains intact, and caring. Those less caring amongst our community must however be policed by laws ensuring that the disadvantaged groups are not harassed. Thus: 'the development of a Black perspective in the school curriculum'; and the promotion of a multiculturalist position.

In the school we take pride in its multicultural composition. We celebrate difference and positively promote the notion that 'it's OK to be different' and yet we are all one happy community, all 'one under the skin' as it were. There are however limits to this that make me feel a little uneasy, as any real challenge to the norm is perceived as potentially disturbing and unsettling. We have, it seems, a hierarchy of acceptable differences and unacceptable ones. A Muslim girl may cover her head but we are less happy with piercings or tattoos, which denote no specific religious group but are seen as simply transgressive. By law homosexuality may not be 'promoted'. And I daily witness black boys in conflict with school discipline; the visible evidence of this is a line of black boys outside the deputy's office at dinner time. And in fact I am unhappy with the notion that we are all the same, since the Muslim girl with her head covered is clearly positioned for me in this context as Other.

In building our community we feel readily able to embrace visible Otherness given our premise of inclusion. There is a risk in this however that it reinforces a sense of a norm that results in fixing the Other firmly in their place. I am uncertain too about our tolerance of the Other when it suits us and not when it shocks us. For example, the covered head represents for me, as a western woman, an unacceptable positioning of the female within this different culture as yet again Other, but I feel a pressure from my western liberal standpoint to accept it because I wish to avoid a Eurocentric bias. How far would my liberal attitude take me? In the case of clitoridectomy, for example, surely I must retreat back towards Europe in horror. So I meet an ideological deadlock here and I need to find a way to resolve it.

A key aspect present in each of the preceding sets of writing is a recognition by the authors that the writing is created as a challenge to their own sense of their professional engagements. They are all in a sense opening themselves up for self-scrutiny in which they seek to locate the masks behind which they are operating. They are examining the 'demands' they are making of the people reading about their research. This results perhaps in the teacher-researchers acting differently but without constructing apparatus that might evaluate whether such new actions are better. The research task in so far as it is located within an enterprise of professional development is not so much about creating improvement *per se* as becoming more sensitive to how specific professional strategies are related to particular supporting rationales. Reflective writing thus provides a vehicle through which teachers can inspect their professional practices with a view to better understanding how external influences (for example, government policy documents, learning theories, personal motivations and so forth) impact on and shape these practices.

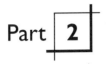

Part **2**

The postmodern turn –
deconstructing the nursery classroom

6

From emancipation to postmodernism: a nursery study

As has been depicted in the preceding chapters we are working with the premise that the practitioner researching in their own classroom brings about changes both through acting in the classroom itself and in producing writing commenting on this classroom practice. That is, descriptions of classroom practice made by the practitioner effect changes in the reality attended to by this practitioner. The writing generated in this process can be seen as both responding to past action and guiding future action. In short, the practitioner, in describing their classroom, affects the way they both see and act in it and, moreover, the way that they subsequently choose to describe it (since it has been changed by their actions). In engaging in this circular hermeneutic process, teacher-researchers pass through a sequence of perspectives each capable of generating various types of writing and each susceptible to a variety of later interpretations.

For us, an essential task of this book centres on how the research process – when it is conceived in these terms – enables the practitioner in organizing the complexity of the teaching situation, with a particular emphasis on how 'monitoring change' can be converted to 'control of change'. But it was this very desire for control, and the difficulties we encountered in trying to document it, which led us into a certain scepticism with our original proposals. We began to question whether this central motivation clouded our vision from the very complexities we sought to capture. What began as an attempt at a reconciliation of the hermeneutic underpinnings of our practitioner research enterprise with poststructuralist analyses turned more into a disruption of our initial assumptions. Thus we switched from a somewhat rationalist focus on effecting productive change through a systematic process, towards moving from premises where initial assumptions are necessarily a little less secure.

The remainder of this Chapter and Chapters 7, 8, 9 and 10 can be seen as an extended case study where efforts are directed at realizing a shift in this focus. The writing is drawn from Liz's doctoral studies and where the central focus was on Liz's teaching practice within a nursery class. Because Liz is principally responsible for the work that follows, the co-authorial 'we' will now be replaced by the 'I' of the teacher-researcher.

My PhD work (Jones 1999) was an extension of a masters enquiry where the aim had been to explore how and in what ways the production of certain education practices were (supposedly) disadvantageous to girls. Such an aspiration was born out of a long-term commitment to both feminism and socialism. As a consequence, the following title and set of aims were drawn up for the PhD proposal in 1994:

Title

The teacher researcher and emerging power relations in the nursery.

Aims

- To provide an account of how children's identifications, as evidenced in their use of language, contribute to their own evolving identity, with particular reference to gender.
- To create a theoretical framework, based on modern social theory (e.g. Habermas 1987), for examining and structuring the teacher's professional engagement, which accommodates personal shifting perspectives.
- To collate examples of children's speech as data in critically examining the social norms governing their classroom activity.
- To create a record of everyday teaching, critically examining the social norms which guide teacher practice, directed at enhancing children's critical capability.
- To develop an action research methodology, which emphasizes textual production as both a monitor and catalyst of professional change.

Specifically, I wanted to investigate:

interactions between children and with their teacher. Concepts of power will be examined and their relationship to emergent identities and particular features of the practice of teaching. The study is directed at examining the ways in which children represent through language their understanding of themselves as social subjects within the dualistic gender order (Walkerdine and Lucey 1989). A key issue will focus on how language empowers and constrains; through language children not only constitute themselves as unique persons in relation to others in the social world but that . . . 'language has a material existence. It defines our possibilities and limitations, it constitutes our subjectivities' (Coward and Ellis 1977). The study examines how attempts to describe the developing linguistic facility of a child become entangled with the evolving linguistic categories of the practitioner's perceptions.

A central tenet of the study is that teaching and learning are social acts. They occur because of and in response to historical circumstances and social contexts. There is a recognition that such contexts are also constituted by acts of teaching and learning. A contention of this study will be that the emergent social identities of the children are in part conferred by society but that the children themselves are active agents in shaping their identities. Through examples of children's language which illuminate the child's perception of her/his social world it will be possible to review how society shapes social identity, and how, simultaneously, the children appear to be resisting aspects of this process. Embedded in the study is the assertion that children are not passive subjects who receive their gender identity as a given, but that they are active participants in the development of self-realisation. The writing will describe the world as the children seem to see it as reflected in the teacher's perception of what constitutes reality.

The theoretical framework, within which the project was to be located, was understood in the following way:

This research project is located within a theoretical framework which asserts that language and the development of language is the central process whereby subjectivity or identity is produced (Urwin 1984). As a practitioner, a task is to discern and describe the child's 'positioning' as implied by her/his language whilst acknowledging that the teacher-researcher's own 'positioning' is implicit in such descriptions. The researcher's 'self', including her perspective, is an essential part of the description being created. This notion draws on poststructuralist accounts (e.g. Coward and Ellis 1977) whereby the self and the situation are not separate but mutually formative and are, as a consequence, part of each other. It also draws on Habermas' theory of communicative action (1987), and his distinction between systemic and life world perspectives on social experience.

The methodology was described in these terms:

By using qualitative methods of research, my aim is to examine the impact of social and cultural processes on the self-identity of a very specific group of young children and to reconcile the findings with the researcher's professional practice. On a practical level this will entail making transcripts of linguistic interactions between the children and their teacher and the children and each other. This task will require understanding the symbolic interactions of the children and the contexts in which those interactions occur. The criteria for selecting certain examples of speech acts will be that they challenge and de-stabilise the researcher's own understandings and assumptions that she brings to social constructs such as 'the child' and 'identity'. In addition, a journal will be kept which will log specific events arising in the classroom which relate to the children's linguistic competence and the social positioning this reveals. This will also be used to record and examine the professional intentions and actions of the researcher in response to the data, as part of a continuing process of interrelating theoretical ideas with practical exigencies (Carr and Kemmis 1986: 145). The written accounts of classroom observations, besides allowing the teacher-researcher to 'capture the moment', will function as an integral part of the research process in that by framing relevant aspects of practice in writing the practitioner can move from mere description to understanding the complexities of such descriptions. The process of monitoring change will thus influence this change, engendering an explicit dialectic between the research process and the object of that research. The study will position itself in relation to recent practitioner research paradigms (e.g. Schon 1983; Elliott 1993b; Brown 1994b; Lomax 1994) with a particular emphasis on teacher narrative as data. The product of this research will not result in statements of practical implications common to all. Rather, it gives an account of a practitioner examining specific issues within her practice and how these were addressed as problems within the research process. The value of the study will be judged through its success in providing a detailed and rich image of professional interpretations and descriptions with which other professionals will find resonance.

Generally speaking, plans or proposals such as the one outlined above become the means for allowing progress. However, rather than making 'advancement' or 'headway', the movements of the resulting thesis could be better characterized by words such as 'toing' and 'froing' and sometimes even 'regression'. Such manoeuvrings can be attributed to certain ambiguities and paradoxes situated within the proposal.

It would seem that what I was proposing to do was to couple and join together two significantly different conceptions of what constitutes identity or subjectivity. In other words, by drawing on poststructuralist theories I was acknowledging a distrust of the idea that the human being can be an independent entity – preferring instead the notion of the individual who is constructed within and a product of social and linguistic forces and is, therefore, a being who is 'always in process' (Weedon 1987).

But, the proposal also indicates an attraction to an 'Habermasian' conceptualization of the subject. That is, one who can use reason, clarity and truth in order to progress (Barry 1995). It is this notion of the subject which finds favour within certain practitioner research paradigms. It was these two notions of the subject which I was attempting to marry together.

Intertwined in this unlikely union are two contrasting views of how language functions. One perception works from the premise that language can first 'capture the moment'. So, for example, I can collect examples of children's talk which will then allow for insights into their social world. Put slightly differently, by hearing what the children say I can then 'know' what they are thinking. Moreover, language, as it is conceived and used within reflective models of action research, can lead to understandings about practice and hence *control* of practice.

By contrast, poststructuralist theories dispute the notion that language is transparent. As a consequence, experiences, including those that occur within the nursery, are open to contradictory and conflicting interpretations and as such the notion that there can be 'control' gets dissipated. However, this does not imply that there is no such thing as meaning. Nor does it mean that the task of applying meanings should be abandoned. Instead, it is a recognition that any interpretations are both temporary and specific to the context or practices within which they are produced. Additionally, poststructuralist theories dispute that identity is either 'natural' or a 'given' entity and, as a consequence, there is, for example, nothing inevitable about contemporary gender arrangements.

The joining together of two such contrasting positions seemed impossible. However, if a coupling or a marriage was not an option could there instead be reconciliations between the two where, as an example, the hermeneutic underpinnings of practitioner research could be aided and abetted by poststructuralist analysis? There were brief attempts to follow this route. However, it quickly became apparent that reconciliation was not the answer, for it involved two incompatible tasks. On the one hand, there was a belief that there were fundamental anchorings to which individuals had recourse, including universal notions of what constituted 'truth' and 'certainty'. On the other hand, poststructuralism worked at dripping a corrosive scepticism on such assumptions.

As a course of action, reconciliations between modernist concerns of practitioner research and poststructuralist theories were abandoned. However, this out of kilter and ill-suited pair were not yet ready for divorce or a complete break. Too much was at stake, including the abandonment of certain personal hopes and desires. Effectively, it was these aspirations which underpinned the aims of the thesis (and this book). That is, I/we still had/have ambitions that practitioner research could/can work towards improving the social conditions of all our lives, including teachers and their pupils. Thus, rather than moving from and breaking with paradigms which drew their strength from liberal humanism the decision was made to remain not 'married' but 'engaged'.

As Stronach and MacLure (1997) point out, there is an embedded paradox within notions of 'engagement', for it can be both a 'commencement of war, or an announcement of marriage' (p. 10). But, as they go on to indicate, both wars and marriages are problematic, for each in their different ways seek closure, whether this is in the form of victory or consummation (p. 11). However, perhaps there are other ways to engage and where the aim is to open thinking up rather than close it down. Indeed, Stronach and MacLure go on to suggest that one can simply 'engage' – that is, 'take part' (p. 11). This then raises the question of how to 'take part'?

The 'how' of taking part is both complicated and paradoxical for it requires remaining within the logic which circumscribes 'teacher as researcher' paradigms while simultaneously trying to take apart the logic which supports and gives strength to such traditions. Clearly, such a move has a knock-on effect. For example, it situates the practitioner-researcher within a conundrum. Thus, work is undertaken which aims at securing equitable relations as well as developing critical thinking so that both the children and the practitioner might then free themselves from dominant and coercive structures. Against this, however, the attempt is to incorporate and interrelate with poststructuralist theories; theories which in very many ways work against and cut across the above concerns.

Both the PhD thesis and this book are attempts at engaging with and incorporating poststructuralism into practitioner research. We have not abandoned our aspirations for emancipation, rather it is these which have become the basis for self-critique. It is our own investments in such aims which both the thesis and this book, theoretically and practically, examine.

Chapters 7, 8, 9 and 10 are attempts at illustrating what some of the repercussions are when poststructuralism is incorporated into practitioner research. First however, some additional notes may be of use.

Loose definitions

As stated previously, poststructuralist theories will not allow for accurate expositions, nor will they tolerate conclusive definitions. However, some definitions of terms may be of use, particularly to other practitioner-researchers who are not, as yet, so immersed in the areas which this book tries to cover. Accordingly, the following definitions are to assist with accessing the work. However, it should be recognized that my own understanding of the terms is ongoing, so the task of fully defining them is an impossible one.

First, throughout the forthcoming chapters, the terms 'poststructuralist' and 'postmodernist' are used more or less interchangeably. This is because, and here I am leaning on Lather (1991), the two terms are sufficiently interrelated and flexible enough to allow me to do this. In a general sense, 'postmodern' is often used to describe 'the larger cultural shifts of a post-industrial, post-colonial era', while 'poststructural' refers to 'the working out of those shifts within the arenas of academic theory' (Lather 1991: 4). This book, however, attempts to work out these shifts within the terrains of practice and theory. Furthermore, while I've used a singular form for grammatical reasons, both should be pluralized to denote the different forms and definitions which are attributed to each.

Second, practices of deconstruction are incorporated into the research processes. This prompts the question, what is deconstruction? Again, this is defined in a number of ways. However, I have found the following definition the most thought-provoking: 'Deconstruction, if such a things exists, should open up' (Derrida in Brannigan *et al.* 1996: 261). At first glance, Derrida's statement seems to be simplicity itself. Thus, I am offered a definition, something which appears tenable and manageable; in other words, something to hold on to. But the words 'if such a thing exists' immediately loosen the grip. So, rather than clarity there is a confusion, a confusion which I have come to believe is a necessary and integral part of being a practitioner-researcher. For confusion means that more pressing questions have to be asked. Hence, deconstruction can open up but not in ways in which I can then definitively claim to know. Rather, it obliges yet another look and yet another set of questions. Moreover, deconstruction can accommodate alternative interpretations. In this way, space is created where particular assumptions and preferred ways of seeing the world can be critiqued.

The final definitions to be offered here centre on 'critical pedagogy'. Before moving into definitions let me first explain why I have come to favour this term over others including 'action research'. My antipathy to 'action research' rests on a number of reasons. For example, action research is premised on the assumption that human beings can become knowledgeable about their own situation (Scott and Usher 1999). Within schools, for example, teachers can improve aspects of practice by means of their own practical actions and by means of their own reflections upon the effects of their own actions. Such reflections can, so it has been argued, have an emancipatory dimension, where internal and external constraints can be challenged and removed (Carr and Kemmis 1986). Construed in these terms, therefore, action research is a collaborative venture, where practitioner-researchers work together to achieve three things: first, a better understanding of themselves; second, a better understanding of their situation; and third, overall changes to a situation. It is Habermas' (1984, 1987, 1991) model of ideal speech which underpins such formulations.

For me, Habermas' model of ideal speech is problematic for two reasons. First, to make it possible language has to be 'undistorted' (Parker 1997). However, for language to be undistorted it would have to be pure and transparent or, as Scott and Usher (1999: 34) put it, 'a language free of the distorting effects of particular practices, readings and interpretations . . . a totally decontextualised language which can fulfil its referential function without vagueness, variation or ambiguity'. Moreover, while action research is committed to challenging a number of dualisms it (or at least many forms of it) does this through a reconciliation of oppositions. There is, as Stronach and MacLure (1997: 117) put it, an 'imperative to resolve, or dissolve, boundary problems in the interest of coherence, wholeness, certainty or singleness of vision'. So while many of the discourses of action research seek to transcend a number of oppositions by favouring a variety of hierarchies (e.g. the practitioner over the researcher, practice over theory), it nevertheless fails to disrupt the hierarchical power of the dualisms. What we have instead is a reversal of dualisms and not a disruption. So while action research can be effective in taking an initial step in order to deconstruct oppressive hierarchical power, it falters when it comes to taking the second step. As Scott and Usher (1999: 39–40) note, it fails to understand that oppositional binaries are 'always present, and indeed necessarily always present, in a conflicting yet interactive way. Each pole of the opposition needs the other, but must always remain 'other'. They continue:

> Thus action research attempts to counter the oppressive hierarchical power of binary oppositions by reconciling the opposites. But in doing this it locates itself in an economy of the same which rejects the otherness or radical alterity which cannot be reconciled. This means that in critical action research emancipation has to be constructed in terms of an economy of sameness, where emancipation becomes the same for all regardless of difference and can only be brought about by processes of rational consensus which converge to the same.

Critical pedagogy

The following chapters can be understood as an attempt to undertake action research differently. The writing does not aim for reconciliations – rather, efforts are directed at trying to disturb and dislocate my own bounded practices.

That said, what meanings am I attributing to 'critical pedagogy'? Let me deal with the latter of the two words first. Why 'pedagogy'? Why not 'teaching', which besides being easier on the tongue, is perhaps more definable?

Perhaps it is because the word 'teaching' and the meanings that are attached to it are so commonplace that there is a tendency to assume that we know what we mean when we say the word. 'Pedagogy' is, by contrast, under-defined. Using 'pedagogy' is, if you like, a way of slowing down those meanings which are or can be readily attached to the more familiar form, 'teaching'. Additionally, I take note of and have heeded David Lusted's (1986) definition of the word. Lusted believes that as a concept 'pedagogy' is important because it 'draws attention to the *process* through which knowledge is produced' (p. 2). He elaborates: '"Pedagogy" addresses the "how" questions involved not only in the transmission or reproduction of knowledge but also in its production (p. 3). He expands further:

> How one teaches is therefore of central interest but, through the prism of pedagogy, it becomes inseparable from what is being taught and crucially, how one learns. In this perspective, to bring the issue of pedagogy in from the cold and onto the central stage of cultural production is to open up for questioning areas of enquiry generally repressed by conventional assumptions, as prevalent in critical as in dominant practices, about theory production and teaching, and about the nature of knowledge and learning.
>
> (Lusted 1986: 3)

Finally, Lusted asserts that 'pedagogy' addresses 'the transformation of consciousness that takes place in the intersection of three agencies – the teacher, the learner and the knowledge they together produce' (1986: 3). Lusted's definition is salutary, I believe, for it resists giving the teacher precedence over the child. However, while taking note of his words, I nevertheless am cautious about his use of the word 'intersection'. My worry is that by using the term Lusted is implying that the meeting or 'intersection' between the agencies can then be said to produce 'truths'. Diagrammatically, the intersection of the three might be seen as shown in Figure 6.1.

However, in the chapters that follow, while there will be crossings or intersections, these will cause destabilizations of assumed knowledge and in so doing create space where it may be possible to rethink thinking. Thus, the proposed 'intersection' might resemble that shown in Figure 6.2.

And what of 'critical'? This refers loosely to those theories which are intended to 'enlighten', 'empower' and 'emancipate' people from oppression. It includes feminism, as well as those educational initiatives

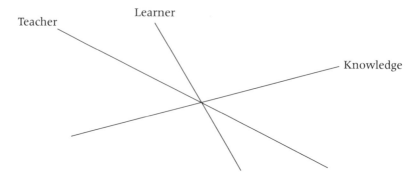

Figure 6.1   'Intersection' of teacher, learner and the knowledge they produce

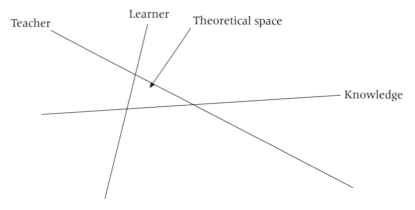

Figure 6.2   Alternative conception of 'intersection'

which are drawn from the critical theory of Habermas, neo-Marxism and liberationist philosophies. It also includes those who in broad terms situate themselves within emancipatory projects but nevertheless seek to incorporate postmodern theories in order to critique and readdress their own emancipatory interests. As such, Figure 6.2 can be seen as a representation of the space which can be made as a consequence of what Giroux (1991: 501) describes as 'border pedagogy'. Thus the opening in Figure 6.2 functions as a 'theoretical space, for creating a discourse capable of raising new questions, offering oppositional practices and producing fresh objects of analysis' (Giroux 1991: 501). In brief, the diagram is a crude and simplistic way of illustrating 'some *other* site' (Derrida quoted in Kearney 1984: 122, emphasis added).

Research context

Empirical work for both masters and doctoral projects was undertaken in my own nursery classroom. The specific focus throughout has been on how children in the nursery classroom become initiated into conventional social practices. In particular, gender relations have been examined in the formation of children's identities. This work has been carried out from the perspective of a teacher-researcher who, simultaneously, has kept an eye on the research process that is being initiated. That is, I was concerned both with the evolution of gender relations in the classroom and with the procedures and structures through which perceptions and research reports are built upon. In doing this, I was bringing into question some of the practices implicit in the cyclical approach underpinning action research (e.g. Elliott 1991), *en route* to developing research strategies which, in my view, were more sensitive to classroom concerns.

My nursery classroom is part of an inner-city primary school in Manchester. The school lies in a district where the assorted ills of urban poverty, including unemployment, are clearly evident. Furthermore, it is an area where certain social structures have undergone changes. The children who attend the nursery reflect these shifts. To give an example – the notion of 'family' within the nursery encompasses those children who are cared for solely by a single parent, as well as parenting by married couples, unmarried heterosexual couples, same-sex (female) couples and foster parents. A core of 20 children attend the nursery full-time while the remaining ten places are reserved for 20 3-year-olds, who because of their young age attend on a part-time basis. At the time of my research there was an even division between these children: ten opted to join us in the morning leaving the remaining ten to attend in the afternoon. I worked alongside a nursery nurse. The children that I focus on in Chapters 7, 8, 9 and 10 all attended school on a full-time basis.

Engaging with poststructuralism and enacting deconstruction: a problematic affair

As already stated, the next four chapters centre on different aspects of the nursery study. It is these aspects which will provide a framework through which a poststructuralist approach is explored. Two theorists, Foucault and Derrida, have been particularly influential in the enquiry and it is their work which underlies much of the analysis in the chapters that follow. However, as indicated, adopting a poststructuralist perspective and incorporating practices of deconstruction into the research practice is neither a straightforward nor an unproblematic affair. Poststructuralism pierces and generally erodes away at the notion of the individual 'coming

to know'. Indeed, poststructuralism, because it renders fragile conceptualizations of subjectivity or identity, creates and imposes a particular
dilemma for one who aspires to being a feminist. In some ways, to
attempt to combine the locations of 'feminism', 'critical pedagogy' and
'postmodernism/poststructuralism' is to tie oneself up in a series of paradoxical knots. Hence, in adopting a feminist stance, as is being attempted
here, it is necessary to criticize the fundamentally homocentric nature
of subjectivity and as a consequence work at expelling the stigma from
notions of 'femininity'. However, is this possible when the (postmodern) subject is conceptualized as splintered and plural? Or, to rephrase
this slightly, is it still conceivable to have a politics of subjectivity when
there is no longer a viable subject? Similarly, can the self achieve
self-determination from the postmodern site of fractured and multiple
selves?

Such questions could lead to resignation, despair and, as a consequence, inactivity. Alternatively, the notions of uncertainty and ambiguity can be set to work to interrogate and interrupt the 'methodological
will to certainty and clarity of vision' (Stronach and MacLure 1997: 5).
What might well then be created is a 'more fluid and less coercive
conceptual organisation of terms which transcends a binary logic by
simultaneously being both and neither of the binary terms' (Grosz 1989:
15). Moreover, writing from a position of indeterminacy may be a more
useful means of unsettling what Spivak (1980: 75) refers to as 'mindset'.
By writing from the premise of 'not knowing' rather than 'knowing' and
by acknowledging the excess of meanings and the endless possibilities
deriving from this may well loosen the ties that ordinarily guide us into
over-familiar and well trodden styles of accounting for what we see. The
challenge, as Stronach (1997: 17) suggests, rests in the 'impetus of not
knowing, in not-ever-knowing but in continuing to learn something of
that "not-ever" of knowing'.

What follows then is a form of self-critique or analysis aimed at first
foregrounding and then disrupting my own paradoxical inscription within
binary logic (cf. Hutcheon 1989). Moreover, practices of deconstruction
are levelled at marking out a number of things including, for example,
those 'realities' which are constructed within the context of the nursery
classroom. Another goal is to foreground how I am immersed in that
which I seek to disrupt. In other words, the critique is mounted from the
confusing position of being and feeling simultaneously the insider/out-
sider and the observer/observed or, as Rhedding-Jones (1996: 24) puts
it, as a 'subject of / in discourse'.

7

A tale of disturbance

As for what motivated me, it is quite simple: it was curiosity – the only kind of curiosity that is worth acting upon with a degree of obstinacy; not the curiosity that seeks to assimilate what is proper for one to know, but that which enables one to get free of oneself. There are times in life when the question of knowing whether one can think differently from the way one thinks and perceive differently from the way one sees, is absolutely necessary if one is to go on looking and reflecting at all. What is philosophy today – philosophical activity, that is – if it is not the critical work that thought brings to bear upon itself? Of what does it consist, if not the endeavour to know and to undertand to what extent it might be possible to think differently, instead of legitimating what is already known?

(Foucault 1985: 8–9)

This chapter describes some of the repercussions of adopting a poststructuralist framework when examining social practices as part of a teacher research enterprise (cf. Jones and Brown 1999). I shall examine some of the tensions which lie between those locations occupied in offering such accounts. These will include those of 'teacher-researcher' and 'feminist teacher'. I shall also consider the ways in which these positions connect/disconnect with poststructuralism. I offer an example of children's play in a nursery school to illustrate an applying of deconstruction, and in so doing indicate how different questions concerned with practice can be opened up.

Deconstructing some children's play

One strategy which is employed within this chapter is to perceive a story, which a group of children tell through the vehicle of play, as an allegory. Conventionally, allegories (whether in the form of a poem, a play, a piece of prose or as in this instance a children's game) operate on two levels. There is the surface plane where there is apparent meaning but below this lie deeper complexities, where the symbols and characters of, for example, a story enacted through play, stand in for and are illustrations of truth, including moral and spiritual truth. However, in this writing allegories are being perceived and used a little differently. Here there is no expectation that by perceiving the children's story as an allegory a truth about the children or their lives will be revealed. Instead, the hope is that as a consequence of reading the children's story as a multi-layered tale and by engaging with deconstruction certain pedagogical beliefs and assumptions will be destabilized, thus creating a space whereby they may be reconsidered, problematized and where personal investments in them can be scrutinized. These points will be extended later.

For a number of years I have kept a journal. This has documented various aspects of classroom life, including my interactions with the children and their social encounters with one another. The writings in the journal, based on my own observations, are hurried jottings which are then used as reference points to allow for subsequent, more extended, reflective pieces. These writings, while clearly subjective, allow an initial rendering of a particular incident such as a description of children's play as complex followed by an opportunity to move beyond making positive and limited assumptions about such complexities. What this entails is a shift from supposedly unproblematic descriptions of a particular incident to offering in its place stories or 'fictional framings' (Hassan 1987: 118) about a constructed world. The journal, as it has been written, does not attempt to 'tell it how it really is'; rather, it has become a means of chartering and articulating some of the tensions and bewilderment, for me, when working within this particular environment. In the subsequent analysis of this material outside of the school context there is a further shift away from seeing the context of the nursery classroom as 'real' towards 'foregrounding how discourse worlds the world' (Lather 1993: 675).

In researching from positions of possibility rather than the positive, and by incorporating deconstruction into the methodology with a view to deliberately blurring certain binary oppositions, such as subject/object and fact/fiction, I depart from more traditional action research paradigms where a prevalent view is that individuals can, as a consequence of empirical enquiry, come to 'know'. The intention here is to illustrate how practices of deconstruction have been incorporated into the practitioner research task within this enquiry, in ways which will allow me to tease out and unravel some of the theoretical and ideological underpinnings of my practice. The intention then is not to destroy or abandon such underpinnings; instead, the deconstructive practices employed here aim to unsettle specific foundations with a view to opening them up, and in so doing create possibilities for rereadings.

Deconstructive enquiry, while more familiar within the field of literary criticism is, additionally, incorporated into the work of several critical education theorists (e.g. Lather 1991; Spivak 1993; Stronach and MacLure 1997). What binds these theorists is that all in their various ways seek to question, disturb and worry those established ground rules which stipulate our ways of cognizing. In other words, they aim to 'challenge the legitimacy of the dominant order' (Lather 1991: xv) while functioning within it. This attitude underpins my task here.

The example of play: journal entry 20.9.95.

Carly is in the home corner. She has on a random collection of dressing-up clothes including one of the battered hats and a too-long skirt. She piles several handbags and shopping bags on to the dolls' buggy. Finally, one of the dolls is placed precariously on top of the heaped bags. She makes her way from the home over to the reading area. Here, the doll is placed on a chair while Carly sets to putting various books into the bags. It would seem that for Carly the reading corner has temporarily become the shops. Meanwhile, Peter and Nathan enter the home and take the tablecloth and one of the cot sheets. They bring these to me and ask to have them tucked into the necks of their jumpers. Cloth and sheet are now capes. Both boys immediately place their arms straight out in front of their bodies in a 'super-hero flying' pose and together they run off to the construction area. At this point, Matthew, Ryan, Colin and Michael enter the home and begin to rearrange the chairs into a straight line. Ryan is the first to sit down on a chair. He puts his arms straight out and it is clear from both the noises he is making and the swaying of his body that he is 'driving'. The other boys imitate him. Perhaps because of the noise and general hubbub the two super-heroes, Peter and Nathan, are drawn back into the home. They now have lengths of Mobilo [construction toy] tucked into the waistbands of their trousers. They take the home's two remaining easy chairs and add them to the existing line of chairs. Now, the only means of getting back into the home is via a small gap. The boys, when sitting, all adopt more or less identical positions. That is, their arms are held straight out in front of their bodies while their hands grip at imaginary steering wheels. They sway from side to side while emitting engine like noises. Colin then leaves his seat and begins to collect different items out of the home. The 'driving' stops as Colin proceeds to give out some of these things:

Colin [passing the kettle to Ryan]: You've got to have the oil – it's special.
Ryan: Yeah, the oil will make my boosters go fast.

[*Ryan gets off his chair and, using the kettle, applies oil to the chair legs.*]
Colin [*giving the teapot to Matthew and the jug to Michael*]: You've got
   to have it – you put it in – it's special.
[*Matthew and Michael also 'oil' their 'cars'.*]

Colin then retakes his position as one of the drivers. As he begins to
drive he calls out 'Mine's fastest – it's got special boosters'. It is as if
he has challenged the other boys. The driving now has a furious
quality; tyres screech and engines roar. It is brought to a halt by
Michael. He stands, faces the boys and pronounces 'Mine's a police
car – it goes fastest 'cos I catch baddies'.

   At this point Carly, pushing her buggy, approaches the home. She
uses the buggy to try to nudge and widen the gap which the boys
have left in the line of chairs. Nathan raises his length of Mobilo
construction toy into the air and simultaneously calls out 'I'm a
Power Ranger [a TV "super-hero"], I'm shooting up high, higher
than the sky [he waves the Mobilo], higher than the moon'.

   Peter, the other 'super-hero' also raises his length of construction
toy. The boys do not address Carly but she appears to be watching
them attentively. The boys on the chairs, having watched Nathan
and Peter, then continue with their 'driving'. Carly makes a couple
more attempts at using the buggy to widen the gap then gives up
and makes her way back to the book corner. After a brief moment
the two caped boys return to the construction area. They are quickly
followed by the rest of the boys.

As has been said, my purpose in perceiving this example as an
allegory is not to see the play as a mirroring of the 'real'; rather, it is
an attempt at revealing certain blind spots of the writer/interpreter's
own conceptualizations (Lather 1991: 91). Hence, the children's story,
which ostensibly concerns itself with a home, some drivers and a mother,
is being seen not as a description or a depiction of life, but as an
inscription. Thus, in writing about the children and their play it is very
likely that I have been prompted into actively selecting, transforming
and interpreting that which I have *chosen* to see (cf. Zeller 1987: 93).
   It is perhaps not accidental that, out of the many stories which the
children act out within the nursery environment each day, the account
provided centres on the ways young children both construct and take up
gender positionings. Because of my own locations including those of
'feminist teacher' and 'woman' the ways in which I focus and the readings that I bring to images are enmeshed in and entangled with those
hopes and desires which I have for the children I teach and for myself as
their teacher. What follows is an attempt to disturb the foundations in
which these hopes and desires are rooted.

An oppositional tale

At this point consider the line of chairs that the boys have constructed as being a representation of a dichotomy. This has, as its underlying paradigm, a male/female opposition with an inevitable positive/negative evaluation (Cixous 1975: 115). Given this, the children's play can be perceived as a series of oppositions where not only are the boys and the girl aligned against one another, so too is the nature of their play; certain characteristics or qualities are positively or negatively valorized. Hence, using the journal entry above, the following two lists of polarities could be created:

(+)	(−)
super-hero cape	long skirt and battered hat
racing cars	buggy
driving	shopping
super-hero	mother
noise	silence
group activity	solitary play
moon	shops
'baddy' capturer	nurturer
swords	shopping bags

One ramification in listing as opposites the play of the children is to produce a heavily stylized and unitary model of gender qualities where certain generalizations and assumptions can be made both about the nature of the play and about the boys and the girl. Hence, it is possible to read the boys' play as being concerned with and centring on an idealized notion of hegemonic masculinity. In creating their characters and positioning themselves as either super-hero or racing-car driver the boys have drawn from, been informed by and relied upon a very prescribed and narrow notion of masculinity. As Davies (1989: 89) points out, a key element in the boys' construction of their male characters is 'the fact that the *idea* of what it is to be male is constructed in opposition to the idea of femaleness'. Davies continues, 'this means that the boys must at least in part position themselves as masculine through oppressive acts of domination and control of their environment and non-masculine others'.

In this story, some of this control of the environment comes, I believe, as a consequence of several symbolic transformations. Hence, various domestic artefacts such as chairs, the teapot and the kettle are altered into cars and oil cans respectively. Additionally, the cot sheet and the tablecloth are metamorphosed into super-hero capes. Such conversions have a double-edged consequence: first, household objects are removed from the traditionally female realm of the home and transferred into the more masculine arena of the pit-stop and garage while, simultaneously, they add to the boy's power. Now, as racing drivers and super-heroes the boys are forceful dynamic agents who have connections with, and perform in, the world outside of the home.

By contrast Carly, with her 'symbols' of 'motherhood' (her baby, bags and buggy) is steeped in and anchored to the private world of the home. The story does indicate that Carly performs several of her own transformations; for example, through donning adult clothes she swaps 'girl' for 'mother' while books are converted into 'shopping'. However, there is a sense, I believe, that those things which give her play both its impetus and its substance also work at tying and constricting Carly in a number of ways. First, as a consequence of them she is fettered to a very particular version of femininity; she is the 'carer' and 'nurturer', in fact the 'good mother'. Positioned as such Carly is the negative 'other' to the boys' positive 'heroes'. Perhaps it is not too surprising that when Carly tries to re-enter her home her attempts are so tentative. In a sense, how can they be otherwise when the one area where her control is assumed and recognized has been disrupted, tampered with and finally incorporated into an opposing discourse. The gap that the boys have left in the line of chairs must, it would seem within this reading of the story, remain a tantalizing space. Thus, Carly can see that which she desires but because of a number of reasons including maybe some sense of her own powerlessness 'it' must remain a dream which lies visible yet just out of arm's reach.

Tantalizing gaps

However, what I now want to propose is that the gap which has been left in the line of chairs be conceptualized as a metaphorical opening or rift in the male/female dichotomy. Here, in this space or gap our aim is to make the familiar unfamiliar. To accept the familiar, oppositional reading of this story is to both assume and accept that the familiarly known is properly known. This is why Derrida is important. He cautions against 'accepted' and 'correct' readings of texts; rather his advice is to (re)examine the minute particulars and in this way come to perceive how our meaning-making has become enclosed within the desire to make the definition coincide with the defined. In short, Derrida urges us to change certain habits of mind (e.g. Derrida 1976: xviii). As Spivak (1987: 78) puts it, we face 'a weave of knowing and not knowing which is what knowing is'. For Derrida, language is structured as an endless deferral of meaning, and as a consequence he rejects both the notion and the desire to seek from a text a 'final, unified meaning that in turn might ground and explain all the others' (Moi 1985: 9) – 'Language bears within itself the necessity of its own critique' (Derrida 1976: xviii).

Making a gap in the oppositional reading of the children's play

An effect of reading the children's game as an oppositional tale is that the children themselves are reduced to singular entities. Carly, immersed as she is within domesticity, can be read and hence understood as a metaphor for an essentialist notion of what constitutes a girl/woman. That is, through the make-believe world of play and through the donning of 'dressing-up' clothes Carly becomes an embodiment for what is 'real' about 'womanhood'. One consequence is that, even though Carly's disguise is both striking and remarkable, its effect is to render her invisible. The text literally stops seeing her while the boys through transformations of the ordinary and the mundane take centre stage and, as is evident from the text, occupy the teacher's gaze.

The gap

When she does re-enter the text, Carly is perceived to be nudging at the gap with the buggy. Given that the teacher has observed Carly leave the home she can perhaps justifiably assume that the girl wants to gain access to the home once again. Furthermore, she could make another justifiable assumption that the reason Carly cannot widen the gap is because the boys intimidate her – that is, their loud voices and raised arms thwart her efforts.

However, there is room here for the play of interpretation. For example, it could be that while Carly may have wanted to return to her 'home' she finds that because of certain symbolic transformations it is now neither hers nor is it a 'home'. Just as Carly was able to change the book corner into a 'shop' and books into 'goods', similarly the boys have made their own switches. It might be that Carly's withdrawal from the home is not because she is 'defeated' but that she has understood the embedded logic of the game. To return to this 'home' is now illogical, as clearly it is no longer a 'home'.

Reading 'solitary play' negatively

Within the oppositional reading of the play, 'solitary play' is read negatively. By deconstructing the notion of 'solitary play' I want to foreground two issues. First, following Derrida I want to assert that dualisms are always both oppositional and hierarchical, never neutral; thus the need to interrogate the conceptual organization which has structured the oppositional reading of the play. Second, deconstructing a sexist world has to be resolved through the dismantling of patriarchal binary thought, because it is here that people are constituted as one part of the male/female dualism and where the 'feminine side' is always seen as the negative, powerless instance.

Gapping 'solitary'

The word 'solitary', while it does have a range of meanings has, I would suggest, within the nursery come to be understood and used in a very particular way. To elaborate, around the word 'solitary' a breadth of meanings revolve. For example, these might include the notion of 'independence' and the reliance on one's own 'resourcefulness'. In the nursery, these traits are regarded as key qualities. However, 'solitary' also comes tinged and tainted with negative meanings. These circulate around acts of separation, often undertaken for punitive and medical reasons, where individuals are deliberately kept away from fellow beings. Hence 'solitary', when used in conjunction with 'play', while denoting an activity undertaken by an individual also works at devaluing both the individual and the activity. Carly's qualities, including her independence and resourcefulness have in this instance been subsumed by the term 'solitary' and consequently are demeaned. This depreciation is further heightened because of the metaphor which Carly has chosen and which is the vehicle for her fantasy. However, this then prompts the question: what are Carly's other metaphorical choices? That is, within the context of the nursery classroom what other metaphorical openings are made available to her and the other children which would allow them to take up multiple positionings and which furthermore would acknowledge that subjectivities are not stable but variable and ever-changing? Before going on to address these questions I want to re-emphasize the point that concerns the fixing of an essential meaning.

The desire to fix a singular meaning

I hope that I have gone some way to illustrate that it is not possible to attach an essential meaning to the children's story. The process of knowing is about moving oneself. An engagement with knowledge processes requires shifts in thinking. It is not about standing on the same spot where reassurance is gained from comforting assumptions and familiar stories.

To read the above story and to privilege an exclusive meaning is in itself a discursive practice drawn from traditional literary criticism theories. At this juncture it is only possible to offer a sketchy simplification of some of the prevailing ideas and features which were regarded as the common bedrock of these theories (Barry 1995: 34). Such characteristics would include the promotion of literature as a vehicle for enabling us to understand the 'truth' about human 'nature'. Additionally, traditional literary texts were characterized by linearity, clear authorial voice and closure. However, because notions of subjectivity or human nature were conceptualized as male this had the inevitable repercussions of creating the conditions for naturalizing the social power relations of patriarchy and hence patriarchal binary thought (Weedon 1987: 139).

However, gestures such as deconstruction seek to undo this logocentric ideology with a view of going beyond the static closure of binary opposition. While working within the system of the logic, one undertaking of deconstruction is to overload and deliberately strain the system by indicating its own paradoxes and ambiguities such that it implodes. This is what I am trying to do, and need to continue to do, with the story of Carly and the boys.

Let me now return to those questions which were left dangling.

Metaphorical gaps and openings

Previously the questions posed were: what other metaphorical openings are made available to the other children which would allow them to take up multiple positionings and allow for shifting subjectivities? What efforts are being made within the nursery to shift dualistic discourses?

There is evidence, I feel, that very real attempts are made to disrupt aspects of the nursery curriculum in the hope that difference and diversity can be accommodated within the classroom and where, additionally, stereotypical and 'sex appropriate' behaviour is discouraged. Similarly, ways are sought to disturb and unsettle attitudes, including complacency, towards the status quo. For example, stories are read with the hope that they will upset some of the children's expectations. The characters in these books are not depicted as uniform and coherent; rather, they display contradictory qualities.

However, while it is comparatively straightforward to move, mix and manage play equipment and resources with the intention of deliberately blurring certain conceptions which are brought to these things, what is much more complex and deeply challenging is the confronting of hierarchical dualistic thinking; particularly within my own accounts. I shall elaborate this point by returning again to the children's story. Specifically, recollect the moment when I helped the boys transform cot sheet and tablecloth into super-hero capes. This is, interestingly, the only point in the story when the children step outside their narrative – asking for some adult help. Could this have been a moment when I might have made a difference? Should I have made a difference? Can I make a difference? Do I have the authority to make a difference? In a sense the answer is yes and no. For there to be a 'yes' answer what has to be disrupted is my own immersion in what Walkerdine (1990: 324–5) refers to as 'pedagogy of choice'. This 'pedagogy of choice' is prevalent both in my classroom and in nursery education generally. It has a long tradition and is underpinned by a belief in rational thought. A central tenet is that the 'freedom' to 'choose' allows for children to develop 'normal and satisfactory emotional development' (Lowenfeld 1935: 324). If not given this 'freedom', so the argument continues, the consequences are severe because those 'forces unrealised in childhood remain as an inner drive, for ever seeking outlets, and lead men [sic] to express them not any longer in play, since this is regarded as an activity in childhood, but in industrial competition, anarchy and war' (Lowenfeld 1935: 324–5).

While many years have passed and too many wars have been waged since these words were written, nevertheless the dream which surrounds the 'pedagogy of choice' can still be found lingering within the classroom. Here the hope is that, if children are left alone to act out stories, they will 'become agents responsible for their own actions, whose interactions are based on rationality alone, having left the irrational behind them' (Walkerdine 1990: 8).

Interrupting this discourse requires that the teacher does not support the boys' 'choice' but interrupts it and attempts to introduce deviations. Perhaps if I had suggested a different use for the cot sheet and tablecloth I might have created the space for the boys to reconsider and hence have the chance to develop a less restrictive metaphor and one that resisted a particular form of idealized hegemonic masculinity. As it was, in helping, I gave the game some kind of tacit approval and unwittingly endorsed the boys' story. What was then missed was an opening where both the teacher and the children could have learned something.

Perhaps postmodernism's greatest potential is that it can serve as a caution to those who find themselves immersed in critical pedagogy. In this way, poststructuralist analysis helps in working at cracking or opening out aspects of the social world of the classroom, particularly my own entrapment within specific discourses. As Shapiro (1991: 120) notes, power is everywhere and exists 'even amongst the forces of liberation trying to overthrow domination'. What is then made possible are opportunities to concentrate on the anomalies or contradictions of practice and to perceive these not as failures but as the breaking down of rational thought. Once fractured, they are then 'the creative source of new understandings, new discourses' (Davies 1989: 139). In seeking, as a teacher, to ensure gender equity within the nursery the task, while clearly involving a disruption of the male/female dualism, cannot be achieved via acts of oppression against the boys. Deconstruction obliges a reconsideration and a reconceptualization of what it means 'to disrupt'. Similarly, more generally, in formulating a research strategy predicated on a desire for 'improvement' or 'knowing better' there is a need to acknowledge the heterogeneity in conceptions of how such objectives might be understood. Gestures, such as deconstructive practices, aim to show how, beneath the text's apparent unity of purpose, lie internal contradictions and inconsistencies, and it is these which defeat endeavours at attaching singular and permanently reliable meanings. So while I still have hopes and dreams that critical pedagogy may work towards greater justice and humanity, postmodernism works at tempering these desires. Is this caution such a bad thing? Not when it is remembered that such dreams and desires have been built upon a universal discourse that, while privileging some, denied many including women, the poor and other subordinate and dominated groups of human beings (see Welch 1985).

Let me conclude this chapter by contrasting the dream of rationality referred to earlier with the moon which the boys sought to reach, and then go beyond. As a metaphor within the logic of binary oppositions the moon was the feminine other to the male sun and as such it was mysterious, poetic and irrational (Cixous 1975: 115). However, what I am suggesting is that under the guise of exploration, development and civilization the western world has robbed the moon of this identity and in so doing has left it stained, tarnished and polluted. Perhaps in aiming for the moon the boys have set their sights on an ignoble scrapyard.

8

Identity, power and resistance

The questions that arise continue to provoke answers, but none will
dominate as long as the ground-clearing activity is at work. Can
knowledge circulate without a position of mastery? Can it be
conveyed without the exercise of power? No, because there is no
end to understanding power relations which are rooted deep in the
social nexus — not merely added to society nor easily locatable so
that we can just radically do away with them. Yes, however, because
in-between grounds always exist, and cracks and fissures are like gaps
of fresh air that keep on being suppressed because they tend to
render more visible the failures operating in every system. Perhaps
mastery need not coincide with power.

(Trinh 1989: 41)

Introduction

Trinh's ground-clearing activities clearly lean on a gardening or horticul-
tural metaphor where laying bare, besides exposing 'roots', will also
allow for air to circulate. This chapter is also concerned with exposure so
that 'failures operating in every system' might then be made visible.
However, my own metaphorical preferences incline towards notions of
performance. Given the above mention of 'exposure' the idea of performance as it is played out within striptease was toyed with. However,
there is a danger that by incorporating the striptease metaphor assumptions might be made that subsequently 'all' would be revealed. The
following strippings are in a sense disappointments because very little
nakedness will be exposed, including the self in the raw or, indeed,
naked truths. Instead, the strip/teases envisaged in this chapter aim to
ruffle and disarrange those ordinary, conventional, frequent and usual
aspects of classroom life. In this way, I might then notice those things
which, because they are so commonplace, go by unnoticed. Having made
the familiar unfamiliar, attention can then focus on the 'failures operating in every system'.

Power relations, as Trinh comments, are deep-rooted. Nevertheless,
this need not necessarily imply that they remain undisturbed. However,

what the forthcoming deconstructions hope to illustrate is that before dominant constraints can be loosened or broken down, attention must be paid to those ways that I routinely address facets of practice. Accordingly, by positioning myself as a postmodernist the intentions are to call into question and displace certain beliefs and practices so that they may be readdressed. Taking this view locates postmodernism not as an oppositional movement; rather, it can be perceived as a means of interrupting and challenging dominance by working within it. Positioned not against but within, postmodernism aims to dis/locate those realities that the children and I create within the location of the nursery classroom with a view to destabilizing them.

Story 1: Journal entry 13.5.96

This story centres on a boy called Ashley (cf. Jones and Brown, in press).

Ashley had arrived in school this morning wearing a T-shirt which had emblazoned across its front the memorable slogan: 'Ashley – Born to be Wild'. Later, I watch him as he runs into the home and takes the tablecloth from the table. He brings the cloth to me and I tuck the ends into the neck of his T-shirt. I ask: 'Who are you now?' In a low and growly voice he replies, 'Batman. I'm Batman.' As soon as the cape is attached Ashley runs off with both arms stuck out straight in front of him. He goes into the construction corner and I move further down the room in order to keep observing him. Carly (a 4-year-old girl) is in the construction corner. She stops building to look at Ashley. He growls at her: 'You're under arrest.' Carly laughs as Ashley approaches her. He still has his arms stuck straight out. She stands up, sticks her arms straight out and both children run out of the construction corner into the centre of the room singing the Batman theme tune; 'da da da da Batman'. Carly leaves Ashley to join some of the other children while Ashley continues to run around the room. His singing becomes louder and I make a decision to stop him. I take him by the hand, lead him to the book corner and (deliberately) read to him the story of 'The Paper Bag Princess.'

'The Paper Bag Princess' is a story about a princess who commits many heroic deeds to save her Prince Ronald. We are told at the beginning of the tale that the two, Ronald and Elizabeth, intend to get married. Despite being saved by Elizabeth from certain death Ronald gives her no thanks; rather, he attacks her with a string of criticisms which centre on how she looks. The scales fall from Elizabeth's eyes and she sees him for what he really is – a 'bum'. They don't get married after all (abstract derived from Davies 1989: viii).

I then asked Ashley the following questions to see whether I could discover which bits of the story he liked best and what he had gleaned or appreciated from the story:

LJ: What do you think of Ronald then? What do you think he should have said to Elizabeth after she rescued him from the dragon?

Ashley [there is a pause]: He's like a girl . . . he likes . . . he just likes dresses.

LJ: What do you mean . . . he's like a girl?

Ashley: Girls like dressing up.

LJ: But you like dressing up. You've got a cape on.

Ashley: But that's Batman . . . girls like dresses.

LJ: Who do you like best in the story?

Ashley: The dragon.

LJ: The dragon. Why the dragon?

Ashley: Because he flies . . . and he's a monster.

This extract raises certain troubling contradictions and the intention here is to try to address them. As a first step in this teasing apart, let me begin where the journal entry starts – that is, with Ashley's T-shirt. We have discussed this elsewhere thus:

> Whilst we are not in any position to offer reasons as to why Ashley was wearing his T-shirt we can offer some thoughts as to why its slogan was for the teacher 'memorable'. As a word, 'wild' is used and can be defined in diverse ways – for example, lions are wild and behaviour that is extremely erratic and out of control can be described as wild. However it seems to me, when retrospectively reading Ashley's story, that at first a somewhat narrow meaning was attributed to the word and second this then had the effect of contributing to the way in which the teacher tried subsequently to position Ashley. In other words, the word 'wild' stood in for and was representative of an essentialist notion of Ashley's identity which in turn resulted in a deterministic reading of his behaviour. Thus, in our view 'wild' was equated with a hegemonic notion of 'power' and the wearing of the T-shirt and its slogan symbolised or represented a statement or fact about masculinity; men are born to be indomitable and they cannot be restrained. In short, they are born to be wild.
>
> (Jones and Brown, in press)

However, if this was the case, why is it that I am to be found helping a boy transform himself into a super-hero? Why am I stuck and unable to move myself and the boy out of repetitive ways of being? Why is he so hooked on such 'goody/baddy' stories? Such stories or myths, including Ashley's 'Batman', are constructed around binary oppositions which, in the case of 'super-hero' play, would include good/evil, attractive hero/ ugly villain and active male/passive female. What super-hero stories do is repetitively play out these characteristics and in so doing mark out and make clear the consequences and thus the logic of such oppositions. As a feminist I ought to oppose the constant re-enactment of such stories. But how?

My 'mindset' comes in part from being so steeped and hence ensnared within the 'pedagogy of choice' (Walkerdine 1990). This phenomenon was briefly discussed in Chapter 7, however because of its impact on me as a teacher more must be said about it. As a discourse, the 'pedagogy of choice' works at fostering the notion that self-control can be nurtured, but in order to encourage its development young children must have opportunities to make choices. This makes choosing a mechanism where-by young children are controlled rather than regimented and where they are given latitude and encouragement to express, rather than be repressed (Walkerdine 1990: 8). However, within the context of the nursery class-room, the very discourse which is intended to liberate children from oppressive over-regulation works instead at providing a space for them to regurgitate stories. A major function of these stories is to both confirm and normalize a binary structuring which positions many, including women and girls, as the negative 'other' (cf. Fiske 1987: 134).

Why then, given that it was very likely that a super-hero character would be materialized from the 'cape' did I agree to Ashley's request? In helping him, was I not simultaneously helping to sustain a particular conceptual framework which positions both me and the girls of the nursery as the negative other to the positive male? It would seem how-ever that, while I perceive myself as in opposition to Ashley, Carly, the little girl that he tries to 'arrest' appears to find Ashley not a threat but a joke. For it may be remembered she does two things when he growls 'you're under arrest' at her. First, she laughs. Second, she neither resists him nor is she pacified. Rather, she sticks her arms out and briefly is not only a 'bat man', but Ashley appears to accept her as such. Both chil-dren, but particularly Carly, seem able to play with the lines which I seem keen to draw.

I read my repetitive actions as an indication of the strength of ration-ality's dream. However, where is the sense in clinging onto this dream? Will Ashley become 'civilized' if allowed to 'get rid' of certain traits through the vehicle of play? Or should more thought be given to devel-oping new discourses where different narrative forms could emerge which might allow for more diverse ways of being? As it was, there is, I think, a certain irony in that having given Ashley permission to position himself as a super-hero I was then obliged to adopt a counter and oppositional position by reading to him a feminist fairy tale, 'The Paper Bag Princess'. Perhaps my intentions by reading the story were intended to negate

Batman's power by repositioning Ashley as 'passive child'. Unable to sustain being the rational teacher I turn instead to using a feminist children's story where it then seems that reading becomes a form of punishment levied because a teacher's values and sensibilities have in some way been offended.

Can the reading of feminist children's stories counter and work in opposition to traditional narrative forms? Is it just a matter of exposing the children to stories where girls are heroes, as in the story of 'The Paper Bag Princess'? Reading this book to Ashley was clearly not a success in that he had difficulties engaging with the characters. However, perhaps the solution is not a case of finding the 'right' character or indeed the 'correct' discourse. Such a move would require dogma in order to defend them. Maybe a better alternative is to combine, recombine and continue to adjust multiple discourses so that Ashley can experience notions of himself in ways that could take him beyond mundane, worn out, stale and hackneyed forms of self, where new forms of social relations and new patterns of power and desire can be explored (cf. Davies 1989: 141).

From my current position, I have come to see the above example as a wasted opportunity. I think that there were moments within it when it may have been possible for me to explore further with Ashley why 'The Paper Bag Princess' was for him an unsatisfactory narrative. While the example indicates Ashley's critical capabilities, he clearly finds the character of Prince Ronald flawed, and he is not given the time to develop this. Instead I ask more questions rather than consider his answers.

Finally, it is only now that I am beginning to have some understanding as to why it is that out of all the characters in 'The Paper Bag Princess' Ashley liked the dragon best. It could be that as the dragon is so evidently not of Ashley's world it signifies a way out of that world and is representative of a desire which I believe is lodged within us all – the desire to be at times someone else, somewhere else.

Story 2: Journal entry 20.11.95

The following extract features two children, Jamie, a 4-year-old boy and Chloe, a girl also aged 4. Its significance for me is that I think it illustrates the ease with which young children can 'combine, recombine and adjust' discourses to allow for multiple subjective positionings.

The children are playing outside in the play area.

Chloe: You're the monster.
[*Jamie makes snarling and growling noises. His arms are held up in front of his body. His hands have been fashioned into claws or talons. He does not*

touch Chloe but she appears to be cowed by both his body language and the harsh sounds he is producing. Chloe runs from Jamie but stops to allow herself to be caught.]

Chloe: You take my hand. You take me to your house.

Jamie: I'm the monster and I take you to the house.

[*Chloe walks by the side of Jamie.*]

Chloe [*calling out as she walks*]: The monster's got me! The monster's
    got me!

[*Jamie leads Chloe to the area where the trees and bushes have been managed to give the children a 'den'. Chloe sits down on a tree log. She smooths her dress and places her hands on her lap. Jamie alternates between keeping his eye on Chloe and facing out to the play area.*]

Jamie [*in a sing-song chant*]: I'm the monster. We're in the house.
    I'm the monster and I've got Chloe.

[*Jamie directs himself to the general mêlée of playing children.*]

Chloe: We've got to have some dinner. You sit down. I'll get the
    dinner.

[*Chloe changes places with Jamie. She piles cherry blossom into two heaps and gives Jamie a stick to use as a spoon. Both children sit to 'eat'.*]

Chloe: I run away and you come after me.

[*Chloe runs away. As she runs she glances over her shoulder to check she has been followed. I observe her slowing down to allow Jamie to catch her. Although she is being held by Jamie, it is Chloe who instigates the move to the large wooden toy train. She sits in the train cab and pokes her arms into two adjacent holes which form the windows of the cab. She now appears to me as if she is sitting in a set of mediaeval stocks. Chloe mimes the finding of the key and then the locking of her arms into the holes. Meanwhile, Jamie has been standing guard. Again, he uses his arms, hands and voice to create a 'monster'.*]

Chloe: You have to look away.

[*Jamie turns to look away and Chloe takes the opportunity to run from the train. She pauses to turn and make a teasing face. She then waits for Jamie to catch up.*]

Chloe [*shouting in an exaggerated, excited voice, just as Jamie is about to
    grab her arm*]: Look behind you!

[*Jamie turns to look and Chloe runs off.*]

Chloe: I've tricked you! I've tricked you!

What I find interesting about this extract are the ways in which different subject positions are created and then taken up by the children. At the beginning of the story Chloe informs Jamie that he is the 'monster'. Using various body parts including his voice, arms, hands and face Jamie fashions for himself a 'monster'. While he can growl, have sharps claws and a scary face, she by contrast is weak and defenceless. However, Chloe, although maintaining the over-arching structure of the monster/victim story works at denting it. This I believe gives her some freedom and a certain resistance. So, while she insists that Jamie stays within a particular persona she herself exchanges and plays with different positions.

At the beginning of the story she is, momentarily, a hapless victim. Within the confines of monster stories Chloe would have to remain in this position unless of course she was rescued by a hero. With the absence of a hero Chloe has to construct her own resolution and she does this gradually. First she moves the monster and herself into the den, remaining in the position of a controlled and passive female. In fact, she seems to embody the essence of obedience – her clothes are smoothed and she sits quietly. But then, by offering to 'get the dinner' she makes several transformations – she exchanges 'helpless victim' for 'cook' and the 'den' shifts from being a place of confinement into a place where dinners are got. In other words, a 'home'.

By introducing a 'home' into their play Chloe can then tap into a range of discursive practices where her appreciation of how to organize meals redefines the relationship between herself and the monster. While in the 'home' the monster's power is subjugated to that of the 'mother/cook' and as a consequence he is obliged to sit and to eat quietly while by contrast Chloe can bustle around getting the meal ready.

However, the decision is made by Chloe to reposition herself once again in the role of 'victim'. She directs Jamie: 'I run away and you come after me'. While it is only possible to hazard guesses as to why Chloe wanted to exchange 'cook' for 'victim', one interpretation could be that she finds it more fun using her wits to develop fresh strategies for outwitting the monster than she does from getting his dinner ready. In order to play again she has to free herself from the constrictions of a domestic discourse where the practices do not include play. In the final scene of the story Chloe, just as she is about to be caught by the monster, uses an age-old trick to effect an escape by urging the monster to 'Look behind you!'

As the teacher of these two children what implications can I draw from this example of play? Let me begin by considering Chloe in relation to the position of the monster. While there may be reasons as to why Chloe 'chose' not to position herself as 'monster', one possible stumbling block which may have prevented her from taking up this position was her own gender. The monster story, while greatly abridged by Chloe, is nevertheless drawn from a patriarchal narrative where femaleness is reduced to an inferior way of being (Davies 1989: 71). Further, although Chloe shows herself to be forceful and powerful she does so either through domestic discourses or by locating Jamie so that it is he that is 'powerful' while she herself is cast as 'victim'. So, while Chloe acts out resistance to Jamie, nevertheless she has learned 'the patterns of power and desire through which the male/female relations are organized' (Davies 1989: 86).

For me, however, a significant feature of the story is the way that both children seemed happy to zig-zag between polarities of behaviour and as a consequence they both overlapped the male/female dichotomy. Both Jamie and Chloe displayed an ease in moving from one discursive framework to another. Jamie for example was able to both recognize and reciprocate appropriately when Chloe moved the play into the 'home'. Additionally, it seemed that Chloe in particular, while clearly playing within the patriarchal order of the monster story, was trying to develop ways of being which resisted the crippling definition to which the story would have her conform. Whether she was 'heroic' is debatable, but it struck me that she displayed a capacity to be both feminine *and* devious, feminine *and* athletic and feminine *and* resourceful. As such, her identity was more mercurial than fixed and unitary.

At this point I would like to introduce the third extract from my journal. Following the analysis I then want to conclude this chapter by returning to the classroom to indicate what some of the repercussions are on practice when stories which are concerned with play are taken seriously.

Story 3: Journal entry 7.11.95

This story concerns two 4-year-old girls, Jane and Kate. The girls have known one another since birth, their mothers having met on the delivery ward of the hospital where the two girls were born. Both mothers are single parents. The two girls are also friends outside of school.

> The story opens with Jane and Kate sitting at a table. On the table the girls have placed four tiny beds. On three of these are lying small wooden, female figures; three to a bed. In the fourth bed are just two figures. I make the assumption that because the figures are in bed that they are all sleeping.
>
> I bend down to the tabletop and whisper to one of the three 'sleeping' toy figures: 'What's your name?'
>
> *Jane:* It's Sophie.
> [*The charade of whispering to each of the figures is repeated, with the girls offering between them eight different girls' names: Tina, Lucy, Sarah, Emily, Susie, Kayleigh, Kirsty and Chelsea. Again, I whisper to the sleeping figures: Why are you so tired?*]
> *Kate:* They've been to a wedding.
> *Jane:* There's been a ball. They've been dancing, now they're tired.

[*I whisper to one of 'the couple' in the fourth bed: 'And what are you called?'*]

Jane: That's Linda. They've got married. They love one another . . . she [*pointing to the 'girl' figure*] loves him [*points to the discernibly male 'Playmobil' figure. I bend and whisper in the ear of the 'he': 'What's your name?'*]

Kate: He's he . . . he's not got a name . . . he's he.

LJ: Can't he have your brother's name?

Kate: No, he's a boy . . . This is a man . . . He's married her [*points to the other figure*].

As a starting point I want to begin with 'Linda' who has, in my view, just become a 'wife'. However, the girls themselves do not use the term 'wife'. This prompts the question: have they an understanding of marriage which does not encapsulate a concept of 'wife'? While there may be very many reasons as to why Jane and Kate do not incorporate the word 'wife' into their story it could be that their omission is in part because of their own domestic circumstances. As referred to in the introduction, the girls themselves are cared for by a single parent, their mother. The girls thus have mothers who are not 'wives'. It could also be that the girls have images of 'wives' and find them lacking.

On a general level, the role and status of a wife is robbed of both glamour and dignity through powerful discursive practices. One example of this is the legal system. It is only comparatively recently that some anomalies associated with the status of 'wife' have been rectified (Holdsworth 1988), but legal discrepancies still exist (e.g. it does appear that wives who commit acts of violence against their husbands can expect harsher custodial treatment than husbands who carry out similar crimes against their wives).

In indicating these discrepancies I am not trying to suggest that these 4-year-old girls have a hold on and fully comprehend such aspects. However my argument is that discourses are powerful, including those that work at denigrating female roles including that of wife. Through language and a process which is known as 'semantic pejoration' those labels which refer specifically to women get devalued over a period of time. Hence, 'wife' both as a position in the social structure and the role that the society expects a wife to adopt can be and is reduced to a narrow stereotype summed up here by Holdsworth (1988: 15) as 'her indoors'. Given all this, perhaps it is not too surprising that the girls have chosen to talk of weddings but not of wives.

However, these are broad and general interpretations which are inevitably glossed by my understandings of the world. It is, however, possible to read the above text more closely, not in order to reveal a 'truth' about the girls but rather to explore how subject positionings and narrative structures interrelate. In particular, I want to try to highlight how the girls seem to have a certain ambiguity in relation to the male/female dualism framework on which much of their story hangs. I then want to foreground how these perceived ambiguities should be considered as creative entry-points and where dominating practices might be eroded allowing for more flexible ways of being.

Let me begin again with 'Linda' who I assumed to be the tired, newly married 'wife' of the 'he' who lies next to her. In their play the girls do not speak of wives or indeed husbands. Instead they focus on the heterosexual practice of weddings and it is this practice and the ways in which schools prepare girls for their insertion into this practice (Walkerdine 1990: 88) that I now wish to explore. Jane and Kate tell of a wedding, dancing, a ball and finally bed. This litany of events is derived from the classic fairy tale. My response to their story is a twofold one. I am both perplexed by it and yet at the same time I find it revelatory. I will try to unravel what it is about the tale that confuses me.

In part, some of my confusion comes because I suspect I am reading the story as if it is some kind of endorsement that the girls think marriage is a 'norm' for women. Clearly, it is not the norm for the mothers of these two girls nor is it for many of the other children in the nursery; out of the 20 children who attend the nursery on a full-time basis, 12 children live with either one parent or with two parents who have chosen not to marry. Within the wider context of society the trend for women between the ages of 18 and 49 to remain unmarried appears to be on the increase, with 29 per cent remaining unmarried in 1992 as compared to, for example, 18 per cent in 1979 (Thomas *et al.* 1992).

The myth that surrounds the notion that for a woman to be a 'complete (happy) woman' she has to be married is an ancient one and its power is maintained through a variety of agencies. Despite the girls witnessing at close proximity the absence of a 'husband', and despite growing up in a society where there are an increasing number of women who remain unmarried, they seem attached to a 'truth' which for them has very little substance. In a similar vein, McRobbie's (1978) study of working-class girls in Birmingham clearly demonstrates that the girls perceived marriage as an indicator of what constituted normality and that a mature woman who remained unmarried was perceived by the girls and by their wider culture as a 'marginal person' (Mungham, in McRobbie 1978).

At school it is children's stories, and in particular the classic fairy tale, where this 'truth' concerning women is both constructed and then relayed to the children. Work by Steedman (1982), Davies (1989) and Walkerdine (1990) reiterates this view. As the girls' teacher I face a dilemma: do I continue to read to my children stories which repeat fantasies rather than truths about women? In telling fairy stories I may be complicit in presenting particular historically derived sets of values and traditions which are established around the male/female dualism. Furthermore, Zipes (1994) has suggested that many fairy stories themselves were written quite deliberately to indoctrinate children and rein in their sexuality. His analysis indicates that the stories were a subversive way of making little girls (e.g. 'Little Red Riding Hood') conform by controlling through threats and by rewarding docility and obedience. That the girls of my class are indoctrinated is questionable, although it would seem from the account above that such stories are powerful in influencing how play is structured and the language that is used when playing.

However, while I might be surprised and troubled by what could be a condoning of a practice whereby the female is in part constituted through the male as a consequence of marriage, the story is also something of a revelation. The revelatory aspect centres on what I perceive as the meshing of two discourses where one interrupts the other. The girls' story is clearly influenced by the classic fairy tale. The tradition of such tales is often to portray women as so passive that they are almost dead (Steedman 1982). However, within this story what I want to suggest is that the girls have as it were 'turned the tables' and by not naming the male they have removed something of the male's essence, in particular his power. Naming gives identity. The name becomes part of the person's individuality and personality. As a society we adopt the practice of not naming people when it is in our own interest not to understand the person as an individual. For example, we will use serial numbers for prisoners. Foucault's work (e.g. 1991) is underpinned by a shift from knowing individuals to regulating suitably classified populations.

In brief, it could be that in telling their story the girls are reforming a discourse concerned with 'femininity'. To fashion their tale they have borrowed from one tradition where 'wives' are inextricably linked with 'husbands' and knitted it with what for the girls is a relatively common cultural practice of women raising children unsupported by a man. For these girls the 'he' although present within a specific fantasy is nevertheless a vague and insubstantial subject and as such cannot be named. What this story indicates are those inherent contradictions and tensions present in all of us between what we know to be 'reality' and what we fantasize and desire (Walkerdine 1990).

A thread of the girls' story is modelled on fairy stories. An option available to me is to counter the inherent message of these tales with stories which present girls as strong and assertive characters. To try 'to make girls a bit more like boys' and vice-versa would, however, still maintain the dominance of male power within the male/female dualism; what would alter is that on some occasions and in some situations girls could be 'token boys'. However, I think to respond merely in this way would be to bring only a partial reading to Jane and Kate's story. In their story the girls gave names to all the female figures but left the male unnamed. In a sense the girls, by naming, have awarded recognition and status. Perhaps this is as a consequence of their own lives where the powerful adult figure is the mother. To a small degree the girls have challenged the essence of the male/female dualism. How can I as the teacher make further inroads towards disrupting traditional oppositions?

Tentative conclusions

In answer let me try to bring the three stories together and in so doing draw some tentative conclusions. In describing and analysing these stories the aim was not to present a clear picture of classroom life or to detail facts about the children. Rather, such tales or anecdotes can, I think, provide an albeit brief opportunity to discern something about those ways that young children set about putting some shape(s) onto their lives. The work of Bettleheim (1976) suggests that storytelling is a means by which young children can classify and order their lives. If this is the case, then how can I as a teacher work at broadening these classifications and ordering systems? How, for example, can the categories of 'boy' and 'girl' be opened up in order to allow for more divergent and creative subjectivities?

By way of answering let me return again to poststructuralist theory. By incorporating theories of poststructuralism I have sought to make clear a number of issues. First, young children's subjectivities are not fixed but in process. An assumption of poststructuralist theory is that the individual is 'no longer seen as a unitary, unproblematically sexed being, but rather as a shifting nexus of possibilities' (Davies 1989: 12). The analysis following the stories makes it difficult to perceive the children as being simply socialized into their appropriate gender roles. They 'positioned' themselves within the available discursive spaces. It was, I think, clear that the children could have multiple subjectivities but only within those discourses that were available to them. I shall return to this point subsequently.

Second, interpreting the stories through a poststructuralist framework emphasized the 'power-knowledge' couplet. Power was not conceptualized as a monolithic, repressive force. Rather, it was seen as producing knowledge rather than repression and as such worked at forming positions for subjects to enter (Walkerdine 1988). Following on from this, the focus was less on who had power and more on defining those patterns of power which worked at ensnaring. Excavating power patterns worked at highlighting my own entrapment in discourses, particularly my deep-rooted attachment to the Enlightenment dream of the rational subject; an attachment which the analysis showed not only circumvented opportunities for resistance but prompted repressive acts through seemingly liberatory manoeuvres. Finally, researching from a poststructuralist position places me both as observer/observed and the researcher/researched, and as such the analysis works at both revealing and problematizing some of my own biased ways.

Postscript

Having written a draft of this chapter I then gave a copy to my colleague Ian Stronach. Ian's comments are both salutary and helpful and I include them here as a way of allowing me to have yet another say. He wrote:

> I didn't like your last reading so much, and thought it a loosely connected politicisation of the data . . . My criticism here – I think – links to some of the past stuff in that you privilege one set of meanings and neglect others because you give too determined (in two senses) a feminist reading of the data and hence, for me, the criticism of reductionism. It's not that I don't 'agree' with the reading that you give your data (re. 'wife', 'her indoors', 'classic fairy tale') but it is a *singular* reading. You ignore a parallel story that runs within and against that one. What astonished *me* (eminently deconstructable purchase here of course) was the man as cipher ('him') who was unnamed. Who was only what women 'love', an object of some passive kind. Who did not even feature reproductively as a possibility (all the children were girls). Your move was to read the 'classic fairy tale' complete with 'ball' as a 'truth' on which tables were turned. But why – on what grounds – is this a Fairy Tale on Top story rather than the other way round? A more interesting question might be: how can such a braiding of myth and symbolic representation of the 'real' be read differently – without a reduction to the singular?

So, how can such a braiding of myth and symbolic representation of the 'real' be read differently without a reduction to the singular? In trying to get to grips with Ian's comments I want to take as a starting point the notion of the male as a 'cipher'. First, I want to comprehend a little more fully what this word means. Second, I am interested in trying to deconstruct Ian's reasonings for perceiving the male doll as a 'cipher'. The hope is that by attempting to occupy or situate myself in Ian's position I might then have some appreciation as to why his perceptions were not readily available to me. Let me begin with definitions of the word 'cipher'. These, I have learnt, include the following.

'Cipher' it seems, is understood as a method of secret writing where letters are both transposed and substituted so that a key then becomes necessary in order to read the message. Moreover, a 'cipher' is a person or a thing of no importance – in other words, a nonentity. In music, a 'cipher' is a defect in an organ resulting in the continuous sounding of a pipe, the key of which has not been depressed. 'Cipher' also relates to numbers, where, for example, it means to perform (a calculation) arithmetically. However, it is also an obsolete term for zero.

By playing with some of the meanings of 'cipher' in relation to the girls' story, my aim is to emulate or echo some of the deconstruction that Ian might have intended as a consequence of using the word. Indeed he has, I think, already alluded to one meaning of the word when he describes the man as 'an object of some passive kind' and where consequently the 'he' of the story is 'a person or thing of no importance'. Clearly, however, Ian would have intended the word to carry more than this. Working from this premise and with this notion as the man as 'cipher' I want to offer further readings of the Jane and Kate story.

The girls do not write, instead they play with some small dolls and toy beds. These playthings can, however, be perceived as a medium which the girls use to communicate aspects of their thinking. However, rather than perceiving the extract as a story which has embedded notions of clarity, perhaps it is more appropriate to discern the play as a complex collage which has woven into it scraps of ideas. A task for me was to try to discern or decode how these might be understood.

One message seems to be relatively straightforward and easy to access: the dolls, it appears, are tired because first they attended a wedding and then there was dancing. However, other bits are less coherent because only shreds or fragments are visible. This means guesswork or deductions have to be incorporated in order to decipher or make some sense of the play.

Let me begin by speculating on the girls' naming of the dolls. Why has the naming designated all but one of the figures as female? Moreover, why have all but one of the dolls been named? Why is there only one 'he' figure? Is it because traditional notions of a wedding stipulate the presence of a bride and a bridegroom? That is to say, the girls, when playing, have to submit to a logic or an underpinning equation – an equation which could be read as:

('groom' + 'bride') = wedding.

However, perhaps what we have here is not so much an 'adding up' but a disturbing of the calculation. Bhabha (1990: 305–6), drawing on Derrida's strategy of the supplement, makes the following observations:

'The supplementary strategy suggests that adding "to" need not "add up" but may disturb the calculation . . . Insinuating itself into the terms of reference of the dominant discourse, the supplementary antagonizes the implicit power to generalize, to produce the sociological solidity'.

So, while the 'he' has to be present, what kind of 'presence' is it? In naming the bride as 'Linda' and yet refusing to name the 'groom' are Jane and Kate accentuating or diminishing 'his' position within the equation? Is 'he' an equal partner? Does 'he', for example, carry the same amount of weight as 'Linda'? Or has there been a tampering with the balance?

Furthermore, while I am informed that the couple 'love one another' the elaborations appear to be one-sided. For though Jane points out that 'she' loves 'him', she stops short of reversing the equation. I am not told, for example, that 'he loves her'. Instead, at the end of the extract, I am informed by Kate that 'this is a man . . . He's married her'.

While it is impossible to answer the above questions with any degree of confidence they are, nevertheless, a means for suggesting some tentative conjectures. It occurs to me that the girls' decision to include a 'he' in their play is couched in a 'necessary ambivalence'. To expand – because they have included a wedding they are, therefore, under an obligation to include a 'he'. But, by withholding a name, something of the male's presence is diminished. Effectively, it appears that 'he' is both present and absent within the story. That is, 'he' is necessary as a feature but meanwhile work is undertaken to render 'him' as characterless or featureless. It is as if 'he' is both needed yet must somehow be kept peripheral. In all, 'he' seems very much a 'sleeping' or passive partner within the marriage. Put a little differently, he is a non-functioning organ.

The above meanderings are attempts at trying to do several things. First, I wanted to try to situate myself differently so that I might then be better placed to challenge habitual and restrictive perceptions. With this in mind, I borrowed and used Ian Stronach's idea that the 'he' of the story could be understood as a 'cipher'. By working with and off some of the meanings that are associated with 'cipher' I then posited ideas concerning the symbolic presence and function of the 'he' within the girls' play. The ambition here was to resist the imposition of my own desires, wishes and aspirations onto the play of the girls. Rather, the hope was that by offering a range of interpretations the play might then be understood as complicated, confusing and complex. Overall, the task became a matter of trying to read differently so that there was not a reduction to the singular.

The above strippings and teasings have failed to suggest solutions or make clear certain answers. As such they are a disappointment. However, perhaps what these inept attempts at undressing, addressing and readdressing do show are those ways by which I try to convince and lend authority to particular meanings and definitions. The above interpretations should, therefore, be seen as the beginnings of a process to shift myself towards that 'becoming space' (Derrida 1981: 27), where thinking and doing may be a little less bounded.

9

Deconstructing the nursery classroom: that will undo nicely, but so what?

I do not believe in decisive ruptures, in an unequivocal 'epistemological break', as it is called today. Breaks are always, and fatally, reinscribed in an old cloth that must continually, interminably be undone. This interminability is not an accident or contingency; it is essential, systematic, and theoretical.

(Derrida, quoted in McCarthy 1991: 99)

Introduction

The concerns of this chapter cover a range of topics including notions of difference, storytelling, narratives and the effects and consequences which certain kinds of play can have on me as teacher. In the main I use two extracts from my teaching journal to examine and discuss these different items.

I make no claim that the extracts I use are attempts at describing reality. Rather, they are the initial writings, or what Derrida (1978: 292) refers to as 'active interpretations' which were prompted by something/s occurring. The extracts being used are the hurried notes written after an event. The more fulsome and subsequent 'active interpretations' come as a consequence of rereadings of the hurried notes.

The aims of this chapter are threefold. First, I want to show that by incorporating practices of deconstruction into the research I am being *responsible*. Second, I want my attempts at playing with texts that are themselves concerned with play to be taken *seriously*. Third, the chapter as a whole aims at *bafflements* rather than understandings. I will expand on this curious statement subsequently.

I have always had certain worries about incorporating practices of deconstruction into the research. I was troubled that the deconstructions I would be offering would in some way work at trivializing the lives of the nursery children. After all, it was from observations of the children that the data and hence the deconstructions emanated. Recently, however,

I have come to the realization that the anxieties, cautions or concerns that I take with me when 'undoing' should and must be an integral part of the deconstructions. I take note here of Derrida's advice that being responsible or taking responsibility is not something that can be systemized:

> Once you know or you think you know in a determinant judgment what your responsibility is, there is no responsibility. For a responsibility to be a responsibility, you must, you should, know whatever you can know; you have to try to know the maximum, but the moment of responsibility or decision is a moment of non-knowledge, a moment beyond the programme. A responsibility must be infinite, and beyond any theoretical certainty or determination.
>
> (Brannigan *et al.* 1996: 223–4)

Deconstruction in itself cannot be 'responsible'. This is because it is neither a tool nor is it a method. Indeed Derrida asserts that it is 'not even an act or operation' (Brannigan *et al.* 1996: xix). Arguably, there are those who would claim that it can be used in a mechanistic fashion. Hargreaves (1994: 39–40), for example, proposes that the researcher can do just this. His suggestion is to adopt a utilitarian strategy towards postmodernism generally but particularly towards practices of deconstruction. Hence, incorporating deconstruction can have some 'methodological advantages' and it is useful as an 'intellectual strategy'. But Hargreaves goes on to warn against postmodernism as a 'theoretical position'. In my view, this proposal whereby the 'bad' bits of postmodernism get dumped while the 'good' aspects are salvaged smacks of trying to make scraps of the movement 'respectable', a concern that was of little interest to me.

However, it is because deconstruction is not a method or a tool that it cannot be made to be 'responsible'. Rather, the onus must be on the one who is applying it to be responsible. For as Derrida comments:

> deconstruction is not a doctrine; it's not a method, nor is it a set of rules or tools; it cannot be separated from performatives, from signatures, from a given language. So, if you want to 'do deconstruction' – 'you know the kind of thing Derrida does' – then you have to perform something new, in your own language, in your own singular situation, with your own signature, to invent the impossible and to break with the application, in the technical, neutral sense of the word. So, on the one hand, there is no 'applied deconstruction'. But on the other hand, there is nothing else, since deconstruction doesn't consist in a set of theorems, axioms, tools, rules, techniques, methods. If deconstruction, then, is nothing by itself, the only thing it can do is apply, to be applied, to something else, not only in more than one language, but also with something

else. There is no deconstruction, deconstruction has no specific object, it can only refer to, apply to, for example, the Irish problem, the Kabbalah, the problem of nationality, law, architecture, philosophy, amongst other things. It can only apply.

(Brannigan *et al.* 1996: 217–18)

Thus, given Derrida's cautionary words, it would seem that there are not necessarily any right ways to 'do deconstruction' – but nevertheless there are wrong ways. I take Derrida's words to mean that deconstruction does not imply a 'free for all' and that it is up to me to accept the responsibilities when applying deconstruction, 'to act in good faith, to try to do the right things' (Brannigan *et al.* 1996: xix).

Those deconstructions that I bring to texts that are concerned with teaching are, I believe, as a consequence of 'trying to act in good faith'. 'Trying to do the right thing' is considerably more problematic and in a sense this constitutes one of the overall aims of the project. The writing that follows could, I believe, be described as enactments of 'trying to do the right thing'.

However, being 'responsible' was not my only concern. As said, I wanted my efforts at playing with texts that are themselves concerned with play to be taken *seriously* and where it would be appreciated that such play was a serious attempt to think and write 'otherwise' in an area that is over-invested with received wisdom and almost invisible ideological inflections.

Clearly, I am occupied with 'play'. It is the children's play which prompts me to write. I then 'play with' these texts and by playing the hope is to deconstruct so as to expose contradictory undercurrents of meaning. 'Play', in this sense, is unquestionably serious. As Stronach and MacLure (1997: 140) warn, 'nothing is more serious in deconstruction than "play"'. They elaborate further: 'Play, in the sense of a certain looseness between mechanisms or meanings, is the condition of and for meaning. Deconstructive play is never kidding'.

The third aim is that there will be some acceptance of 'bafflement' rather than 'understanding'. That is, there will be an appreciation that the deconstructions offered here will not amount to solutions, answers or advice. However, they might, as Johnson suggests, open up 'meaning as a question, as a non-given, as a bafflement' (1988: 39). In other words, the deconstructions of the data are important to me as both practitioner and researcher. Because of its absence the data matters because it offers no secure meanings or descriptions of self-realizations. The writing, because it will remain open-ended, will beg further questions and this is what matters. So, while 'bafflement' might be a somewhat incongruous position to adopt in a research project, nevertheless the suggestion is that it is potentially creative.

As Derrida indicates, practices of deconstruction need not imply a complete break or a 'decisive rupture' with particular ways of being. However, what this chapter tries to indicate is that deconstruction obliges me to position myself so that I can question those boundaries that are established around me and which I have erected around myself. Enactments of deconstruction work at troubling these boundaries and dominant structures, and while I may not become fully free of them I can nevertheless work at troubling them. As Derrida reminds me, I can only work on the 'old cloth' but here I can make tears and rents in order to find some place *between*:

> *Between* can be an exposed location, open to attack from any direction. *Between* also opens up fissures in our habitual certainties of (self-) definition. Moreover, *between* is the site of application leading from one discourse to another, which modifies each in turn and turn about. Without *between* there is no self and no other: and it is the *sine qua non* of transmission, for without the space *between* you cannot send anything across to anyone (without *between* there would be no one there) or to be anywhere (without *between* there would only be here).
>
> (Brannigan *et al.* 1996: xx)

As practitioner-researcher my efforts have been and are directed towards thinking about and rethinking those habitual and taken for granted aspects of teaching. Applying deconstruction to aspects of practice requires, I believe, a revisiting, where the less than obvious can claim some attention. Rather than take, for example, a child's game 'as read' or 'comprehended' the move is to look for those things which are not 'precisely' present. These cannot directly impart meaning, however they can invoke and provoke potential meanings and/or different perspectives. So for me it is not a matter of attempting to change actual practice. Rather, through my writing the hope is that there may be opportunities to ask 'new and different questions' (Hebdige 1989: 226) which arguably is both an act of responsible education and a form of intervention. The hope is that through rereadings I will practise stripteasings yet again. In this chapter the focus is on addressing, undressing and readdressing the 'so what' part of the title.

Example 1: A meaningful tale

The following example evolves around Jonathan, a 4-year-old, who at the time was playing outside in the nursery play area. In the account Jonathan is joined by a boy called Kyle who is also aged 4. Again, the following extract is based on notes which were written up moments after the events occurred.

Jonathan brings me a stone.
He tells me it's a music stone.
He holds it to my ear.
I make an 'Oh'.
I give back the stone and ask, 'What kind of music is it playing?'
Jonathan holds the stone to his ear and hums. Kyle joins us, he's
  interested by the stone.
Jonathan offers him the stone, telling him that it's a 'music stone'.
  Kyle listens to the stone. Then looks puzzled.
He hands the stone back to Jonathan.
Jonathan: 'It's now a hero stone.'
Kyle runs off.

Rereading the story, what is it about? Such a question may seem beguilingly simple but it is possible, I believe, to move it from being a straightforward and unproblematic proposition to one that is ambiguous and multiple. First, it would seem that I have decided that it is *about* Jonathan. Arguably, it could also be *about* 'a stone' or *about* 'Kyle' or *about* the 'me' who is the onlooker/participant. This story is without a knowable subject but it can, I suggest, become a means by which I can discuss subjectivity.

Additionally, *about* can suggest time and space but in ways which confound the above story further. Take the idea of time. The above extract describes an incident which happened at a point in time. Then there is the time of writing. Between these two is a space. Here all manner of slippages and movements can occur including those involving observations and memory as well as language and meaning. In a sense the 'incident' is displaced and distanced by the writing. In asking 'What is this story about?' it seems I am about to tell more stories about a story that has already been told. Interestingly, the writing could serve as a passe-partout – a frame within a frame, 'which sets off the picture from its ostensible frame, and thence frames its distance from the outside' (Robbins 1996: 43). Interestingly, the passe-partout is not a pure containment. It does not impose limits on either what may be seen or in this case what may be written. For as Derrida warns us: 'The internal edges of a pass-partout are often bevelled' (1987: 13), which allows for reflections and refractions.

All this implies is that there is much which prevents 'What is this story about?' from being a simple question. Arguably, it is a simple story and a single, over-arching explanation could be attached to it. However, what this chapter wants to assert is that to do this would be misguided. Better perhaps to both read and interpret the story as layered, often ambiguous and inevitably inconclusive, but nevertheless prompting curiosity. Subsequently, the writing will explore whether, as a consequence of bringing a range of meanings to a child's narrative that result in an unstable, disorderly and complex (dis)array of meanings, it is possible to challenge certain pedagogical practices which, because of being habitual or mechanistic, are held as 'truths'.

It is perhaps inevitable that the double undoing of play and teaching results in a blurring between the intellectual borders and boundaries which surround 'education' and 'culture'. To take something such as play and treat it seriously when on a level it is so clearly not serious is ambiguous. This ambiguity exists outside school – for example, play is sold at 'Early Learning Centres' and is both packaged and read as 'educational', while within school it is very much understood in terms of which theoretical and ideological baggage is brought to it. In general terms, the parental attitudes of the children that I teach are also ambivalent, with a propensity towards defining play as 'not work' and as a consequence its presence in school is 'not serious' and hence perhaps 'not appropriate'.

My choice is to view play as one medium through which the tensions and interplay which lie between the two sites of education and culture can surface and be investigated. A further suggestion is that while this story cannot reveal a 'truth', including a true 'self', nevertheless it can be a medium by which the fragmented selves of both teacher and child can be discussed. Better perhaps to problematize and take seriously such complexities than look to a single point – for example, the National Curriculum. Here, it seems to me, there are clear-cut provisos and definitions, where teaching and learning are understood in terms of 'processes', 'attainments' and 'targets'. Adopting what McRobbie (1993: 133) refers to as a 'strategy of unsettlement and an embracing of the idea of difference' may or may not 'improve standards'. However, what I believe it will allow for is an unpicking and a revealing of how certain practices work at repressing and marginalizing and as a consequence are inhibiting.

Perhaps the first point that should be considered is whether the above story can be called a 'story', or a 'tale' or a 'narrative'. Throughout this chapter I use the word 'story' and sometimes 'tale' or 'narrative', and these are used because I know of no other suitable terms. On a level these words suffice. However there are, I would suggest, too many loose ends for this story to be described as a 'complete' and 'finished' story. It does not, for example, have an ending where I am left with a sense of fully understanding what has gone on. This is, I believe, the tale's strength. It is in the peripherals of the story – that is, in its gaps, omissions, lack of ending or incomplete structure – where creative possibilities lie. Jonathan's story is important because I could neither predict its opening nor can I anticipate its ending. In a number of significant ways this runs counter to accustomed expectations of research. In general, it is anticipated that research will tell a complete story. Thus the imperative of the search is to describe and explain, to search for origins so that a satisfactory conclusion can be established. It is not feasible nor, in my view, is it desirable to use Jonathan's story in this way. As Benhabib (1992: 83) notes 'we have to explain how every human infant can become the initiator of a unique life-story, of a meaningful tale – which certainly is only meaningful if we know the cultural codes under which it is constructed – but which we cannot predict even if we knew these cultural codes'. What I can attempt, however, are rereadings where different questions can be posed.

Rereading the story

So Jonathan brings me a stone and informs me 'It's a music stone'. Effectively, Jonathan has undertaken several transformations and displacements. First, he has taken a natural object, a stone, and transformed it into a cultural artefact, the 'music stone'; a change which moreover necessitates merging fantasy and truth and the real and the unreal. Furthermore, by holding the stone to my ear, he invites me to move from being an observer to a participator. So in various ways Jonathan enacts a series of transgressions between different binaries and in so doing breaks with a customary form of logic.

Is it significant that Jonathan chose to 'share' the stone with me, his teacher? It could well be that in selecting to show his teacher a 'music' stone Jonathan is indicating both an awareness of and complicity with a specific set of discursive practices concerned with schooling which include in this instance the telling of a certain kind of story for a specific audience. Jonathan, in telling his music stone story to me perhaps does so in the knowledge that it will be accepted and appreciated and, while there is a brief attempt to try out the music stone story on a peer it is quickly exchanged for a more palatable idea – a 'hero stone'.

Or, is it conceivable that Jonathan, having used the stone to upset several dichotomies, then tries once again to use it to displace our respective positionings as adult/child? It could be that by placing the stone to my ear he was inviting me to cross the boundary which separates children's culture, including play, from that which is associated with being an adult. However, my pragmatic question: 'What *kind* of music is it playing?' puts me back in the role of questioning teacher and/or the inquisitive researcher, where Jonathan is then obliged to 'categorize' or 'explain' his music. However, there is a resistance to do this. Instead of explaining or naming his music he 'hums' a reply.

When Kyle enters the scene Jonathan tries briefly to include him in the play. Kyle, however, is merely puzzled and appears unpersuaded by the fantasy. In response, it seems that Jonathan then attempts another transformation. Now the stone is no longer a 'music' stone; rather it has metamorphosed into a hero stone.

I can attach several significations to this particular transformation. For me, it is as if there is a switching of registers ranging from an implicit high culture, with Jonathan and I sharing acts of creativity including making music, to that of low culture, where the image of popular and mass-produced super-heroes is evoked by the speedy transformation of the stone. I say for me, because clearly the signification that 'hero' is being awarded within this story (by me) comes as a consequence of other stories that are played out in the nursery; my reading of 'hero' within the context of the nursery has become narrow and relatively specific on the basis of meanings derived from preceding stories. To expand, the word 'hero' within this story becomes a powerful signifier. It is not used, I don't believe, as a claim on Jonathan's part for personal status, but rather it signals a familiarity with the discursive practices of a particular game, that of 'super-hero' play.

It is, I think, possible to read this story as an attempt on Jonathan's part to articulate 'difference'. In a sense, what is happening within the tale is a 'juggling with different values' act. I have an impression of Jonathan trying on the one hand to connect with the values of school and in particular with those of his teacher while, on the other hand he is obliged to alter his stone from 'music' to 'hero' in order to reconcile with more local values of community. It could be that Jonathan has an understanding that if the stone is to be used as a ticket allowing him to travel from solitary to social play then the stone has to be invested with an identity which is immediately recognizable and has charisma, thus making it desirable. Given this reading, the stone becomes a representation of Jonathan himself. I suspect also that the word 'hero' is akin to being a password which could allow Jonathan membership of a collective. Like a great number of social groups or clubs, super-hero play has rules but the rules of hero play are rooted in a dualistic patriarchal framework with a total reliance on the logic of 'either or'. As a consequence, there is no toleration of difference, hence the narrative or storyline of super-hero play is fixedly repetitive; it is about goodies fighting baddies and baddies are always vanquished. Power can only be, and hence is always, defined as male physical strength.

There is then a suggestion that the stone is representative of both the security of belonging while simultaneously hinting at (perhaps) the desire for difference. Here Elspeth Probyn (1993: 2), writing from the perspective of a gay woman, develops this ambiguous notion:

> in common usages, the term belonging moves from being the property of someone, something to the sense of 'fitting in socially', 'being a member', and that 'belongings' designates 'possessions' and 'baggage'. Belonging for me conjures up a deep insecurity about the possibility of really belonging, truly fitting in. But then, the term

'belongings' also forefronts the ways in which these yearnings to fit in will always be diverse: at times joyous, at times painful, at times destined to fail. Perhaps more immediately, belonging brings forth images of leaving, carting one's possessions and baggage from place to place. Thus, while belonging may make one think of arriving, it also always carries the scent of departure – it marks the interstices of being and going.

The 'hero stone' story is a vague affair. Clearly, it is not hard-edged evidence nor can it be replicated or verified. However, its strength is that it hints at possibilities rather than indicating understandings. There is no way of establishing why Jonathan initiated the exchange with me, but what is unusual about the exchange is that the child was informing the teacher about a phenomenon – that is, there was no way of me 'knowing' that the stone was a music stone or indeed what kind of music it played; I had to be informed. This I believe to be rare. Young children, within the context of schooling, very rarely have the opportunity whereby they are able to inform adults. Stories such as Jonathan's, told through signs and symbols, become for me remarkable moments. They interrupt and disturb me and, consequently, prompt me to ask more 'so what' questions.

So what if the boys play super-hero games, and so what if Jonathan wants to abandon one kind of game for another? As must now be very apparent, one of my central aims within the nursery is to explore what opportunities there are for denting the traditional form, whereby men and women are fantastically presented as unified – almost to the point of being robotic – subjects. That said, however, there is still cause to pause in all this and to question whether I have given a too hasty reading to 'hero'. Maybe it is because I am keen to diminish, if not completely outlaw, a particular narrative form that it seems I insist that 'hero' is to be equated with the 'super-heroes' that dominate children's television shows. Perhaps it is because I have lulled myself into an untimely satisfaction with the word 'hero' that I am then unable to use my own creativity which might then allow Jonathan to continue dis-cussing his stone with me. Maybe Jonathan senses or he has learnt that while I might be interested in a 'music stone' there would be little point in trying to engage me with a 'hero stone'. In part this might explain why the story peters out.

So in what ways do these writings of Jonathan and his stone impact upon practice? Do they alter, change or shape future practice? As a consequence of working with Jonathan's story, am I better prepared? Will I behave differently next time? For me, the notion of behaving differently is caught up with wanting to resist resolution which merely repeats previous actions or strategies. Rather, I enter the next situation with residues of past experiences and it is these traces which prevent me from feeling complacent or satisfied with aspects of practice. So while I do want to feel satisfied, nevertheless dissatisfaction can be seen positively in that it triggers a renewal of action rather than relying on mechanistic ways.

Example 2: Gun play

At this juncture I want to turn to the next example of data which centres on gun play. This is an issue which has challenged and perplexed me ever since I have worked in the nursery and I have previously made some attempts to write my way to some understandings about it (see Jones 2001). For example, in a piece written in 1995 I wrote:

> Why was it that four year boys, when presented with construction equipment such as Mobilo or Lego, invariably constructed guns, and in so doing broke the decision by the nursery teaching team to ban guns from our room? Why was it that even gentle Paul, who often played in the 'Home Base', performing the domestic tasks that this area allowed for, would also build guns? And as our embargo on guns was so obviously not working, why did we persist in parroting our rule?
>
> (Jones 1995: 6)

It seems at this point I was preoccupied with the following issues:

- Gun play appears to be a gender-specific activity in that it is the boys who construct and play with guns.
- There is, however, a 'no gun' rule which circulates within the nursery and which includes those that children construct from play equipment. Clearly, the children do not have 'free choice' when it comes to playing with construction materials.
- Gun play is not just isolated to 'rough' boys because 'even gentle Paul' will make and play with guns. Why is this?
- It would seem that 'no guns' as a rule was:
  (a) being 'parroted' by the staff; and
  (b) found to be ineffective because the boys continued to make and play with guns.
- This would imply that the words 'no guns' hold no meaning for either the staff or the children. As a consequence 'no guns' is a powerless expression. It leaves the adults 'parroting' the rule while the children ignore it.

However, before elaborating further on these issues, another journal extract will be introduced. This foregrounds how ideology can work at fixing a teacher's repertoire. The move is then to unsettle and displace the writing by locating those oppositions which work at strengthening and structuring specific positions. Moreover, in rereading the piece the attempt will be made to weave in and address the points raised above.

Journal entry 11.9.95. (notes made at break time)

> Ben, Dean and Nathan were in the construction base using some wooden sticks to make guns. I was conscious of this but for a while resisted stopping them. However, the play began to get more wild. 'Guns' were being raised and waved and the noise level increased. At this point I intervened. There were two visitors in the room and I was conscious that I didn't want to make this kind of play visible.
>
> What did I do with the boys?
>
> I put away the sticks and got out the 'Duplo' farm. I then took the three boys with me to the easel. Here I pointed out that all the colours mixed that day were all 'autumn' colours. I made a point of naming each of the colours. The boys were then asked to 'do me a painting about autumn'.
>
> The three boys brought me their pictures when they had finished. I was conscious that I gave each of the paintings a cursory comment, e.g. 'That's a lovely picture'. The boys were then 'invited' to join me at the table where I was working. However, my tone of voice and facial expressions indicated that there was no choice in the matter. While we were cutting, gluing etc. I asked the boys if they knew why I had taken them away from the construction sticks. All three, almost in unison, chanted, 'Because we were making guns'. I then informed the boys it was not just the gun-making which had made me 'unhappy' but both their shouting and stick waving were objectionable. It might even, I suggested, frighten some of the children, especially the younger ones. I then led the three back to the construction area. Here a mixed gendered group were playing with the Duplo farm. The three boys were instructed to 'Watch these children for a bit'. A minute later I asked: 'Are these children shouting? Are they waving the toys around so they might hurt someone? Do you think you could play properly now?' Not too surprisingly, all three answered 'No' to questions 1 and 2 and 'Yes' to the third.

Locating the oppositions

> If one is always situated in ideology, then the only way to demystify these ideological operations . . . is to occupy the interstices of contesting ideologies or to seek the disjuncture and opposing relations created within a single ideology by its own contradictions.
>
> (Ebert 1988: 27)

What I want to suggest is that the above scenario could be conceptualized as a series of oppositional moves where the teacher in particular contrives to keep the upper hand by using her adult/teacher authority. However, while the boys' behaviour might have been contained, in effect nothing has changed. The boys' acquiescence is a hollow affair. Their responses come as a consequence of habit and repetition and are reminiscent of the tried and tested replies that the audience is obliged to make at the Christmas pantomime. As the teacher, I am left feeling both despondent and trapped. I am trapped because the options seem so limited. It seems that either I let the boys go their way, in which case they will continue to make guns and act out stories that centre on the gun, or I can organize and construct the classroom to the extent where I can have more or less complete surveillance and where the boys' play is both monitored and checked. While this may put a brake on gun play there is clearly a price to pay for such actions. For example, it negates any notions of autonomy where children themselves can make some choices about the nature of their play. Furthermore, it would preempt attempts on my part to explore why it is that I find constructing and playing with guns problematic or offensive.

What follows is an attempt to show how change, including changes in attitudes, will not be achieved until certain fundamental dichotomies which currently regulate aspects of classroom life have been shifted. In denting these what might then be available is space, perhaps some place *between*, where different discourses can be produced and where actions and subjectivities can be read and understood differently (Walkerdine 1990: 9).

'Undoing' gun play

The intentions here are to first identify certain oppositions which are embedded in the above journal extract. Following on from this an attempt will be made to explore what has shaped and fashioned these oppositions. The third move is to posit whether there may be alternative, non-oppositional ways of positioning myself.

The oppositions

Perhaps the most obvious dichotomy centres on gender, where not only does gun play appear to be a 'boys only' activity but where its presence is in opposition to the wishes of the female teacher. However, the dichotomy can be extended to include other polarizations. For example, it includes the disparity between adult/child and teacher/pupil relations as well as the split between those who make and keep the rules, and transgressors. Additionally, the following lines appear in the extract:

'There were two visitors in the room and I was conscious that I didn't want to make this kind of play visible'. This suggests that there are certain tensions around what 'outsiders' can and cannot see of the 'inside' world of the nursery. There are, for example, specific aspects of children's play which can be made 'visible' (e.g. playing with the Duplo farm and painting) while others, such as 'gun play', should remain hidden. Perhaps this is because the first two are seen as being 'creative' and 'constructive' while gun play, although a fantasy, is nevertheless read as being both 'destructive' and consequently 'in/appropriate'. Moreover, besides being kinds of play which the outsider can and cannot look at there are also forms which have the propensity to make me either 'unhappy' or 'happy'. Similarly, it seems that gun play has the capacity to 'frighten' some of the younger children.

Above, I used the word 'offensive' to describe my reactions to gun play. Curiously, it would appear that in order to stop the gun play I mounted my own offensive against the boys. First I put away the materials from which the guns materialized. I then transferred the boys from one area of the room to another where they had to paint a picture. Following this, the boys were obliged to do further creative activities with me before being returned to the construction area in order to witness other children 'playing properly'. Beneath these physical strategies lie further emotional moves where there is a sense of the boys being 'guilt tripped' into submission. Thus, the boys are meant to understand that gun play not only makes me 'unhappy' but it could also 'frighten' the younger children.

What underpins such an offensive and what has been achieved? The answer to the latter part of the question is 'very little', but disentangling the ideology which supports or guides my actions is a little more complex. In the next section the intention is to try to delve into some of these complexities.

Performance, production and playing properly

> It is common in some psychoanalytic discourses, for example, to counter pose 'fantasy' and 'reality', yet it is this division that appears most questionable . . . It is not necessary to counter pose fantasy to reality but to demonstrate how fantasies themselves are lived, played out and worked through their inscriptions in the veridicality of discourses and practices.
>
> (Walkerdine 1990: 140–1)

If both the 'teacher' and the 'child' are considered as performers it then becomes possible to explore those expectations which feed into the performance of each. Here my aim is twofold. First, I want to try to show how these expectations are rooted in particular historical conceptions of what constitutes the production of 'the teacher' and 'the child'. Second, via the journal extract I want to indicate my own immersion in these expectations.

There are two specific performances that I want to pay attention to which interact and interrelate with the scenario that the journal entry depicts. The first centres on the production of the nursery teacher as 'the mother made conscious', while the second is the 'the child-centred teacher'. Both these productions, I shall argue, are part of the machinery geared at producing the ideal, that is the rational, subject: 'the ideal teacher is like "a mother made conscious"' (Froebel, quoted in Steedman 1992: 179).

Historically, nursery classrooms were both conceived and constructed along specific feminized lines where 'mothering' and 'nurturing' were vital and salient concepts. Under the philosophical guidance of certain key 'founding fathers', including Froebel, from the late nineteenth century onwards an ideology grounded in notions of 'naturalness' took root. Classrooms, for example, were conceptualized as places where young children could touch, explore and as a consequence, 'flower' (Williams 1979). Similarly, women were construed as *ideal* for the teaching of young children because they were imbued with *natural* qualities. As Froebel observed, the onus on the 'teacher-as-mother' was to:

> waken and develop in the Human Being every power, every disposition . . . Without any Teaching, Reminding or Learning, the true mother does this of herself. But this is not enough: in Addition is needed that being Conscious, and acting upon a Creature that is growing Conscious, she do her part Consciously and Consistently, as in Duty bound to guide the Human Being in its regular development.
> (Herford 1899: 34–5)

It is clear from this quotation that 'childhood' is being described and understood in terms of developmental stages. Froebel was among the first to establish a theory of individual child psychology and to describe childhood in terms of developmental stages. As Steedman notes, child analysis inherited this psychology, not so much as a psychology in itself, but rather as a generalized cultural perception of childhood (Steedman 1992: 188).

It is this nineteenth-century ideology which still underlies current pedagogical practices. Obviously, the twentieth century developed it further. For example, the nursery class, besides being a place to 'flower', came to be envisaged as an arena where working-class children could be 'compensated' for their supposed cultural deficit. In recent times this has required that teachers, besides supporting the emotional needs of their charges, have also had to work at lessening the cognitive gap, particularly linguistic deficits, which was said to exist between middle- and working-class children. The hope was that by filling working-class children with 'rich experiences', schools might endeavour to 'fill the emptiness, make up for the "noise, crowding and physical discomfort" of the child's home, in which "the usual" (i.e middle-class) parental role of tutor and guide is largely lacking' (Edwards, quoted in Steedman 1992: 191).

These 'rich experiences' were and are shaped and fashioned by the discourse of developmental psychology, for it is here that the notion of 'natural' development is secured (Henriques *et al.* 1984). It is, therefore, essential that young children should learn to 'express' rather than 'repress' in order to 'self-regulate'. Practices such as 'choosing' become essential in allowing for the development of the 'normal' and 'natural' child. As Walkerdine (1990: 8) puts it:

> The pedagogy of 'choice' is the tool in the production of the rational ideal. Rationality, rational choice and decision-making are the ideal, the goal of the pedagogy. It assumes (following Piaget and many others) that the rational individual can be produced by leaving children alone to 'grow-out of' their base animal sexuality, their aggression – that is, the non-rational.

This then is the ideological legacy which underpins current practices. Using this albeit brief sketch it is now possible to reread the journal extract and in so doing foreground how the fantasies which underlie the production of 'teacher' and 'child' work at oppressing both.

Oppressive acts, repetitive behaviour
The journal extract begins at the point where I noticed that the boys were playing with guns. However, rather than stop their play I chose instead to ignore it. Obviously several reasons could be posited which might go some way to explain my action. Ignoring 'bad' behaviour yet praising 'good' is, for example, part and parcel of the routine behaviour of teaching. For instance, bad behaviour is conceived of as attention seeking. To respond to it is to reward it. Therefore the injunction is usually to ignore it. But I think this 'ignoring' is more complex, and in this case made more so because it was a feature of a scene that was being played out in front of visitors. Maybe for these observers (two mothers of children who were to join the nursery the following term) the sight of boys playing make-believe games with guns was both natural and expected, and what would be more surprising would be for the teacher to intervene in something which, in their terms, constituted 'normal behaviour'. Or, perhaps it is the case that the mothers did not even notice the gun play because it is such a common and familiar aspect of boyhood culture. This then prompts me to ask whether it was because the boys were playing 'like boys' that I both noticed the play and wanted to put a stop to it? Was I reading the boys' play from a feminist standpoint where the boys' fantasy is understood as an early expression of male domination? Is it then the case,

however, that because of the ideology of the 'progressive teacher' I am unable to respond to my feminist positioning? That is, the dual positioning of 'feminist' and 'progressive teacher' causes a temporary standstill where stopping the boys (a feminist act) would be to circumvent their freedom to choose (a central tenet of progressive pedagogy). Is this what lay behind and prompted my hesitation?

Interestingly, when I do act it appears that my actions were in response to the general hubbub that the boys were making. Was this because I wanted to make my actions ostensibly understandable to the watching mothers? Was it that I was trying to project the 'mother made conscious' image – that is, the 'mother' who 'intuitively senses' that it is time to move the children from one activity to another? However, I did not ask the boys what they would like to do. Rather, I set them the task of painting pictures.

There are some interesting anomalies caught within this sub-scenario of the boys painting. As noted, I made the boys trade in guns for paint brushes. Was this because I wanted to reposition the boys back into the fantasy of the 'natural, creative and flowering child' and thereby appease my own positioning as 'progressive teacher'? Perhaps by using painting I tried to achieve a double guise. That is, the feminist teacher has put a stop to gun play while the progressive teacher tries through painting to provide a 'creative' outlet.

Bronwyn Davies argues that, in general terms, young children, while sometimes resisting both female and male adult power, will mostly go along with it. She goes on to say that children are adept at 'finding ways to achieve their ends despite adult control, often achieving what they want by conforming to what adults want them to be' (1989: 89). Davies, writing from a poststructuralist standpoint, postulates that those arenas in which boys practise constituting themselves as masculine (dominant and oppressive) are 'generally independent of powerful adults and inside a discourse different from adult-child discourse' (p. 89).

Like Davies I agree that it is mainly within specific arenas that the boys play at being 'powerful males'. In general terms, within the teacher/child couplet the children tend to adhere to my authority. I think the journal extract shows this. The boys offered no resistance to my orders to tidy away the sticks. On the contrary, they quickly positioned themselves as docile acquiescent small children in relation to my powerful adult. The boys' play is not so much an act of resistance against the over-arching femininity which is prevalent in the construction and organization of the room. Rather, it is a means of acting out a particular mutation or notion of masculinity; a notion which is constructed in opposition to a specific version of 'femaleness'.

However, 'ideas', as Foucault's work has shown, are not impervious to change. He proposes that through 'practices of the self' individuals can transgress specific structures which stipulate ways of being. He writes: 'I am interested . . . in the way the subject constitutes himself in an active fashion, by the practices of self, these practices are nevertheless not something which the individual invents by himself. They are patterns that he finds in his culture and which are proposed, suggested and imposed on him by his culture, his social group' (1998: 11).

In Foucault's terms transgressions are not envisaged as transformations, where, for example, boys could become 'like girls' imbued with all those qualities which traditionally are associated with being female (e.g. caring, nurturing etc.). All this would entail would be exchanging one fantasy of the stable self for another. Rather, the task is perceived as destabilizing those 'truth effects' (Butler 1990) which work at perpetuating the idea of oppressive masculinity. As Butler writes: 'If the inner truth of gender is a fabrication and if a true gender is a fantasy instituted and inscribed on the surface of bodies, then it seems that genders can be neither true nor false but are only produced as the truth effects of a discourse of primary and stable identity (1990: 337).

So if gun play is an external manifestation of an internal fantasy, does it matter that it happens? The answer has to be 'yes' because as a fantasy it is fixed and powerful and therefore considered as 'natural'. To quote Butler (1990: 339): 'it seems crucial to resist the myth of interior origins . . . Only then, gender coherence might be understood as the regulatory fiction it is – rather than the common point of our liberation'.

Encouraging diversity: deconstructing unitary notions of subjectivity

Resisting 'the myth of interior origins' requires both persistent creativity and persistent critique of one's ways of knowing and doing. Previously, equity work in the nursery had been directed at eradicating negative aspects of masculinity and femininity – for example, girls were given opportunities to play with pieces of equipment that were habitually favoured by the boys (e.g. large construction toys, the climbing frame etc.) and boys could experience themselves as gentle and caring. So by mixing and merging furnishings and other paraphernalia more play was sustained by boys within areas such as the home. However, such steps, while encouraging movement across the male/female divide do not deconstruct fixed notions of masculinity and femininity. Effectively the children are given temporary membership of a category where sometimes boys can be *more like* girls and vice versa.

More recent initiatives have focused on diversity where the children have been actively encouraged to experiment with roles that are contra-dictory rather than coherent. So, for example, a recent spate of boys constructing swords from Mobilo led to a mini-project on the Vikings. Here, while we didn't attempt to gloss over the cruelty of the Vikings, we nevertheless did ensure that all the children appreciated that in addition to fighting, Viking men also wrote poetry and moreover loved to make and wear jewellery. In this way, while swords were still constructed so too were bracelets, crowns and necklaces. Such items gave the boys opportunities to move away from play where they were dependent upon a limited notion of masculinity. Wearing a necklace meant that a boy could slip from being a warrior into being a pop star, where singing and dancing was then admissible. As such he could be *both* a fighter *and* a dancer. In this way he was freed from those obligations which are imposed by a notion of subjectivity, which is conceived as being fixed and coherent. It is this practise, whereby all the children are given opportunities to practise multiple notions of self that currently occupies the staff and which taxes their creativity. We are encouraged to continue because it does appear that by extending notions of subjectivity the children's imaginary worlds are extended.

Transgressive agents: an optimistic possibility?

the agency denoted by the performativity of 'sex' will be directly counter to any notion of a voluntarist subject who exists quite apart from the regulatory norms which she/he opposes. The paradox of subjectivation (*assujetissement*) is precisely that the subject who would resist such norms is itself enabled, if not produced by such norms. Although this constitutive constraint does not foreclose the possibility of agency, it does locate agency as a reiterative or rearticulatory practice, immanent to power, and not a relation of external opposition to power.

(Butler 1993: 122)

Postmodern critiques of essentialism which challenges notions of universality and static overdetermined identity within mass culture and mass consciousness can open up new possibilities for the construction of self and the assertion of agency.

(hooks 1989: 28)

Introduction

In general terms, this chapter occupies itself with the notions of agency and transgression and whether there are possibilities for these ideas to be accommodated within the postmodern subject. Interrelated with these issues are conjectures which are concerned with 'choice'.

The chapter opens with a discussion on those meanings that can be attributed to both 'agency' and 'transgression'. Drawing on Bronwyn Davies' (1996) work, a model of agency is sketched out. It is a model which stands outside of traditional or 'common-sense' assumptions of agency. Perhaps, however, scare quotes should be placed around 'model'. Generally speaking, 'models' are conceived as being relatively fixed and stable. This is their supposed 'beauty'. But, by contrast, Davies' suggestions are more fluid and imbued with flexibility. Following on from this, notions of 'transgression' are explored using a Foucauldian perspective.

Following these two explorations, an extract from my teaching journal is introduced. Briefly, this centres on three of the girls in the nursery who, when greeting me at the beginning of the school day, 'play' with my name. The experience has prompted several analyses which have been written at different points in time. I see the writing of this chapter as another opportunity to open out texts concerned with the experience in ways which prompt further enquiries. A particular focus, when rereading, is to ascertain whether the children can be described as having agency and whether it is this that allows them to transgress. Considerations are also given to my own responses. These, it would appear, are characterized by a need to police particular boundaries which surround pupil/teacher relations.

The final part of the chapter considers whether becoming a 'transgressive agent' is an integral and necessary part of resituating or relocating emancipatory education.

Defining agency

In outlining out her proposal for a model of agency Davies (1996) begins by making clear her position with regards to language. This is specified as being poststructuralist and as a consequence the 'common-sense' view of language as being transparent and simply a tool with which to describe the 'real' world is refuted (1996: 342). According to Davies, this understanding of the relation between the individual, language and society is itself a discursive production. Put simply, we think that way because we talk about it that way.

Poststructuralism works at undermining realist notions of language and meaning. Poststructuralism perceives language acquisition as going hand in hand with initiation into those discourses which constitute the social world. Thus, in learning to talk, 'each person gains access to what it means to be a person within each of the discourses available to them, and in practising them becomes the kind of speaker who is implicated in and made sense of through such practices' (Davies 1996: 342). Davies goes on to extend this position by drawing attention to the individual's, 'accumulated personal history' (p. 342). This 'history', she suggests, is what each person brings to any social episode. It is their: 'sense of themselves not only as they are positioned in the present moment but also of themselves as persons who can or cannot be positioned in that way, i.e. as one who is located in certain ways within the social and moral order, who is known to act and feel in certain ways, whose life is explicable within known story lines' (p. 342).

Central to Davies' enquiry is the connection between 'agency' and 'choice'. She asks: 'What is it of one's own, then, that can stand outside of and beyond the collective?' (1996: 432). In order to answer her question, Davies looks to Bakhtin ([1931] 1981). According to Bakhtin, language lies on the 'borderline between oneself and the other'. In other words, meaning is established through dialogue. Everything we say and mean is modified by interaction and interplay with another person. Here Bakhtin ([1931] 1981: 342) elaborates:

> The word in language is half someone else's. It becomes 'one's own' only when the speaker populates it with their own intention, their own accent, when they appropriate the words, adapting it to their own semantic and expressive intention. Prior to this moment of appropriation, the word does not exist in a neutral and impersonal language (it is not after all from a dictionary that the speaker get their words), but rather it exists in other people's mouths, in other people's contexts, serving other people's intentions: it is from there that one must take the word and make it one's own. And not all words for just anyone submit equally easily to this appropriation, to this seizure and transformation into private property: many words stubbornly resist, others remain alien, sound foreign in the mouth of the one who appropriated them and who now speaks for them; they cannot be assimilated into one's context and fall out of it; it is as if they put themselves in quotation marks against the will of the speaker. Language is not a neutral medium that passes freely into the private property of the speaker's intentions; it is populated – over-populated – with the intentions of others. Expropriating it, forcing it to submit to one's own intentions and accents, is a difficult and complicated process.

Within this model, meaning arises through the 'difference' between the participants in any dialogue. The 'other', in short, is essential to meaning (Hall 1997). Conceived of in these terms, notions of agency is a shifting affair, open to argument and contestation. As a model it is in sharp contrast to traditional sociological models (Parsons 1937), where agency is conceptualized as an individual matter in which 'any individual conceives of a line of action, knows how to achieve it and has the power and right to execute it' (Davies 1996: 343).

For Davies (1996: 343) the person is a person by virtue of the fact that they use the discursive practices of the collectives of which they are a member:

> Each person can only speak from the positions made available within those collectives through the recognised discursive practices used by each collective. Their desires are formulated in the terms that make sense in each of the discourses available to them. Embedded within those discursive practices is an understanding that each person is

one who has an obligation to take themselves up as a knowable, recognisable identity, who 'speaks for themselves', who accepts responsibility for their actions, that is as one who is recognisably separate from any particular collective, and thus as one who can be said to have agency.

Transgression

In a number of significant ways Foucault sought to disturb the confident assumptions of Enlightenment thought. Through his analysis of the clinic, madness, prisons and sexuality he was able to mount a sustained critique of those assured dualisms which inform and effect our common-sense conjectures about what truth is, how we discover truth, the superiority of reason over emotion, objectivity over subjectivity, mind over body (Ramazanoglu 1993: 23).

Foucault did not advocate the replacing of one episteme by another or the establishment of another truth to replace a discredited one. Rather, he sought to show how deeply unsatisfactory the notion of the 'humanist subject' was and how under various guises humanism worked at 'subjectifying' (Fraser 1985: 178). Foucault, by asking different questions about subjectivity, sought to show that individuals are social selves, formed by powerful relations and coercions that act upon the body (1977a: 138). In other words, the structures and processes of the social world are recognized as having a material force, a capacity to constrain and to shape.

Foucault's theories are of particular interest because embedded within them is the notion that individuals have the potential to change. With Foucault's analysis there is no obligation to perceive the individual as a social construction which results in some relatively fixed end-product. Instead, subjectivity can now be understood as being constituted and reconstituted through a variety of discursive practices. Given this, there is the space to 'promote new forms of subjectivity through the refusal of this kind of individuality which has been imposed on us for several centuries' (Foucault 1983: 216).

Similarly, Butler (1993) following Foucault, situates resistance and the possibilities for transforming the status quo within the discursive field which produces both existing power relations and forms of subjectivity. As Weedon comments: 'There is no possibility within this model of either fully autonomous subjectivity or a space beyond power from which to act. Agency can, however, transform aspects of material discursive practices and the power relations inherent in them' (1999: 123).

All this prompts the question: how can individuals implement changes or alterations? In other words, how can subjects break with or from those restrictions, coercions and social structures that work at governing notions of subjectivity? Foucault's suggestion is to 'transgress'.

The idea of transgression which Foucault sought to develop is not dependent upon some notion of transcendence (Boyne 1990: 81). Rather, there is a recognition that individuals can inhabit or occupy no space other than their own social space and that because this is not fixed there are possibilities to open it up and exceed or tamper with its limits and limitations. In Foucault's terms, transgression is the experience of the limit, where 'transgression has its entire space in the line it crosses' (Foucault 1977b: 34). He writes:

> Criticism indeed consists of analysing and reflecting upon limits. But if the Kantian question was that of knowing what limits knowledge has to renounce transgressing, it seems to me that the critical question today has to be turned back into a positive one: in what is given to us as universal, necessary, obligatory, what place is occupied by whatever is singular, contingent, and the product of arbitrary constraints? The point, in brief, is to transform the critique conducted in the form of necessary limitation into a practical critique that takes the form of a possible transgression.
>
> (Foucault 1984a: 45)

As a consequence of transgressive acts, individuals by their own efforts can trespass those boundaries which make us perform in habitual ways. Boundary work is not undertaken in the hope that a new, better or more coherent self will be located. Nor will transgressions allow for a rebirth of self. However, there are possibilities for regeneration of selves; selves which are 'always in process, producing . . . in response to and being produced by the contingent antagonisms and alliances that constitute the social' (Schrift 1995: 39). To transgress entails 'embracing the skilful task of reconstructing the boundaries of daily life, in partial connection with others, in communication with all ourselves' (Haraway 1990: 181). In particular, transgressions can be a means of breaking and entering those dualisms in which we have explained ourselves and which oblige us to perform in repetitive ways. Transgressions interrupt and as a consequence create an uncertain space where boundaries, including those that shore up notions of self, are made insecure.

At this juncture I want to introduce an extract from my teaching journal. As inferred above, the extract has already prompted previous writings. My intentions here are twofold. First, old writings will be reread and woven into the subsequent analyses. Second, I will address the piece through a Foucauldian perspective, where the girls' actions and mine can be understood as 'practices of self' (Foucault 1998: 11). In this, the girls' behaviour in particular can be seen as a 'kind of playful struggle' (Allan 1997: 1) with those positionings that they are obliged to take up within the teacher/pupil relationship and the adult/child couplet.

Story

The example of children's talk which is used in this extract occurred at the beginning of the school day. It features three 4-year-old girls: Hannah, Jessica and Amanda. As a point of interest, it is one of the rare pieces of talk between myself and the children that I managed to successfully tape-record.

The nursery, at the start of the day, is quite a hectic place in that the parents and carers of the children are present in the room helping to sort and settle them. My practice, when welcoming the children, was to sit. Sitting down had, I had found, several advantages. For example, an apprehensive child could gain some comfort and security from sitting on my knee. Also, it physically brought me down to the children's height which made listening easier. Additionally, I had come to consider that by sitting I was making myself more approachable and a little less formal to the children. These notions of 'being more approachable' and being a 'little less formal' will be picked up in the analysis.

The children that feature in the extract regularly played together. I had often observed and been impressed by their imaginative dexterity when playing. They were, for example, good at using both themselves and paraphernalia from the room, such as dressing-up clothes, furniture and play equipment, to construct vivid and inventive stories. On the morning when the particular incident occurred it was Hannah who arrived in the room first. She came straight to where I was sitting to greet me. Her two friends, Jessica and Amanda, were, however, following close behind and as a consequence could hear the initial exchange between Hannah and myself. To appreciate the dialogue between me and the children fully, it must be remembered that my surname is Jones.

Journal entry 18.2.96

Hannah: Morning Mrs Dones.
LJ: Good morning Hannah.
Hannah [*grinning broadly*]: Good morning Mrs Dones Lones.
LJ [*also grinning*]: Good morning Lanna Danna.
Hannah [*now concentrating*]: Good morning Mrs Dones Lones Bones.
LJ: Good morning Lanna Danna Shanna.
Hannah [*in a giggly, excited rush*]: Good morning Mrs Jonesy Bonesy.
LJ: Good morning Mrs Hannah Panna.

Hannah [*looking crestfallen*]*:* I'm not a pan. You cook in a pan.

LJ: Well, I'm not just bones. I'm skin and bones.

Hannah [*smiling once again*]*:* Mrs Jones skin and bones. Mrs Jones skin and bones.

LJ: What else can we think of to rhyme with your name? I know, you can make Hannah and banana sound nearly the same.

Amanda: Do 'it' with my name. Make my name say something.

LJ [*in a sing-song voice*]*:* Amanda panda.

Hannah: There's a picture of a panda, Amanda [*she points to the A–Z wall frieze where there is displayed a picture of a panda to illustrate and accompany the letter 'P'*].

Jessica [*rhythmically*]*:* Jessica messica pessica. Pessica messica Jessica.

LJ: That sounds like a train moving.

[*I repeat Jessica's phrases and as I say the sounds I move my arms in a train motion. The three girls, Jessica, Hannah and Amanda, take off round the room, arms moving train-like, chanting Jessica's phrase.*]

Transgressions of the pupil/teacher relationship

I want to begin this section by considering Hannah's opening sentence: 'Morning Mrs Dones'. With this opening line I think Hannah wanted some fun. My initial and troubled response was establishing what the nature of this 'fun' was and what my response should be. Was she inviting me to share her fun or was she making fun of me?

It could well be that Hannah was eliciting fun from my name and indeed she might well have been making fun of me. However, in this analysis I want to work from the premise that Hannah was *playing* with my name and as a consequence she was also *playing* with certain discursive practices which work at regulating social relations between the adult and the child and the teacher and the pupil. To expand: Hannah, by playing with my surname, also plays with those usual forms of address by which children address teachers when in school. As Foucault's work (1977a) has demonstrated, practices which would include how teacher and children address each other are an execution of 'surveillance' through which teachers and pupils regulate themselves and one another in the interests of 'governmentality'. Foucault writes:

> for although surveillance rests on individuals, its functioning is that of a network of relations from top to bottom, but also to a certain extent from bottom to top and laterally; this network 'holds' the whole together and traverses it in its entirety with effects of power that derive from one another: supervisors perpetually supervised. The power in the hierarchized surveillance ... functions like a piece

of machinery . . . it is the apparatus as a whole that produces 'power' and distributes individuals in this permanent continuous field. This enables the disciplinary power to be both absolutely indiscreet, since it is everywhere and is always alert . . . and constantly supervises the very individuals who are entrusted with the task of supervising; and absolutely 'discreet' for it functions permanently and largely in silence.

(1977a: 177)

Forms of address within institutions are very much part of the regulatory processes and within school they work at maintaining the hierarchy which exists between teacher and pupil. Given this, can Hannah's transgressions with my name be understood as an attempt at playing with the order and structures embedded in the teacher/pupil relationship? My suggestion is that it can.

Interestingly, Hannah maintains the title of 'Mrs'. This, I think, achieves several things. It secures my positioning as adult but at the same time it throws into the air certain questions which surround the investing of titles. The use of titles is an interesting cultural phenomena. Within Victorian households, for example, the bestowing or taking away of titles was one of the means by which social distance was maintained between the masters and mistresses of the household and their servants, with the latter being referred to by surname only. Servants, on the other hand, had to always use a title when addressing their employers because this marked respect. Hannah, while she uses a title, effectively diminishes its social significance by spoiling its effect with her use of 'Dones'. It is as if with one hand she gives me respect while with the other she withdraws it. Hannah's greeting of 'Morning Mrs Dones' can, I think, be read as an attempt on her part to play with the line which works at separating out the teacher from the pupil and the adult from the child. Effectively, she positions herself 'in between' (Stronach and MacLure 1997: 59); she is neither the passive child to my powerful adult nor is she a complete renegade or delinquent who stands outside the boundaries of convention. Rather she presents herself as a 'trickster' (Haraway 1990) and one who plays in between.

How am I affected by Hannah's misnamings? I think that my responses to Hannah can be perceived as a series of struggles and, in the main, these are a struggle concerned with teacher identity. Effectively, by disfiguring a routine exchange Hannah dislocates my perceptions of her. By failing to act 'properly' as the child she obliges me to question my teacher identity. She makes me unsure about myself. In part, I think this is why my initial response is a formal one. Maybe by saying 'Good morning Hannah', I was choosing to ignore something in the vain hope it would go away. More significantly however, perhaps it was an attempt to re-erect the boundaries between us, situating Hannah back on the 'right' side of the teacher/child dichotomy.

Why then, if I felt perturbed, did I not either rebuff or rebuke her? To do this would, I believe, require tampering with certain other boundaries which I both erect around myself and are imposed upon me. Using the same extract of data, my intentions here are to undertake further boundary work.

As is evident from the transcript, Hannah is not deterred in her play; instead, she first grins and then extends and elaborates the name play. Furthermore, I make the decision to join in. There are, I think, several ways of interpreting this. One reading would be to describe my actions as an act of transgression where I had decided to make the move from being the serious adult to being one who is willing to join in the fun. However, I suspect this is too easy a reading and one which misses much.

There are, if we look back at the transcript, several things to note about the exchange between Hannah and myself following my 'Good morning Hannah'. First of all, Hannah grins broadly. Is this grinning an indication that she recognizes what my intentions are geared towards and she grins as a way of both acknowledging and resisting my move? Second, Hannah imitates and incorporates my formal 'Good morning' but immediately detracts from it by adding 'Lones' to 'Dones'. Thus, by using a mix of grins and formal and informal address, Hannah still plays at some point in between the divide which lies between us. It is this divide which I think I try to attend to when I enter the game.

Walkerdine and Lucey (1989) and Walkerdine (1990) would suggest, I think, that I enter the game because of my own regulation, a regulation which would include the notion of being an 'approachable and sensitive teacher'. Having failed to reposition Hannah by the subtle use of a 'proper' and 'correct' form of address I then have to seek other covert ways of regulating her transgressions. I cannot openly rebuke her, for this would be both insensitive and furthermore it would involve squashing her creativity, a creativity which within the discourse of child-centred pedagogy is understood to be 'natural'. Additionally, Hannah is a working-class child whose language skills, while they might be perceived as different, cannot and indeed should not be perceived as deficient. But, as Walkerdine and Lucey (1989: 21) point out, perceiving Hannah's talk as 'different' 'frees us from one trap only to reensnare us in another, and that trap is to remove any idea of exploitation and oppression, to end up with a liberal pluralism of difference'.

Given this, Hannah is a 'normal' child who is being creative in her own particular way. My task is not to damn, suppress or prevent this. Rather, I must carefully and sensitively guide Hannah, and in this way all aspects of her growth will be both regulated and developed. With this reading, while Hannah's play might be understood as an attempt at boundary transgression, my play can be understood as a symptom or a demonstration of my own regulation. Joining in the game means that I can then exercise control over the child. Take, for example, the question: 'What else can we think of to rhyme with your name? I know, you can make Hannah and banana sound nearly the same'. This, I think, produces several effects. First, it gives the game an 'educational' veneer, and second it takes the 'heat' off *my* name.

Let me expand on the second point first. Prior to this question being asked, one of Hannah's addresses had been, 'Good morning Mrs Jonesy Bonesy', to which I replied, 'Good morning Mrs Hannah Panna'. This seems to perturb Hannah because she says, 'I'm not a pan. You cook in a pan'. My curiosity is over why I both called her a 'panna' and why I gave her the title of 'Mrs'. Was I trying to score a point off Hannah because she, in referring to me as 'Bonesy', had come a little too near for comfort? But, in order for me to 'legitimately' retaliate, Hannah and I had to be 'evenly matched', hence the 'Mrs'. If this is so, was I momentarily crossing a divide between Hannah and myself, but then was obliged to reconsider the move because it seemed to cause offence? Is this why I offer up both my skin and my bones as compensation for a sleight, but in doing so recognize that I have reached some kind of limit? In other words, it is time to turn the play into a pedagogical activity – that is, give the whole scenario an 'educational veneer'. In asking what turns out to be a rhetorical question – 'What else can we think of to rhyme with your name? I know you can make Hannah and banana sound nearly the same' – I contrive to situate all the children back into the familiar territory of the teacher/pupil couplet. Here, I can control the children in a number of ways.

First though, it is interesting to note the inclusive 'we'. This suggests that the task of finding rhyming names is one that can be equally shared between the teacher and the children. That is, together we can act in reasonable ways to find solutions to problems. But by supplying the answer myself I reduce the notion of the collective 'we' to a sham. Perhaps the prospect of Hannah or one of the other girls coming up with an 'improper' reply is too risky a business. Supplying answers to my own questions can, I suggest, be one of the oblique ways by which the children learn what constitutes a 'correct' or 'proper' response. Given this, it is not too surprising that Amanda, recognizing the practice, moves from passive spectator to participant. She can now join in because the 'play' is embedded firmly back into a known nursery discourse where, for example, names can be made to 'rhyme'. Amanda's request is: 'Do "it" with my name. Make my name say something'. This allows me opportunities to bring all the children into the secure boundary of the discourse. For example, I sing 'Amanda panda' and perhaps thereby press home to all the children (and Hannah in particular) that they are nursery-aged children who, when at school, are expected to behave in certain ways. It would seem that Hannah has read, understood and succumbed to the regulation for she turns from playing with names to making 'educational connections' between Amanda's name and the alphabet frieze that is displayed on the wall. Finally, Jessica allows me to consolidate the 'educational' worthiness of the play. She says both her name and other 'words' rhythmically. I pick up on this and suggest the idea of a train.

It is possible, I think, to bring different readings to this contribution of a 'train'. Previously, I had suggested two readings. I wrote:

> One reading could be that I'm building on from Jessica's contribution and that I am helping the children to extend and develop their ideas. What the children and I have established is a partnership which allows us to collaborate and pool ideas. However, there is an alternative reading. It could be that through introducing the idea of a train my intention was not to collaborate rather it was to direct and as a consequence assume more control. The 'train' effectively took the girls' attention away from rhyming words and put an end to the game. Furthermore, the 'train' added a physical dimension and as a consequence removed the focus from a verbal one.

To this I can add some further thoughts. Perhaps the journal extract might best be understood as a paradoxical tale where complexities are woven together in terms of what it means to be a teacher and a child. We are both caught up in a network of desires and needs which at times are in conflict. Hannah wants to talk to me in ways which the current teacher/child discourse does not allow for. I, on the other hand, work at subjugating her desire for pedagogical reasons and needs. In short, both teacher and pupil want to surmount barriers, but the question of how to do this remains. In other words, how can transgressions be effected?

Hannah: transgressive agent

Can teachers, by developing various strategies, teach children to transgress identities and categories? Allan (1997), for example, is enthusiastic about this suggestion and has evolved a number of strategies. These include teachers taking up the challenge of listening to pupils to ensure that their voices are not silenced by teachers' own 'professional discourses'. Allan's particular research focus is special education. Within this terrain, Allan perceives those professionals involved, including teachers, as being enmeshed within 'discourses of needs'. Allan then goes on to suggest that teachers 'need to be able to express what they understand to be the needs of the individuals, based on their experience and professional judgments'. However, rather than see these as 'contradictory demands of desires and needs', a more constructive move would be to acknowledge 'needs' and 'desires' as 'separate layers, from which solutions can be found'. Finally, Allan premises the success of these strategies on 'dialogue between teachers and pupils' (1997: 17).

Allan's research centred on secondary-aged pupils who, in a variety of ways, made efforts to transgress out of, or conversely, into 'disabled identities'. Within the secondary setting it is possible to envisage teachers and pupils developing dialogues and in such instances teachers can play a very real role in helping pupils to 'explore their sense of self expressed as desires rather than needs'. Allan's notion of dialogue, as it is presented, strikes me as being relatively conventional, where teacher and student are either talking in a one-to-one relationship or in a small group situation, a practice which within the context of the nursery would, from my experience, have very little success. However, that is not to say that 'dialogues' do not or cannot take place in the nursery; rather, they have to be envisaged a little differently.

For Davies, classroom practice is not only a collaborative venture between teachers and students in which they constitute themselves and each other as such (see Davies 1983), but additionally it is 'a complex weaving together of contradictory beliefs about the rights of the individual and the collective, about what it means to be gendered, about what it means to be a teacher or a student' (Davies 1996: 342).

All this begs certain questions. How, for example, can 'contradictory beliefs' be confronted and dealt with? Similarly, what if my desires or Hannah's desires go against the grain of those discourses which stipulate and define what desire 'is'? How can she or I, caught as we are within powerful discursive practices, resist or redefine them? Can discourses be modified? Are there choices of discourse available where subjectivity could be experienced in a number of ways? In other words, what positionings are currently available and what could be made available?

Davies (1996: 346) believes that the key to the dilemma of agency can be found in two ideas:

The first is a recognition of the fact that some discursive practices constitute some speakers as agents. In being constituted as such they have the opportunity (discursively produced but nonetheless real in its effects) to make choices. The second is a recognition of the constitutive nature of discursive practices, along with an attention to the conversational and textual analysis of those practices such that we might learn to recognise the personal and social implications of each discursive practice in which we are caught up – either as speakers or as hearers. This allows the possibility of refusal of any particular discourse or one's positioning within it, the possibility of choices between discourses, or the bringing to bear of one set of discursive practices on another to modify them and the positions being made available within them.

Having first mapped out a theoretical definition of agency and the dilemmas that are located within it, Davies then tries to address how notions of agency can be developed within the classroom. According to Davies (1996: 360), 'agency' requires the following resources.

Discursive resources

1 The discursive construction of the individual as existing not only as a member of one or more collectives, but somehow independently of those collectives.
2 A definition of the individual as one who actively makes sense of, rather then passively receives, the meanings available within discourses used by the groups of which they are a member (and thus as one who can refuse discourses, or positions within discourses, who can stand outside of any particular discursive/interactive practices, who can take these practices up as their own, or not, as they choose).
3 Access to recognized/recognizable discursive practices, in which a range of alternative ways of seeing and being are available, such that the positionings one currently finds oneself in are not experienced as inevitable.

Personal resources

1 Access to the means by which alternative positionings can be brought about. These include knowledge resources, personal skills and the ability to mobilize the relevant discourse (i.e. to use the discursive practices and to be recognized as legitimately doing so).
2 The desire to be agentic – that is, a sense of self as one who both can and should position themselves in that way, make the relevant choices, carry them through and accept the moral responsibility for doing so.

Social resources

1 Access to interactive others, along with the appropriate discourse and the appropriate context, who will take up as legitimate the positioning of oneself as agent. This is very similar to the ability to mobilize the relevant discourses, but shifts the focus from the discursive practices to the interactive others.

The 'relocation' of emancipatory interests and agency

Davies' ideas of 'agency' accommodate two important shifts. First, agency in Davies' terms is not dependent on a notion of self who is essentially determinate with an enduring rational nature. Nor is language considered as being stable or transparent. As such, Davies is rejecting the idea that relations of power can be rejected if individuals engage in ideal, transparent speech acts.

Having said that, however, I am still uncertain about some of her statements. For example, what is meant by the second point in the list given under 'Discursive resources', above? How does one go about 'actively making sense' so that particular discursive practices or subjective positionings might then be refused? Similarly, how do you develop and make available 'a range of alternative ways of seeing and being' (point 3, above).

One of the problems I have when reading Davies is getting rid of a particular way of defining terms including, for example, 'making sense'. I have to recollect that Davies' position regarding language and meaning is a poststructuralist one. Hence, 'making sense' does not refer to a notion of mastery where individuals can fully comprehend or know. Rather, it is more akin to Foucault's notion of permanently critiquing ourselves where the endeavour is not to seek 'to assimilate what is proper for one to know, but that which enables one to get free of oneself' (Foucault 1985: 8).

I have come to consider that Davies' conception of 'agency' has much in common with Foucault's notion of resistance. As a consequence, it is a conception which, for me, is characterized by the struggle to remain ever mindful of 'one's present status and condition so that one might see it more intensely, and to know one's circumstances deeply in order to recognise recurring games of truth' (Pignatelli 1993: 418).

Above I have made attempts to both outline and analyse an example of social exchange between myself and three girls. As a consequence of trying to unravel the piece my attention has been drawn to those mundane ways in which teacher and children are coerced. The piece, having been worked upon, goes some way to show how power circulates through commonplace and insignificant techniques. These include forms of address used within school between teacher and pupil. Such power works at producing and sustaining the 'obedient subject'.

Nevertheless, there are, I would suggest, possibilities for individuals to be agentic, where they can transgress boundaries and hence resist. However, this is not resistance which can be found embedded within the 'grand narrative' of human liberation which is premised on and fortified by belief in the coherent and autonomous individual. Nor is it to be found within communicative action where individuals, by engaging in ideal, transparent speech acts can seek to avoid relations of power (Pignatelli 1993: 416).

To an extent, both Davies and Allan go some way to mark out possibilities to envisage notions of agency which are outside of these narratives.

However, notions of agency can be extended further. More adjustments can be made which in addition to developing notions of agency also affect certain conceptions concerned with emancipatory education. The following proposals are drawn from Parker's work (1997). He envisages certain shifts, modifications and deviations to ideas of agency. In the following extract he sets out some of his thoughts regarding individual actions and how these might then work at relocating emancipatory education. He begins by establishing deconstruction, or deconstructive readings, as central to the task of reconceptualizing notions of emancipation: 'Teachers and student teachers will become deconstructive in their readings of educational texts, in their situating of received wisdom, in their creation of values, in their evaluation of courses and of the statements of bureaucratics and politicians' (1997: 142). He then goes on to mark out certain requirements:

> This will require, though in practice may need to proceed, the development of institutions in which teachers and students will be encouraged to become ironic in reconciling the foundationless status of their beliefs and commitments – and the commitments of others – with the desire to create, develop and defend them. Possession of this ironic attitude – this unstable, dynamic oscillation of the rhetorical forces of deconstruction and position, or reactivity and creativity – is the signature of the postmodern voice and a central characteristic of emancipation in postmodernity.
>
> (Parker 1997: 142)

While I feel that Parker may be in some danger of positing postmodernism as another 'grand narrative' there is nevertheless much in the above few lines which intrigues. The process of 'reconciling the foundationless status' of certain 'beliefs and commitments' with 'the desire to create, develop and defend them' finds resonance within this project. However, have I, or indeed have the children, got an ironic attitude? And if we have not, then what are the possibilities for developing it? By way of trying to answer this let me return once again to the exchange between myself and the three girls. In returning, I want to take with me this notion of an 'ironic attitude', as well as those ideas concerning 'dialogue' which Allan posited.

Wanted: a transgressive agent with an ironic attitude

Perhaps it should be made clear that the return to the extract is not undertaken with the expectation that I will find what I want. In other words, this next reading will not guarantee prescriptions or solutions. Nor will an 'exemplar of agency' emerge. However, what I am hopeful of is that another rereading might prompt more relevant questions. I will return to the subject of questions and questioning in due course.

Above I referred to Allan's notion of developing 'dialogues' between teacher and pupils. I also indicated that within the nursery the idea of dialogue would have to be extended beyond conventional dialogue scenarios. At this point I would like to offer another reading of the extract; one where it is perceived as a 'dialogue' between the teacher and the children and where additionally irony might already be at work.

First, however, let me consider what 'irony' means. It is defined as the humorous or mildly sarcastic use of words to imply the opposite of what they normally mean. An instance of irony would be where attention is drawn to some incongruity or irrationality. That is, incongruity between what is expected to be and what actually is.

Having made efforts to define 'irony' what can now be said about the extract? In calling me 'Dones' Hannah 'chose' to break with, but not completely away from, a convention. In a relatively minimal way she chose to interrupt the repetitive way in which young children and their teachers 'normally' greet one another. In so doing, she caused a certain amount of consternation within me. Thus, those discreet mechanisms which work at both stipulating and safeguarding my position within the room were momentarily dislodged. In other words, Hannah, in behaving in unexpected ways, disturbed the hierarchy of the teacher/pupil relationship. The embedded irony in all of this is that while I seek and have a desire to be free of coercive structures, including oppressive hierarchies, I can nevertheless be seen as mending or restructuring those that Hannah has tampered with.

Thus, although Hannah and I did not have a dialogue in the sense that is implied by Allan's work, nevertheless the exchange can be understood as an opportunity whereby Hannah was both testing and pushing at those boundaries which circumscribe pupil/teacher relations. Following Parker, the suggestion is that by playing ironically with those normal exchanges which occur between pupil and teacher Hannah was momentarily upsetting the power which is awarded to adults within such structures. A further suggestion is that the play was not intended to humiliate; rather, it can be understood as an invitation or an opening for both teacher and child to indulge in dramatic irony, where under our new guises of 'Dones' and 'Lanna' we could then behave in ways which currently fall outside of the prescribed discourse.

At the moment it would seem that teacher agency is being both construed and played out along therapeutic or even technicist lines, where despite (or maybe because of) well-meaning progressive agendas all the children are 'guided' or 'prompted' back into particular ways of behaving. In other words, they are coerced into being obedient subjects.

However, to end on an optimistic note, perhaps all the perambulations and meanderings which my thinking has undertaken in response to Hannah are a necessary element in developing agency, where becoming aware is 'a deep and broad reckoning of one's official discursive positions and professional status as nodes or loci of power maintained by the production of knowledge about oneself, one's peers, and one's students' (Pignattelli 1993: 421). For as Pignatelli (p. 421) goes on to point out:

> teachers exercise their agency caught within a typically modern, complex paradox of knowing subject and manipulated object. Ironically, if teachers test the limits of 'regimes of truth' – for example, by asking not, 'Is it true?' but rather, 'Who wants it to be true? What are the effects of saying this is true and not that?' – they erode the authoritative ground upon which they speak. Asking such questions forces teachers to recognise that they are not only critically engaged with, but are also constituted within, these regimes.

This chapter reflects an attempt to critically engage. The writings have, I believe, unsettled certain power configurations. Furthermore, they have worked at making the banal and the routine both remarkable and extraordinary. As such the writings have cleared some space for alternative ways of thinking and being. Perhaps there may even be an opening for the transgressive teacher with an ironic attitude.

Conclusion

Critical pedagogy in a postmodern world

These 'new times' are also reflective of the narratives we live by. They mirror the stories we tell ourselves, stories that shape both the ecstasy and terror of the world, disease our values, misplace our absolutes, and yet strangely give us hope, inspiration, and framework for insights. We can't escape narratives but I believe we can resist and transform them.

(McLaren 1995: 89)

Every power to exert symbolic violence, i.e. every power which manages to impose meanings and to impose them as legitimate by concealing the power relations which are the basis of its force, adds its own specifically symbolic force to those power relations.

(Bourdieu and Passeron 1977: 4)

It might be suggested that teacher competence or performance does not appear to be especially elastic in terms of its responsiveness to research findings. Research predicated on possible improvements in practice will probably continue to be disappointed with its general impact. When did we start thinking that research into education improved our teaching? What sorts of success can we claim since then? Teacher practice is probably governed to a much greater extent by social norms and the policies generated within these. As such it may be more appropriate for research to focus on how these norms constitute what we teach and how it is taught. While practitioners may always be able to develop their own practice as a teacher or teacher trainer the setting of policy on a broader scale entails rather different rules of engagement. We feel we need to step back to ask what function research serves and how it aims to guide our actions. Presently, practitioners have a tendency to expect the research task to tell them 'how it is' so that they can then plan new strategies for the creation of new outcomes. It is this very attempt at a singular dominant account that we wish to question.

In this book so far we have sought to examine ways in which practitioner-researchers can break into their habitual ways of seeing things with a view to considering alternative understandings of their practice.

While emancipatory quests can be seductive, a recognition that such quests ordinarily get redefined through the passage of time can assist us in building a reflective sense of how such quests are formulated and how alternative conceptions of professional practice might emerge. For example, in Chapter 3 we encountered a teacher whose early research work was built around an aspiration to be more child-centred, yet later on she was able to see this as just one discourse circulating in relation to her practice. Liz's project described in the later chapters can be seen as a more sustained examination of the discourses shaping practice. While we may hold onto guiding principles such as being a socialist, a feminist, a critical educator or whatever, we need to recognize that such concepts are evolutionary, as are the people they predicate; that these evolutions are a function of the narratives we provide about them; and that there is no such thing as a 'straight' narrative.

An ambivalent embrace . . .

Thus, is it a matter of choosing between emancipatory aspirations or postmodernism? Can the Enlightenment heritage be sustained or do we reject its assumptions and beliefs? If we pursue a more postmodernist approach we might ask what is the point of research if it merely creates rather than solves problems? Perhaps, however, this mode of argument need not be the only way of proceeding. Carr (1995), for example, argues that postmodernism should not be regarded as a threat to emancipatory education but as an indispensable aid to the future accomplishment of its goals. He accepts that postmodernism has seriously undermined our modern understanding of what role education fulfils in a democratic society. His move is to look back to the work of Dewey in order to reconstruct the relationship between education and democracy so as to effectively resist the challenge that postmodernism has posed. For as Dewey states: 'it is no longer possible to hold the simple faith of the Enlightenment that assured advance of science will produce free institutions by dispelling ignorance and superstition – the sources of human servitude and the pillars of oppressive government' (Carr 1995: 75).

Carr details how in very many ways Dewey encompasses a number of ideas and notions that can loosely be described as complementing postmodernism (Carr 1995: 87). He concludes (p. 89):

> Dewey's educational philosophy should now be read as an early twentieth century example of what educational philosophy must become in a late twentieth century democratic society: a society that is 'democratic' precisely because it has finally recognised that it is free to make and remake itself without resorting to universal truths drawn from some external authoritative source.

There is, however, a more radical response being made from an emerging body of 'cultural workers' (Lather 1991). Fox (2000), for example, suggests that research, including action research, can be undertaken in such a way as to accommodate certain features which have become associated with postmodernism. Such research, he argues, should be informed by three principles: first, the pursuit of knowledge must be recognized as being a local and contingent process; second, research activity must be constitutive of difference; third, theory-building should be adjunct to practical activity (p. 2). In Fox's view, action research has both the potential and the capacity to 'transgress, challenge or subvert existing conceptions'. His vision acknowledges the very many shortcomings which more traditional and mainstream action research displays. As Stronach and MacLure point out, such approaches fail to recognize:

> the necessary failure of methodology's hope for certainty, and its dream of finding an innocent language in which to represent, without expiating or distorting, the voices and ways of knowing its subaltern 'subjects . . . such work tries to practise what could be called a methodology, and a politics of disappointment – not (or not just) as a state of resignation about the impossibility of escape from the 'crisis of representation', but as a strategic act of interruption of the methodological will to certainty and clarity of vision.
>
> (Stronach and MacLure 1997: 4)

We may aspire to engaging in research targeted at improvement of our professional practices, and so much research is predicated on the assumption of research findings being the stuff of control technology. We have however suggested that this is unlikely to happen in a straightforward manner. There are too many conflicting conceptions of improvement. The disappointment that Stronach and MacLure identify can however be used to both confront and complicate the relations *between* those binary oppositions (see Stronach and MacLure 1997) which, under the guise of the language of social advancement, exploration, development and civilization, subjection and subordination were incorporated (Hall 1992). In other words, it may be possible to use this disappointment to trouble boundaries and to open fissures in our habitual certainties.

However, because our embrace with postmodernity is neither fulsome nor wholehearted it is perhaps better conceptualized as ambivalent and uncertain (MacLure 1994: 283). Like Lather (1991: 1) we are unsure of the politics of postmodern thought and practice. But maybe, as with 'disappointment', this 'uncertainty or 'ambivalence' can be put to work as a way of 'interrogating the limits and powers of postmodern discourse' (Hutcheon 1989: 8). Further, 'ambivalence' could serve as a useful antidote to complacency and hence oblige us to move 'back and forth among the various contestery discourses of neo-Marxism, feminisms, minoritarianisms and poststructuralisms in order to interrupt one another' (Lather 1991: 39).

As McRobbie points out there is and can be a politics of postmodernisms which 'does not eliminate the subject or the self but finds it in operation as a series of bit parts in the concrete field of social relations. Politics must therefore imply subjectivities in process, interacting and debating' (1993: 138). We have adopted what could be called a 'postmodernism of resistance' (Huyssen 1990: 270) where efforts have been made to move out of a dualistic logic. As such, the project has been an attempt at thinking otherwise, where habitual ways of being and doing are unsettled.

We will explore this just a little further in the context of our own personal base domains, namely nursery education for Liz and mathematics education for Tony. These may provide two different sorts of example of what this attitude might look like in teaching and research practices.

The nursery: a place to grow

The notion of the school as being a 'place to grow' has over time been understood in a variety of ways. Froebel, for example, conceptualized schools as gardens where young children could develop 'naturally'. His romantic vision stemmed from the belief that because young children were 'natural' it followed that they were inherently 'good': 'The idea is that "evil" happens to the child from the outside, in the form of unhealthy environments, poverty, bad upbringing, and so on. Evil is therefore not natural; it is a deviation from the natural state. If man is inherently anything, then he is inherently good' (Hultqvist 1998: 91).

As such, schools in general but nurseries in particular were envisaged and structured as places for laying down foundations for the ultimate victory of 'good':

> The preschool should be a blossoming garden for children. The child is compared to a plant, which with the proper care will grow into the beautiful flower it was meant to be. The metaphor structures the educator's job of being gardener in God's nature. The educator nourishes the plant and pulls out all the weeds that threaten to invade the garden . . . The Froebel child is set into a moral order in which the goal of human development is perfection, in fact, to reach God under earthly conditions.
>
> (Hultqvist 1998: 101–5)

With the advancement of developmental psychology the 'natural' child became ceded to and embedded in the constitution and construction of the 'normal' child. Schools, in all manner of ways, became (and continue to be) places where the battle for what is 'good' and 'right' for the child is waged in terms of 'normalization' (Walkerdine 1990). In varying degrees, evidence of these two constructs can be located within the nursery. Inevitably, being situated within any discourse has certain repercussions. Using an extract from Liz's teaching journal our aim is to foreground what the limitations are when children and teachers are constrained within a discourse of normalization.

The 'normalization' of Andrew: journal extract 6.3.95

> practices that systematically form the objects of which they speak . . . constitute them and in the practice of doing so conceal their own invention.
>
> (Foucault 1977a: 49)

The following journal extract centres on a boy called Andrew, who at the time of writing was aged 4. As a consequence, this was his final term in the nursery class.

> Andrew struggles to choose his name card. I smile, encourage and congratulate him when he chooses the right one. I show Andrew how to hold the pencil. Later, my hand covers his and I guide him through the process of writing the letter 'A'. We practise many times and I add a running commentary of directions: 'Down, up, down again and now across'. It becomes something of a chant as it is repeated with each attempt at writing the letter. We momentarily abandon pencil and paper in favour of tracing the letter in the air. Again, I direct him. First I set his arm and hand in motion and then I release him to continue on his own. He makes one successful manoeuvre, then he peters out. We return to writing on paper and Andrew has a stab at writing an 'A' on his own. Two random lines appear that as yet do not resemble 'A'. We trace the letter in the air, on the tabletop and finally I 'finger write' the letter on his back. I ask: 'Can you feel it Andrew?' Andrew nods and smiles. He repeats the game on my back. I feel lines and I make encouraging sounds but his fingers have failed to make an 'A'. I make the decision to abandon writing the letter. Instead, we concentrate on making a simple zig-zag writing pattern.

It is probably fair to say that the above extract was prompted because certain assumptions that Liz held regarding Andrew had been destabilized. She had presumed that giving Andrew the task of copy-writing his name would have been relatively straightforward. However, as the extract indicates, Andrew found the activity a struggle. An immediate question that arises from the scenario is: how did Liz arrive at these misconceptions concerning Andrew's capabilities? In other words, why did she set an activity which the child was not ready for?

The notion of 'readiness' is very significant within the nursery and, because it is so important, it is not left to chance. Various practices and procedures are staged which ensure that the children are, first, developing and second that this development is along the 'right' lines. So during the course of the year, Andrew's progress will have been monitored, recorded and evaluated. As an example, Andrew's progress and facility in using language will have been regularly assessed to ensure that this was commensurate with the norm. Similarly, examples of drawings will have been kept as another means of illustrating his developing competence and as a somewhat crude guide to his inherent abilities. So while Andrew's early representations of figures were random scribblings his more recent drawings of people included facial features and body parts. As such, there was 'clear evidence' that Andrew's general development was normal and as a consequence he was ready for the task of writing his name.

Preparing or 'getting the children ready' for mainstream education is a concern throughout the child's time in nursery. Understandably, it becomes more of a consideration during the final term. Effectively, by copy-writing his name, Andrew would have demonstrated that he was ready for the transition from being a 'preschool' child to a 'schoolchild'. Thus, being able to 'do' paper and pencil tasks is evidence of Andrew's evolution where essentially completion of the task would have indicated a movement up in the hierarchy of knowledge and skills. By copy-writing, Andrew would have signified that he had moved on from 'play'. Moreover, his proficiency would have been a manifestation of Liz's competence in helping him make the move between the two locations of nursery and Reception class. In a sense, by writing, Andrew would be fulfilling some of Liz's needs. Perhaps this goes some way to explaining why the pronoun 'we' is used so regularly in the journal extract and it appears that the struggle to write the name is a shared one.

In some ways, Andrew's inability to write his name means that both Andrew and Liz are robbed of an opportunity to celebrate Liz's teaching and Andrew's learning. It would seem that despite the constant regulation, monitoring and evaluating of Andrew he has, on this occasion, 'failed' to conform. So, rather than a sense of victory we have, if not complete failure, then at least a sense of deficit. Clearly, Liz might feel that somewhere along the 'line' of Andrew's learning she has been remiss and, consequently, he is not equipped to meet the challenge imposed by the regulation of the 'norm'. Such a situation raises certain questions. For example, in what ways could Liz strengthen the foundations of Andrew's learning so that he might grow in all areas of his learning including that of writing? In effect, how may Liz become a better and more effective teacher?

But is there a problem? After all, problems emerge when there is discord between a particular theory and practice. As Parker notes: 'It is only because of the adoption of a particular theory that one is able to describe some aspect of the manifold relations obtaining between the elements of the unique context as anomalous or problematic. The problem gets its significance *qua problem* only by virtue of the role which a prior theory has prepared for it' (1997: 40–1). Parker continues: 'Problem-setting, then, is the construction of a perspective on a situation the description of which precipitates anomalies. Problems, in turn, are parasitic for their existence on the chosen descriptions; they are, we might say, theory relative; and the adoption of a different theory – a different paradigm – will have the result of some problems being dissolved while others are created'.

Andrew's story could be understood as a representation of a modernist model for knowledge. As such, individuals are conceptualized as rational unitary beings who can, as a consequence of following a particular route, then have knowledge and understanding. Like trees, the nursery children grow along and develop within a limited number of paths (Deleuze and Guattari 1983). However, perhaps it is time to make a break with ways of thinking that are inflexible, habitual and, as a consequence, mechanistic. What might then emerge are more creative routes where teaching could be imaginative rather than being reduced to a matter of 'chanting' directions at a child.

From a practitioner research perspective, Liz is using these observations as a way of critiquing her practice and some of the habitual patterns inherent within it. But this scrutiny also includes an examination of the learning theories that Liz presupposes within her practice and how these theories shape the stories Liz offers in respect of her practice. In so doing Liz opens the possibility of questioning how she conceptualizes her own professional development seen in terms of helping Andrew progressing more 'efficiently' down a 'pre-specified route'.

Researching mathematics education

Tony recalls an episode from his own PhD research diary (Brown 1987) and questions his original claim to it being research data. At the time he was undertaking a large number of observations in school lessons in Dominica. His particular declared research interest was how children interacted with each other in the context of mathematical activities. He was carrying out this research in classes being taught by teachers who were assigned to him within a college training programme.

He describes Clifford, a 6-year-old, whom he had observed on a number of occasions alongside some of his classmates. Tony's reading of a particular situation was that Clifford was imitating the superficial actions of his friends:

He held his pen in a purposeful manner, he moved the counting sticks in front him, periodically he looked intently at the blackboard, he said non-committal things such as 'that there' when he pointed. To the teacher he seemed largely invisible in that his overt actions broadly aligned him with the norm activity, taking place around the room.

But to Tony's motivated eyes Clifford's actions made no sense. Tony believed that he himself had some insight into the teacher's objectives yet he could not see how the child's actions connected with these.

In so far as this was a significant observation that connected with many of Tony's other observations we now wonder what sorts of research attitude could be built around observations of this nature. Where are Tony's eyes coming from? What is built into his assumptions? What alternative research perspectives might he assume? What alternative conceptions of mathematics underpin these? In which research agendas would this observation be noticed as being of significance?

To some extent we imagine that as a researcher Tony was motivated by a belief that research might lead to the improvement of practice. That is, his observations were motivated, and his subsequent research statements were shaped by, how he imagined they might fit within some over-arching strategy for developing practice. At the time Tony's motivations were related to the children's teachers within the college programme, and in turn how these teachers might develop their teaching in response to appropriate instruction from him. But how are such notions of improvement developed and understood and how do they serve as motivations for teacher and researcher practices?

In the particular situation described, Tony could assume a number of social roles in delineating his research perspective on the classroom situations he observed. He also had a number of strategies relating to these available to him to convert a research observation into a spur for professional action. Any research perspective can be seen as being shaped by the purpose it is seen to be connected to. Tony identified four such perspectives:

- *Teacherly:* Tony could talk to the particular child and assist them in connecting either with his own sense-making or the specific ideas Tony thought the teacher had in mind.
- *Advisory:* Tony could talk to the teacher and advise them on how they might teach the child.
- *Policy:* Tony could advise a change of curriculum to adjust the sort of task being set. (Bizarrely, as a 25-year-old expatriate volunteer Tony was given the dubious privilege of rewriting the Primary National Curriculum for Mathematics. Although the curriculum was published and implemented, in such evolving development contexts this sort of initiative had a shelf life of some two years!)

- *Sociological:* as a PhD student Tony could assume a disinterested 'interesting' overview and talk about how things 'are'. In this perspective Tony could assume the privilege of being fairly vague about policy implications at any level. Or by putting himself in the shoes of a social commentator, he could analyse policy impact from various perspectives.

However, cutting across any of these perspectives is the nature of the political motivation underpinning the research enterprise, whether this be an instrumental implementation of policy, or an emancipatory attitude in which the purpose of research is to liberate children from an oppressive regime, or a more fatalistic attitude in which the relationship between policies and their implementation is weaker. The attempt to describe mathematics in a curriculum, for example, inevitably results in a caricature of traditional understandings of mathematics as a discipline. However, this caricature can be viewed in various ways, as suggested earlier, as a serious but imperfect attempt to describe mathematics to guide school instruction, *or* as a cynical ploy to make teachers and children more accountable according to a particular institutionalized account of mathematics, *or* as a reconfiguration of the discipline itself to meet contemporary needs.

Analysis of teaching situations in mathematics, for example, cannot be restricted to discussions of the failures of classrooms to meet supposed ideal versions of mathematics through supposed ideal versions of teaching, since many of the demands placed on school mathematics are regulated within a more restrictive domain (e.g. of getting sums right). For example, Herscovics and Linchevski (1994: 59) speak in terms of 'dismal results' generally in our mathematics teaching (and how we need to improve), as though there were some universal against which to measure. But what other sorts of presupposition underlie claims of this sort? Very often demands for improved standards result in a retreat into accountability and the styles of mathematics more readily accounted for. For example, within the UK we have to reconcile being classified as being a country of below average mathematical achievement in international comparisons while simultaneously being among the best at problem solving and one of the most successful in the world economically. Such comparisons only serve to confirm the impossibility of creating a neutral test or vantage point. How far can we subscribe to an idealized version of what mathematics is? Is there a 'correct' view of mathematics? If there is, it may still also be true that this is only a subordinate part of the experience of most people present in the classroom and that many tests only locate involvement in this in a fairly oblique way (see Cooper and Dunne 1999). It seems unhelpful to regard this inevitable state of affairs as a failure, since these cultural pressures are an essential element in the constitution of mathematics as understood in the world lived in by most ordinary people. It is impossible to specify what mathematics is as a discipline outside of the governing social parameters and the specific understandings of what these parameters are.

Elsewhere Tony, with some colleagues, has addressed these issues explicitly in the context of mathematics education research:

> teaching devices (e.g. geometric or balance models as aids in under-
> standing linear equations), which derive from alternative accounts
> of teaching and learning, can be understood as contributing to the
> necessary and inevitable temporal dimension of the constitution of
> the ideas we seek to address in our teaching. That is, they can be
> seen as emplotments that highlight or analogise particular features
> and then organise and sequence them . . . So for a child seeking to
> negotiate a perceived boundary one might understand the need for
> a plot that sees them across, connecting old emplotments, which
> have lost some of their old meanings, with new emplotments residing
> in the extended domain. It is this sort of process through which the
> metaphorical sense of any mathematical form is challenged to open
> up new ways of seeing. Mathematics is mediated and articulated
> through such teaching devices. These devices however should not
> be seen merely as a means to an end, since such embedding is
> crucial to the constitution of the ideas being studied within 'school
> mathematics'. Such constructions of mathematics however also result
> in associated constructions of the students working through math-
> ematics construed in this way. That is, the student is seen as 'high'
> or 'low' ability, at a particular 'developmental stage', 'ready' for a
> particular style of teaching, 'mathematically intuitive', an 'interpreter'
> or a 'doer', etc. These terms predicate particular learning theories
> or evaluation strategies, and the particular characteristics they
> value. Nevertheless, proficiency with concretisations is integral to
> the broader proficiency of moving between concrete and abstract
> domains, a proficiency which lies at the heart of mathematical
> endeavours (at least in schools). Indeed, one might suggest that for
> many students and many teachers proficiency in specific concret-
> isations forms the backbone and principal motivation of activity
> pursued within the classroom.
>
> (Brown *et al.* 1999b: 67–8)

Whose interests might we be serving, and how, in asserting particular understandings of mathematics? Mathematics teachers are all more or less concerned with the child's need to participate in a key social skill – i.e. mathematics. For many it is also important to share with children the intrinsic pleasures of mathematics as a discipline in its own right. The teacher's professional purpose is often specified in terms of such objectives. Similarly, researcher's often construct their own social purpose in terms of highlighting possible improvements towards these objectives, whether this be liberation through a 'campaign for real maths' or through a 'back to basics' campaign. But despite mathematics education objectives being seen in terms of improvement over many years, in which ways are we able to quantify actual improvement? In physics we can measure some sort of advance – they can send people to the moon, something they couldn't do in 1900. But mathematics education is predicated on supporting ever-changing forms of life. Are the intellectual challenges faced by an individual now more complex than their counterpart in an earlier era? In what sense is today's 18-year-old grappling with more sophisticated material than their 1960s counterpart? Hegel was not less sophisticated than Derrida in the context of his specific historical lot. There is no absolute improvement, just a recharging of life. What then is the research enterprise in mathematics education? To get there to . . . , to emancipate, to improve, to preserve? But it never seems to work, yet we maintain our conviction with projects motivated by some sort of ideal.

Apparently, deficit models predicated on terms such as 'dismal results' and 'failure' seem to have strong appeal. We declare such starting points and we feel obliged to say what we are going to bring about – to support personal need maybe – even though we know (as history has shown us) that we never get there. Looking back over what we have done, how would we evaluate the results? What is our history? What are its features? How do we 'story' the past? In a postmodernist age, how do we define research projects in education? What task does action research face in stimulating educational change?

Narrating into the future

Are we offering a model for learning? What are the alternatives to linear models of learning? What are our other metaphorical choices besides the modernist tree of knowledge? Patti Lather (1993), while still drawing on nature, favours the rhizome. Rhizomes defy the regularity of linear growth. They do not have a central or main trunk. Nor do they emerge from a single root. Instead, with their underground stems and aerial roots, they upset all preconceptions which are brought to notions of growth (Lather 1993: 680). Therefore, to behave or 'function rhizomatically' (Lather 1993: 680) involves having a disregard for prescribed order and patterned ways of being. In place of 'the smooth unfolding of an orderly growth' (Lecercle 1990: 132–3) there is an appreciation of haphazard and random growth. Rather than travelling in one direction, the rhizome seeks multiple openings:

Rather than a linear progress, rhizomatics is a journey among intersections, nodes, and regionalizations through a multi-centred complexity. As a metaphor, rhizomes work against the constraints of
authority, regularity and common sense, and open thought up to
creative constructions. They are 'on the ground', immanent, with
appeal not to transcendental values but to 'their content of possibilities, liberty or creativity'. The 'new', however, is not so much about
the fashionable as it is the creativity that arises out of social practices, creativity which marks down the ability to transform, to break
down present practices in favour of future ones.

> (Lather 1993: 680, quoting and drawing
> upon Deleuze 1992: 163–4)

As such, the supposed failure to copy-write a name or to perform
some mathematical algorithm cannot be understood against some fixed
and generalized notion of the young child and their learning. Rather, it
is a 'complexity of problematics' (Lather 1993: 680) which, having been
uprooted, can be seen to be 'connected to a mass of tangled ideas'
(Pefanis 1991: 22).

To 'function rhizomatically' as a teacher is both a scary and yet an
invigorating notion. To develop in this way might be seen as the product
of engaging reflexively with practice where practices of deconstruction
are enacted on stories concerned with teaching. The scariness comes as
a consequence of trying to let go of a comforting story which held that
the self was essentially rational, and moreover that language was able
to transparently represent reality. On the other hand, to act without
recourse to general and overarching theories is an exhilarating thought
for it means, among other things, that there is no longer the need to ask
general questions. For example, the question of the possibility of emancipation in situations of inequality requires that there is some general
theory of equality to which an appeal can be made. As Parker (1997:
143) notes:

> this is precisely what cannot be written, any more than can a gen-
> eral theory of inequality. What can be written – what any putative
> general theory would actually be – are particular stories about this
> or that situation in which judgments about inequality and equality
> are made, questioned, discussed, supported, opposed, through the
> interplay of a common, local cultural and rhetorical currency.

Parker continues:

> That there will be descriptions of the situation in which there are
> inequalities (of power, wealth, status, beauty etc.) is as unsurprising
> as that there will be descriptions that document characters, roles
> and events that are non-identical. Just as the relationships between

characters can only be understood by engagement with the narrative of which they are characters – the story among possible stories, in which their lives are emplotted – relations of inequality can be understood only through engagement with the vocabulary within which the relevant distinctions are drawn, and *that vocabulary* is itself meaningful only within the local narrative textile.

We are keen to avoid the suggestion that in nudging towards a postmodernism we are privileging text over people, narrative over life (see McLaren 1995: 64). Our emphasis on reflective writing is with it being a research instrument through which teachers hold up a self-portrait against which they check out how they feel. Throughout this book we have seen reflective writing as an instrument through which successive and alternative conceptions of practice are marked and preserved for scrutiny. The examination of the practice of such writing becomes an aspect of the research enquiry in so far as we need to build a sense of how this writing acts as a filter through which professional work is critically examined. That is, part of the research task is to understand how practice gets to be encapsulated in pieces of writing and how such framing in writing becomes instrumental in shaping subsequent practice. The focus on writing has sought to emphasize how practitioner-researchers present themselves through this medium in reporting on or devising professional strategies. We are not seeking to locate the researcher's 'true' self. As some of the teachers in Chapter 5 put it, in spelling out their practice in particular ways they are making a 'demand' that you accept what they are saying even though they may be aiming somewhere else. And it may be part of their research enquiry to understand how and why they are doing this. In producing reflective writing they create a reality in writing which resonates with their actual practice in some way, but photographic style representation in this writing may not be the most generative approach in challenging the habits of practice. In Chapter 4 we spoke of how Ricoeur sees linguistic experimentation as producing stresses and strains in our normal meaning of words, resulting in a novel effect in encapsulating our actions. Reflective writing can, we hope, provide a way of seeing practice in a fresh way which in turn can lead to different ways of acting. As McLaren (1995: 92) puts it:

> Narratives help us to represent the world. They also help us to remember and forget both its pleasures and its horror. Narratives structure our dreams, our myths and our visions as much as they are dreamt, mythified and envisioned. They help us share our social reality as much by what they exclude as what they include. They provide the discursive vehicles for transforming the burden of knowing to the act of telling. Translating experience into a story is perhaps the most fundamental act of human understanding.

In many respects the process described within the practitioner writing we have outlined is to inspect the narratives we inhabit, discern the influences on them and experiment with alternative formulations through both delineating them and living them, each time holding the attempt up against the way it was expressed in its conceptualization and in its evaluative reflection. This might be seen as inspecting the discourses that interpellate me and how they make me what I am. In a journal entry dated May 2000, Janice England provides a final example as someone reflecting on her practice, and her research conducted in relation to this, after some four years of engaging with this sort of process. She seeks to unfold the multiple layers to the successive stories she has told:

> Looking back at this writing now, I wish to challenge my own account. What construct am I now offering? I have presented one version of what's going on in this narrative. It is dependent on a certain representation of myself which isn't tenable any more. To what extent can I be as honest as I set out to be about myself when inevitably the vision I have is partial? Why have I told this story in the way I did? How is it distorted? I have a personal need to tell this story in a way that makes me feel good about myself. The construction I offer of my personal identity is apparently very revealing. I present myself initially as a powerful figure. I admit to a feeling of pride in a disarmingly honest way. I then humble myself and admit to my vulnerability also. I feel self-congratulatory with my frankness and warm about my humanity. I need you to know about my strength, but look, I am strong enough to show my weaknesses too. You can't help but respect my honesty, admire my strength and love my inner child can you? And even as I come clean now, what veil am I drawing over your eyes? I admit to my feeling of academic inadequacy, hoping that you will read this account and then deny this even more vehemently because I have declared it myself first. Is it a kind of arrogance perhaps that has the cheek to say 'I know nothing . . . and yet . . .'?

> (England, personal communication)

The product of practitioner research does not result in statements of practical implications common to all. Rather, it gives an account of an individual practitioner examining specific issues within their practice and how these were addressed as problems within the research process. The practitioner, with their perspective and their way of working, is an essential part of the situation being described. In our account, the self, and the situation the self is in, are non-dualistic but, rather, are mutually formative, as part of each other. Further, the self/situation has an essential time dimension understood by the individual through engagement in their situation. To understand the situation involves an appreciation of how the self/situation and the decisions faced evolve, and how this evolution might be seen in different ways. An account of this cannot be given except by an individual addressing specific professional concerns at particular times. As researchers the mirror image we create of ourselves is built through successive interpretations of engagements in the world. But these interpretations are in turn a function of the language we share in the broader community, and of our access to 'the hidden pathology, of collective behaviour and entire social systems' (Habermas 1976: 349). For other practitioners reading the research report the loss of supposed 'objectivity' is replaced by an account of what might be seen and how to see it – a traveller's guide rather than a map or an encyclopaedia entry. It remains for the reader to assert their right to tell stories about how the research report connects with their own practice. Theories meanwhile:

> are not just about seeing the world in different ways, some truer than others, but about *living in particular ways . . . all theories presuppose a narrative intentionality* as well as an empirical social outcome. That is, all theories have a story to tell about social life and an attitude towards it: theories reflect the theorist's situatedness in a particular way of life.
>
> (McLaren 1995: 93)

But how do we understand the person setting out to achieve this research attitude? And how do they understand themselves? A unified subject is implied; a thinking subject who therefore is (Descartes' *'cogito ergo sum'*). This is an idea treated with a certain disdain by poststructuralist writers, in so far as it supposes any 'completed and finished identity, knowing always where it is going' (Coward and Ellis 1977: 108–9). Derrida, for example, would, we imagine, reject the binary opposition between individual and social perspectives. Lacan (1977: 1–7), meanwhile, stresses the importance of Descartes' notion, but places much more emphasis on the formation of the thinking subject in the reflexivity of the thinking done. Nevertheless, the thinking subject may not be aware of this theoretical perspective on their actions and so assumes they have more control over their own destiny than may be supposed in poststructuralist readings (see Brown 1997).

Philosophy and self-narrative are not the same thing (Steedman 2001). It is, however, this sort of intention that is held in the narrative product of practitioner-oriented research. This points to a close relationship between a person's identity and the things they say and write. Indeed is this not the function of psychoanalytic sessions; an assertion of self against which ones lives? It is this person built through narrative product rather than any essential static (even just for now) self that props up more emancipatory inclinations. Not so much 'I think therefore I am' but rather 'I speak therefore I am what I assert I am'. But what we speak

is polluted with all sorts of culturally derived assumptions that comprom-
ise any claim to individuality. And it is through such assertions that
we present ourselves and the place we see ourselves occupying within
our community. This place however both constrains and enables our
conceptions of the job of work we face.

Here there is no sense of an endpoint having been reached. More new
opportunities are opened up for inspecting how the present and future
might be understood in relation to alternative constructions of the past,
as derived from past narrative constructions. There is no quest for the
essential self. There is no Freudian/Habermasian search for the un-
oppressed society, free of the hidden exercise of force, after which language becomes clear. But rather an endless succession of accounts against
which realities are held for learning about the self in practice and how
that self might be encouraged to make future choices. As Ricoeur (1981:
246) puts it: 'we carry on with patience the endless work of distancing
and renewing our historical substance'.

'Finally', we take heart from Derrida when he declares, 'never to give
up on the Enlightenment'. But, as he cautions, this requires: 're-reading
and re-interpreting . . . to raise new questions . . . disturb stereotypes and
good consciences, and to complicate or rework, for a changed situation'
(Derrida 1994: 34).

Bibliography

Adler, S.A. (1993) Teacher education: research as reflective practice, *Teaching and Teacher Education*, 9: 159–67.

Alcoff, L. (1988) Cultural feminism versus post-structuralism: the identity crisis in feminist theory, *Signs: Journal of Women in Culture and Society*, 13(31): 405–37.

Allan, J. (1997) Actively seeking inclusion: pupils with special educational needs and their 'practices of self'. Paper presented to the *British Educational Research Association Conference*, York, September.

Aronowitz, S. and Giroux, H. (1986) *Education Under Siege*. London: Routledge.

Askew, M., Brown, M., Rhodes, V., Wiliam, D. and Johnson, D. (1997) The contribution of professional development to effectiveness in the teaching of numeracy, *Teacher Development*, 1(3): 335–55.

Bakhtin, M. ([1931] 1981) Discourse in the novel, in M. Holquist (ed.) *The Dialogical Imagination*. Austin, TX: University of Texas Press.

Barry, P. (1995) *Beginning Theory*. Manchester: Manchester University Press.

Barthes, R. (1972) *Mythologies*. London: Paladin.

Baudrillard, J. (1995) *The Gulf War Did Not Take Place*. Sydney: Power Publications.

Beattie, M. (1995) New prospects for teacher education: narrative ways of knowing teaching and teacher learning, *Educational Researcher*, 37(1): 53–70.

Benhabib, S. (1992) Feminism and the question of postmodernism, in *The Polity Reader in Gender Studies*. Cambridge: Polity Press.

Berne, E. (1964) *Games People Play: The Psychology of Human Relationships*. Harmondsworth: Penguin.

Bettleheim, B. (1976) *The Uses of Enchantment: The Meaning and Importance of Fairy Tales*. London: Thames & Hudson.

Bhabha, H. (1990) DissemiNation: time, narrative and the margins of the modern nation, in H. Bhabha (ed.) *Nation and Narration*. London: Routledge.

Boaler, J. (1997) *Experiencing School Mathematics: Teaching Style, Sex and Setting*. Buckingham: Open University Press.

Bottery, M. and Wright, N. (1996) Cooperating in their own deprofessionalisation? On the need to recognise the 'public' and 'ecological' roles of the teaching profession, *British Journal of Education Studies*, 44(1): 82–98.

Bourdieu, P. and Passeron, J. (1977) *Reproduction in Education, Society and Culture.* London: Sage.

Bourdieu, P. and Wacquant, L. (2001) NewLiberalSpeak: notes on the new planetary vulgate, *Radical Philosophy*, 105: 2–5.

Bowles, S. and Gintis, H. (1976) *Schooling in Capitalist America.* London: Routledge.

Boyne, R. (1990) *Foucault and Derrida: The Other Side of Reason.* London: Routledge.

Brannigan, J., Robbins, R. and Wolfreys, J. (1996) *Applying: To Derrida.* Basingstoke: Macmillan.

Brown, T. (1987) *Language Interaction Patterns in Lessons Featuring Mathematical Investigations.* PhD thesis, University of Southampton.

Brown, T. (1994a) Creating evidence of classroom activity, *Research in Education*, 51: 33–40.

Brown, T. (1994b) Constructing the assertive teacher, *Research in Education*, 52: 13–22.

Brown, T. (1996) Creating data in practitioner research, *Teaching and Teacher Education*, 12(3): 261–70. Copyright 1996, Elsevier Science Ltd. Selected extracts reprinted with kind permission from Elsevier Science Ltd, The Boulevard, Langford Lane, Kidlington, OX5 1GB, UK.

Brown, T. (1997) *Mathematics Education and Language: Interpreting Hermeneutics and Poststructuralism.* Dordrecht: Kluwer.

Brown, T. and Roberts, L. (2000) Memories are made of this: temporality and practitioner research, *British Educational Research Journal*, 26(5): 649–59.

Brown, T., McNamara, O., Jones, L. and Hanley, U. (1999a) Primary student teachers' understanding of mathematics and its teaching, *British Educational Research Journal*, 25(3): 299–322.

Brown, T., Eade, F. and Wilson, D. (1999b) Semantic innovation: arithmetic and algebraic metaphors in narratives of learning, *Educational Studies in Mathematics*, 40: 53–70.

Bryce-Clegg, A. (2000) *Becoming a Head Teacher.* MA in Teaching dissertation, Manchester Metropolitan University.

Buchmann, M. (1987) Teacher knowledge: the lights that teachers live by, *Oxford Review of Education*, 13: 151–64.

Butler, J. (1990) Gender trouble, feminist theory, and psychoanalytic discourse, in L. Nicholson (ed.) *Feminism/Postmodernism.* London: Routledge.

Butler, J. (1993) *Bodies That Matter.* New York: Routledge.

Carr, W. (1995) Education and democracy: confronting the postmodernist challenge, *Journal of Philosophy of Education*, 29(1): 75–91.

Carr, W. and Kemmis, S. (1986) *Becoming Critical: Education, Knowledge and Action Research.* London: Falmer Press.

Cavarero, A. (2000) *Relating Narratives: Storytelling and Selfhood.* London: Routledge.

Cixous, H. (1975) *La Jeunne Nee.* Paris: Inedit.

Collingwood, R. (1994) *The Idea of History.* Oxford: Oxford University Press.

Connelly, F. and Clandinin, J. (1988) *Teachers as Curriculum Planners: Narratives of Experience.* New York: Teachers College Press.

Cooper, B. and Dunne, M. (1999) *Assessing Children's Mathematical Ability.* Buckingham: Open University Press.

Coward, R. and Ellis, J. (1977) *Language and Materialism.* London: Routledge.

Cryns, T. and Johnston, M. (1993) A collaborative case study of teacher change: from a personal to a professional perspective, *Teaching and Teacher Education*, 9: 147–58.

Dalla Costa, M. and James, S. (1975) *The Power of Women and the Subordination of the Community*. Bristol: Falling Wall Press.

Daly, M. (1978) *Gyn/Ecology: The Metaethics of Radical Feminism*. Boston, MA: Beacon Press.

Davies, B. (1983) The role pupils play in the social construction of classroom order, *British Journal of Sociology of Education*, 4(1): 55–69.

Davies, B. (1989) *Frogs and Snails and Feminist Tales*. Sydney: George Allen & Unwin.

Davies, B. (1996) Agency as a form of discursive practice: a classroom scene observed, *British Journal of Sociology of Education*, 17(1): 341–61.

Dearden, R. (1968) *The Philosophy of Primary Education*. London: Routledge.

Deleuze, G. (1992) What is Dispositif? in *Michel Foucault: Philosopher*, trans. T. Armstrong, pp. 159–68. New York: Routledge.

Deleuze, G. and Guattari, F. (1983) *On The Line*, trans. J. Johnstone. New York: Semiotext(e).

Derrida, J. (1976) *Of Grammatology*, trans. G. Spivak. Baltimore, MD: Johns Hopkins University Press.

Derrida, J. (1978) *Writing and Difference*. Chicago: The University of Chicago Press.

Derrida, J. (1981) Positions: interview with J.L. Houdebine and G. Scarpetta, trans. A. Bass, in J. Derrida, *Positions*. Chicago: University of Chicago Press.

Derrida, J. (1987) *The Truth in Painting*, trans. G. Bennington and I. McLeod. Chicago: University of Chicago Press.

Derrida, J. (1992) Differance, in A. Easthope and K. McGowan (eds) *A Cultural and Critical Theory Reader*. Buckingham: Open University Press.

Derrida, J. (1994) Deconstruction of actuality: an interview with Jacques Derrida, *Radical Philosophy*, 68: 28–41.

Dewey, J. (1933) *How We Think: a Restatement of Reflective Thinking to the Education Process*. Chicago: Henry Regenery.

DfEE (Department for Education and Employment) (1998) *High Status, High Standards*, Circular 10/98. London: DfEE.

DfEE (Department for Education and Employment) (1999) *Social Inclusion: Pupil Support*, Circular 10/99. London: DfEE.

Dockar-Drysdale, B. (1991) *The Provision of Primary Experience*. London: Free Association Press.

Dolar, M. (1992) A father who is not quite dead, in S. Zizek (ed.) *Everything You Wanted to Know About Lacan but were Afraid to Ask Hitchcock*. London: Verso.

Dooley, L. (1994) *Autonomy and Independence*. MA dissertation, Manchester Metropolitan University.

Dunn, T. (1997) *Michel Foucault and the Politics of Freedom*. Thousand Oaks, CA: Sage.

Eagleton, T. (1983) *Literary Theory: An Introduction*. London: Blackwell.

Easthope, A. (ed.) (1992) *A Critical and Cultural Studies Reader*. Buckingham: Open University Press.

Ebert, T. (1988) The romance of patriarchy: ideology, subjectivity and postmodern feminist cultural theory, *Cultural Critique*, 10: 19–53.

Eger, M. (1992) Hermeneutics and science education: an introduction, *Science and Education*, 1: 337–48.

Elliott, J. (1987) Educational theory, practical philosophy and action research, *British Journal of Educational Studies*, 2: 149–69.

Elliott, J. (1991) *Action Research for Educational Change*. Buckingham: Open University Press.

Elliott, J. (ed.) (1993a) *Reconstructing Teacher Education*. London: Falmer Press.

Elliott, J. (1993b) The relationship between 'understanding' and 'developing' teachers' thinking, in J. Elliott (ed.) *Reconstructing Teacher Education*. London: Falmer Press.

England, J. (1999) *Promoting Inclusivity for Disaffected Pupils*. MA dissertation, Manchester Metropolitan University.

England, J. and Brown, T. (in press) Inclusion, exclusion and marginalisation. *Educational Action Research*.

Fay, B. (1987) *Critical Social Science*. Ithaca, NY: Cornell University Press.

Finn, G. (1982) On the oppression of women in philosophy – or whatever happened to objectivity? in G. Finn and A. Miles (eds) *Feminism in Canada*. Montreal: Black Rose Books.

Fiske, J. (1987) *Television Culture*. London: Methuen.

Flax, J. (1990) Postmodernism and gender relations in feminist theory, in L. Nicholson (ed.) *Feminism/Postmodernism*. London: Routledge.

Foucault, M. (1972) *The Archaeology of Knowledge*. London: Routledge.

Foucault, M. (1977a) *Discipline and Punish*. London: Penguin.

Foucault, M. (1977b) A preface to transgression, in D. Bouchard (ed.) *Language, Counter-memory, Practice: Selected Essays and Interviews by Michel Foucault*. Oxford: Basil Blackwell.

Foucault, M. (1981) *The History of Sexuality, 1: An Introduction*. Harmondsworth: Pelican.

Foucault, M. (1983) Why study power? The question of the subject, in H. Dreyfus and P. Rabinow (eds) *Beyond Structuralism and Hermeneutics*. Chicago: University of Chicago Press.

Foucault, M. (1984a) What is enlightenment? in P. Rabinow (ed.) *The Foucault Reader*. Harmondsworth: Penguin.

Foucault, M. (1984b) On the genealogy of ethics: an overview of work in progress, in P. Rabinow (ed.) *The Foucault Reader*. Harmondsworth: Penguin.

Foucault, M. (1985) *The Use of Pleasure*. New York: Pantheon.

Foucault, M. (1988) Power and sex, in L. Kritzman (ed.) *Michel Foucault: Politics, Philosophy, Culture: Interviews and Other Writings, 1977–1984*. London: Routledge.

Foucault, M. (1998) Technologies of the self, in L. Martin, H. Gutman and P. Hutton (eds) *Technologies of the Self: A Seminar with Michel Foucault*. London: Tavistock.

Foucault, M. (1991) Politics and the study of discourse, in G. Burchill, C. Gordon and P. Millar (eds) *The Foucault Effect: Studies in Governmentality*. Hemel Hempstead: Harvester Wheatsheaf.

Fox, N. (2000) Social research in postmodern mood: reflexivity, collaboration and transgression. Paper presented to 'Current Issues in Qualitative Research' conference, University of East Anglia, 24, 25 July.

Francis, D. (1995) The reflective journal: a window to pre-service teachers' practical knowledge, *Teaching and Teacher Education*, 11: 229–41.

Fraser, N. (1985) Michel Foucault: a young conservative? *Ethics*, 96: 165–84.

Fraser, N. and Nicholson, L. (1988) Social criticism without philosophy: an encounter between feminism and postmodernism, in A. Cohen and M. Descal (eds) *The Institution of Philosophy: A Discipline in Crisis?* Totowa, NJ: Rowman & Littlefield.

Freire, P. (1972) *Pedagogy of the Oppressed*. Harmondsworth: Penguin.

Gadamer, H-G. (1975) *Truth and Method*. London: Sheed & Ward.

Gallagher, S. (1992) *Hermeneutics and Education*. Albany, NY: State University of New York Press.

Giroux, H. (1983) Theory and Resistance in Education: A Pedagogy for Opposition. Amherst, MA: Bergin & Garvey.

Giroux, H. (1991) Democracy and the discourse of cultural difference: towards a politics of border pedagogy, *British Journal of Sociology of Education*, 12(4): 501–19.

Gould, T.K.W. (1995) *We Need to Talk: Developing Home-School Relationships*. MA dissertation, Manchester Metropolitan University.

Gray, J. (1995) *Liberalism*. Buckingham: Open University Press.

Grimley, S. (1995) *Communicating Professional Agendas in the Field of Emotional and Behavioural Support*. MA dissertation, Manchester Metropolitan University.

Grosz, E. (1989) *Sexual Subversions*. Sydney: Allen & Unwin.

Grosz, E. (1990) *Jacques Lacan: A Feminist Introduction*. London: Routledge.

Groundwater-Smith, S. (1988) Credential bearing enquiry-based courses: paradox or new challenge? in J. Nias and S. Groundwater-Smith (eds) *The Enquiring Teacher*. Lewes: Falmer Press.

Habermas, J. (1972) *Knowledge and Human Interests*. London: Heinemann.

Habermas, J. (1976) Systematically distorted communication, in P. Connerton (ed.) *Critical Sociology*. Harmondsworth: Penguin.

Habermas, J. (1984) *The Theory of Communicative Action*, vol. 1. Cambridge: Polity.

Habermas, J. (1985) Modernity: an incomplete project, in H. Foster (ed.) *Postmodern Culture*, pp. 8–15. London: Pluto Press.

Habermas, J. (1987) *The Theory of Communicative Action*, vol. 2. Cambridge: Polity.

Habermas, J. (1990) *Moral Consciousness and Communicative Action*, trans. C. Lenhardt and S. Nicholsen. Cambridge, MA: MIT Press.

Habermas, J. (1991) *Communication and the Evolution of Society*. Cambridge: Polity.

Hall, S. (1992) The question of cultural identity, in S. Hall, D. Held and T. McGrew (eds) *Modernity and its Futures*. Cambridge: Polity Press.

Hall, S. (1997) *Representation: Cultural Representations and Signifying Practices*. Milton Keynes: The Open University.

Hall, S., Held, D. and McGrew, T. (1992) *Modernity and its Futures*. Cambridge: Polity Press.

Hallberg, H. (1992) Feminist epistemology: an impossible project, in S. Hall, D. Held and T. McGrew (eds) *Modernity and its Futures*. Cambridge: Polity Press.

Hanley, U. and Brown, T. (1996) Building a professional discourse of mathematics teaching within initial training courses, *Research in Education*, 55: 39–48.

Hanley, U. and Brown, T. (1999) The initiation into the discourses of mathematics education, *Mathematics Education Review*, 10: 3–12.

Haraway, D. (1990) A manifesto for cyborgs: science, technology, and socialist feminism in the 1980s, in L. Nicholson (ed.) *Feminism/Postmodernism*. London: Routledge.

Hargreaves, A. (1994) *Changing Teachers, Changing Times: Teachers' Work and Culture in the Postmodern Age*. London: Cassell.

Hartsock, N. (1987) Rethinking modernism: minority vs. majority theories, *Cultural Critique*, 7: 187–206.

Harvey, D. (1989) *The Condition of Postmodernity*. Cambridge: Polity Press.

Harvey, D. (1992) The conditions of postmodernity, in S. Hall, D. Held and T. McGrew (eds) *Modernity and its Futures*. Cambridge: Polity Press.

Hassan, I. (1987) *The Postmodern Turn: Essays in Postmodern Theory and Culture*. Columbus, OH: Ohio State University Press.

Hatton, N. and Smith, D. (1995) Reflection in teacher education: towards definition and implementation, *Teaching and Teacher Education*, 11(1): 33–49.

Hebdige, D. (1989) *Hiding in the Light*. London: Routledge.

Hegel, G.W.F. (1967) *The Phenomenology of the Mind*, trans. J.B. Baillie. New York: Harper Torchbooks.

Hekman, S. (1990) *Gender and Knowledge*. Cambridge: Polity Press.

Henriques, J., Hollway, W., Urwin, C., Venn, C. and Walkerdine, V. (1984) *Changing the Subject*. London: Methuen.

Herford, W.H. (1899) The student's Froebel, quoted in C. Steedman (1992) *Past Tenses*. London: Rivers Oram Press.

Herscovics, N. and Linchevski, L. (1994) A cognitive gap between arithmetic and algebra, *Educational Studies in Mathematics*, 25: 59–78.

Heywood, D. (1999) *Interpretation and Meaning in Science Education: Hermeneutic Perspectives on Language in Learning and Teaching Science*. PhD thesis, Manchester Metropolitan University.

Holdsworth, A. (1988) *Out of the Doll's House: The Story of Women in the 20th Century*. London: BBC Books.

hooks, b. (1989) *Talking Back: Thinking Feminist Thinking Black*. Boston, MA: South End Press.

Hultqvist, K. (1998) A history of the present on children's welfare in Sweden: from Froebal to present-day decentralization projects, in T. Popkewitz and M. Brennan (eds) *Foucault's Challenge: Discourse, Knowledge and Power in Education*. New York: Teachers' College Press.

Hutcheon, L. (1989) *The Politics of Postmodernism*. New York: Routledge.

Huyssen, A. (1981) The search for tradition: avant garde and post modernism in the 1920s, *New German Critique*, 22: 23–40.

Huyssen, A. (1990) Mapping the postmodern, in L. Nicholson (ed.) *Feminism/Postmodernism*. London: Routledge.

Jagger, A. (1983) *Feminists, Politics and Human Nature*. Totowa, NJ: Rowman & Allanheld.

Jennings, L. and Graham, A. (1996) Exposing discourses through action research, in O. Zuber-Skerritt (ed.) *New Directions in Action Research*. London: Falmer.

Johnson, B. (1981) Translator's introduction, in J. Derrida, *Dissemination*, pp. vii–xxxiii. London: The Athlone Press.

Johnson, B. (1988) The frame of reference: Poe, Lacan, Derrida, in J. Muller and W. Richardson (eds) *The Purloined Letter: Poe, Lacan, Derrida and Psychoanalytic Reading*. Baltimore, MD: Johns Hopkins University Press.

Jones, E. (1999) *Critical Pedagogy: An Impossible Task*. PhD thesis, Manchester Metropolitan University.

Jones, L. (1995) Wanted, new scripts for boys' play, *Language and Learning*, March: 6–8.

Jones, L. (1996) Young girls' notions of femininity, *Gender and Education*, 8(3): 311–21.

Jones, L. (2001) Trying to break bad habits in practice by engaging with poststructuralist theories, *Early Years*, 21(1): 25–33.

Jones, L. and Brown, T. (1999) A tale of disturbance and unsettlement: incorporating and enacting deconstruction with the purpose of challenging aspects of pedagogy in the nursery classroom, *Teachers and Teaching: Theory and Practice*, 5(2): 187–202, extracts reprinted with kind permission of Taylor & Francis Ltd. PO Box 25, Abingdon, Oxfordshire, OX14 3UE.

Jones, L. and Brown, T. (in press) Reading the nursery classroom: a Foucauldian perspective. *International Journal of Qualitative Studies in Education*.

Jones, L., Brown, T., Hanley, U. and McNamara, O. (2000) An enquiry into transitions; from being a 'learner of mathematics' to becoming a 'teacher of mathematics', *Research in Education*, 63: 1–10.

Kearney, R. (1984) *Dialogues with Contemporary Continental Thinkers: The Phenomenological Heritage*. Manchester: Manchester University Press.

Kearney, R. (1986) *Modern Movements in European Philosophy*. Manchester: Manchester University Press.

Kemmis, S. (1985) Action research and the politics of reflection, in D. Boud, R. Keog and D. Walker (eds) *Reflection: Turning Experience into Learning*. London: Kogan Page.

Lacan, J. (1977) *Ecrits: A Selection*, trans. A. Sherridan. London: Tavistock.

Lapsley, R. and Westlake, M. (1996) From *Casablanca* to *Pretty Woman*: the politics of romance, in A. Easthorpe (ed.) *Contemporary Film Theory*. London: Longman.

Lather, P. (1991) *Getting Smart*. London: Routledge.

Lather, P. (1993) Fertile obsession: validity after post-structuralism, *The Sociological Quarterly*, 34(4): 673–93.

Leader, D. and Groves, J. (1995) *Lacan for Beginners*. Cambridge: Icon.

Lecercle, J-J. (1990) *The Violence of Language*. London: Routledge.

Levi-Strauss, C. (1969) *The Raw and the Cooked*, trans. J. Weightman and D. Weightman. London: Jonathan Cape.

Lodge, D. (1988) *Modern Criticism and Theory: A Reader*. London: Longman.

Lomax, P. (1994) Action research for professional practice. Paper presented at conference of British Educational Research Association, University of Oxford.

Lowenfeld, M. (1935) *Play in Childhood*. London: Gollancz.

Lusted, D. (1986) Why pedagogy? *Screen*, 27(5): 2–16.

McCarthy, T. (1982) Rationality and relativism, in J.B. Thompson and D. Held (eds) *Habermas – Critical Debates*. London: Macmillan.

McCarthy, T. (1991) *Ideals and Illusions: On Reconstruction and Deconstruction in Contemporary Critical Theory*. Cambridge, MA: MIT Press.

McLaren, P. (1995) *Critical Pedagogy and Predatory Culture*. London: Routledge.

McLennan, G. (1992) The Enlightenment Project revisited, in S. Hall, D. Held and T. McGrew (eds) *Modernity and its Futures*. Cambridge: Polity Press.

McLeod, J. (1997) *Narrative and Psychotherapy*. London: Sage.

MacLure, M. (1993) Mundane autobiography: some thoughts on self-talk in research contexts, *British Journal of Sociology of Education*, 14: 373–84.

MacLure, M. (1994) Language and discourse: the embrace of uncertainty, *British Journal of Sociology of Education*, 15(2): 283–300.

McNamara, O. (1995) Saussurian linguistics revisited: can it inform our understanding of mathematics education? *Science and Education*, 4: 253–66.

McRobbie, A. (1978) Working class girls and the culture of femininity, in Centre For Contemporary Cultural Studies Women's Group (eds) *Women Take Issue*. Birmigham: CCCSWG.

McRobbie, A. (1993) Feminism, postmodernism and the real me, *Theory Culture & Society*, 10: 127–42.

Manchester Metropolitan University (1994) *MA in Teaching: Review Document*. Manchester: MMU.

Martusewicz, R. (1992) Mapping the terrain of the post-modern subject, in W. Pinar and W. Reynolds (eds) *Understanding Curriculum as Phenomenological and Constructed Text*. New York: Teachers College Press.

Mason, J. (1992) *Noticing: A Systematic Approach to Professional Development*. Milton Keynes: Open University.

Millett, A. (1996) The implementation of 'using and applying mathematics': individual and collective uncertainties and conflicts. Paper presented to the conference of the *British Educational Research Association*, University of Lancaster.

Moi, T. (1985) *Sexual Textual Politics*. London: Routledge.

Nye, A. (1988) *Feminist Theory and the Philosophies of Man*. New York: Routledge.

Olson, M.R. (1995) Conceptualising narrative authority: implications for teacher education, *Teaching and Teacher Education*, 11: 119–35.

Parker, S. (1997) *Reflective Teaching in the Postmodern World*. Buckingham: Open University Press.

Parsons, T. (1937) *The Structure of Social Action*. New York: McGraw-Hill.

Pearce, J. and Pickard, A. (1994) Becoming oneself: revisiting a course rationale. *Chreods*, 7: 33–9.

Pefanis, J. (1991) *Heterology and the Postmodern: Battaille, Baudrillard and Lyotard*. Durham, NC: Duke University Press.

Perry, A. (1994) *An Exploration and Examination of the Conceptual Foundations of my Teaching*. MA dissertation, Manchester Metropolitan University.

Peters, R.S. (1966) *Ethics and Education*. London: Routledge & Kegan Paul.

Pignatelli, F. (1993) What can I do? Foucault on freedom and the question of teacher agency, *Educational Theory*, 43(4): 411–32.

Poster, M. (ed.) (1988) *Jean Baudrillard: Selected works*. Cambridge: Polity Press.

Probyn, E. (1993) Queer belongings, in E. Grosz and E. Probyn (eds) *Sexy Bodies*. London: Routledge.

Rabinow, P. (1991) *The Foucault Reader*. London: Penguin.

Ramazanoglu, C. (1993) *Up Against Foucault: Explorations of Some Tensions Between Foucault and Feminism*. London: Routledge.

Rasmussen, D. (1990) *Reading Habermas*. Oxford: Blackwell.

Rhedding-Jones, J. (1996) Researching early schooling: post-structuralist practices and academic writing in an ethnography, *Journal of Sociology of Education*, 17(1): 21–37.

Ricoeur, P. (1966) *Freedom and Nature: The Voluntary and the Involuntary*. Evanston: North Western University Press.

Ricoeur, P. (1981) *Hermeneutics and the Human Sciences*. Cambridge: Cambridge University Press.

Ricoeur, P. (1984) *Time and Narrative*, vol. 1. Chicago: Chicago University Press.

Ricoeur, P. (1985) *Time and Narrative*, vol. 2. Chicago: Chicago University Press.

Robbins, R. (1996) 'But one thing knows the flower': Whistler, Swinburne, Derrida, in J. Brannigan, R. Robbins and J. Wolfreys (eds) *Applying To Derrida*. London: Macmillan.

Roberts, L. (1997) *Insider-Outsider Discourses: Self and Human Agency in Educational Establishments*. MA dissertation, Manchester Metropolitan University.

Rushdie, S. (1990) *Haroun and the Sea of Stories*. Harmondsworth: Granta Books.

Russell, B. (1914) *Our Knowledge of the External world*. London: George Allen & Unwin.

Safstrom, C. (1998) On the way to a postmodern curriculum theory moving from the question of unity to the question of difference. Paper presented at the *British Educational Research Association Annual Conference*, Belfast.

Sanger, J. (1994) Seven types of creativity, *British Educational Research Journal*, 20: 175–85.

Sanger, J. (1995) Five easy pieces: the deconstruction of illuminatory data in research writing, *British Educational Research Journal*, 21: 89–97.

Saussure, F. ([1959] 1974) *Course in General Linguistics*, eds C. Bally, A. Sechehaye and A. Reidlinger, trans. W. Baskin. London: Fontana.

Savill, M. (1999) *Issues Arising for Me in the Evolution of a New School*. MA dissertation, Manchester Metropolitan University.

Schon, D. (1983) *The Reflective Practitioner*. London: Temple Smith.

Schrift, A. (1995) Reconfiguring the subject as a process of self: following Foucault's Nietschean trajectory to Butler, Laclau/Mouffe, and beyond, *J'Accuse*, 25: 28–39.

Schütz, A. (1962) *The Problem of Social Reality*. The Hague: Martinus Nijhoff.

Scott, D. and Usher, R. (1999) *Researching Education: Data, Methods and Theory in Educational Enquiry*. London: Cassell.

Sears, P. and Feldman, D. (1976) Teacher interaction with girls and boys, in J. Stacey (ed.) *And Jill Came Tumbling After: Sexism in Education*. New York: Dell Publishing.

Shapiro, S. (1991) The end of radical hope? Postmodernism and the challenge to critical pedagogy, *Education and Society*, 9(2): 112–22.

Siegel, H. (1988) *Educating Reason*. London: Routledge & Kegan Paul.

Silcock, P. (1994) The process of reflective teaching, *British Journal of Educational Studies*, 3: 273–85.

Simon, S. and Brown, M. (1996) Teacher beliefs and practices in primary mathematics. Paper presented at the conference of the *British Educational Research Association*, University of Lancaster.

Singh, P. (1995) Voicing the 'other', speaking for the 'self', disrupting the metanarratives of educational theorizing with poststructural feminisms, in R. Smith and P. Wexler (eds) *After Postmodernism*. London: Falmer Press.

Smart, B. (1985) *Michel Foucault*. London: Tavistock.

Spivak, G. (1980) Revolutions which as yet have no model, in D. Landry and G. McLean (eds) *The Spivak Reader*. London: Routledge.

Spivak, G. (1985a) Interview with Barbara Creed, Freda Freilberg and Andrea McLaughlan (introduction by E. Gross), *Art Network*, winter: 20–7.

Spivak, G. (1985b) Three women's texts and a critique of imperialism, *Critical Enquiry*, 12: 243–61.

Spivak, G. (1987) *In Other Words: Essays in Cultural Politics*. New York: Methuen.

Spivak, G. (1993) *Outside the Teaching Machine*. London: Routledge.

Steedman, C. (1982) *The Tidy House*. London: Virago.

Steedman, C. (1992) *Past Tenses: Essays on Writing Autobiography and History*. London: Rivers Oram Press.

Steedman, C. (2001) I want to tell you a story, *Radical Philosophy*, 105: 45–8.

Stenhouse, L. (1975) *An Introduction to Curriculum Develoment and Research*. London: Heinemann.

Stronach, I. (1997) Crisis, what crisis? Dissolving insoluble problems in representing the crisis of representation. Unpublished paper, Manchester Metropolitan University.

Stronach, I. (1999) Shouting theatre in crowded fire, *Evaluation*, 5(2): 173–93.

Stronach, I. and MacLure, M. (1997) *Educational Research Undone: The Postmodern Embrace*. Buckingham: Open University Press.

Taylor, M. (1987) Descartes, Nietzsche and the search for the unsayable, *New York Times Book Review*, 1 February: 3.

Thomas, M., Goddard, E., Hickman, M. and Hunter, P. (1992) *General Household Survey Series* (GAS no. 23). London: HMSO.

Thompson, J. (1981) *Critical Hermeneutics*. Cambridge: Cambridge University Press.

Thompson, K. (1992) Social pluralism and post-modernity, in S. Hall, D. Held and T. McGrew (eds) *Modernity and its Futures*. Cambridge: Polity Press.

Titley, S., Pollock, L., Ross, L. and Tait, L. (1999) Progress' pilgrim: a critical narrative of research in progress, *Journal of Advanced Nursing*, 29(5): 1221–7.

Trinh, M.T. (1989) *Woman, Native, Other: Writing Postcoloniality and Feminism*. Bloomington, IN: Indiana University Press.

Urmson, J. and Ree, J. (eds) (1989) *The Concise Encyclopedia of Western Philosophy and Philosophers*. London: Unwin Hyman.

Urwin, C. (1984) Power relations and the emergence of language, in J. Henriques, W. Holloway, C. Urwin, C. Venn and V. Walkerdine (eds) *Changing the Subject: Psychology, Social Regulation and Subjectivity*. London: Methuen.

Walkerdine, V. (1988) *The Mastery of Reason*. London: Routledge.

Walkerdine, V. (1990) *School Girl Fictions*. London: Verso.

Walkerdine, V. and Lucey, H. (1989) *Democracy in the Kitchen: Regulating Mothers and Socialising Daughters*. London: Virago.

Weber, S. (1993) The narrative anecdote in teacher education, *Journal of Education for Teaching*, 19(1): 71–82.

Weedon, C. (1985) *Feminist Practice & Poststructuralist Theory*. Oxford: Blackwell.

Weedon, C. (1999) *Feminism, Theory and the Politics of Difference*. Oxford: Blackwell.

Welch, S. (1985) *Communities for Resistance and Solidarity*. New York: Orbis.

Williams, R. (1979) *The Country and the City*. St Albans: Paladin.

Winter, R. (1989) *Learning from Experience: Principles and Practice in Action Research.* Lewes: Falmer Press.

Wittgenstein, L. (1961) *Tractatus Logico-Philosphicus.* London: Routledge.

Young, R.E. (1989) *A Critical Theory of Education: Habermas and our Children's Future.* Hemel Hempstead: Harvester Wheatsheaf.

Young, R.E. (1992) *Critical Theory and Classroom Talk.* Clevedon, OH: Multilingual Matters.

Zeller, N. (1987) 'A rhetoric for naturalistic inquiry', unpublished dissertation, Indiana University.

Zipes, J. (1994) *The Trials and Tribulations of Little Red Riding Hood.* Aldershot: Gower.

Zizek, S. (1989) *The Sublime Object of Ideology.* London: Verso.

Zizek, S. (1991) *Everything You Wanted to Know About Lacan but were Afraid to Ask Hitchcock.* London: Verso.

Zizek, S. (1993) *Tarrying with the Negative.* Durham, NC: Duke University Press.

Zuber-Skerritt, O. (ed.) (1996) *New Directions in Action Research.* London: Falmer.

Index